_Y

THE LIFE AND WORKS
OF THE GREAT SON
OF THE HUNGARIAN HIGHLAND

Lessons to be drawn
from the events of a stormy period in European history,
to facilitate the efforts for the achievement
of a lasting and peaceful cooperation
among the peoples of the Danubian basin

by

Dr. Gabor Szent-Ivany

Published by

DANUBIAN PRESS, INC.

Astor, Florida 32102 U.S.A.

Published by

DANUBIAN PRESS, INC.

Astor, Florida 32102 U.S.A.

In cooperation with the

NATIONAL COMMITTEE OF HUNGARIANS

FROM CZECHOSLOVAKIA

Little Library, Volume No. 2

Translated from the Hungarian original

by Laszlo Dosa

Copyright 1989 by Dr. Gabor Szent-Ivany

Library of Congress Catalog Card Number: 89-81318

ISBN: 0-87934-034-7

"Let us develop a peaceful and constructive cooperation, based on equal rights, among the peoples and nations which mutually depend on each other. This is equally in the interest of the Hungarians, Germans, Slovaks and Ruthenians who have lived here for centuries."

From an address by Janos Esterhazy before the Central Committee of the Hungarian Party, June 22, 1942.

Dedicated to the blessed memory
of my beloved wife
Eva Balajthy

Acknowledgments

I wish to extend my grateful thanks to all who have assisted, in one form or another, in the preparation of this work. Above all, The Reverend Kristof Hites; to Baroness Malfatti, nee Countess Alice Esterhazy, and her brother, Count Janos Esterhazy, Jr., for their kindness in providing documents pertaining to this work from the legacy of the late Countess Louise Esterhazy, sister of their late father, Count Janos Esterhazy; Professor Edward Chaszar, Ph.D. and Professor Karoly Vojatsek. Also, Karoly Berenyi, Karoly Esterhazy and Dr. Peter Simek; Countess Istvan Karolyi in Washington and Leslie Balas of the Library of Congress. I also wish to thank Laszlo Dosa for the editing, translating and typesetting of this book, and Pal Takacs for designing its cover. And last, but not least, I am much indebted to Francis S. Wagner who kindly undertook the task of reading the entire manuscript with the eyes of an expert in the problems of the Danubian Basin.

TABLE OF CONTENTS

iv

Esterházy János gróf
szül. 1864, deczember hó 6-án.
† 1905, szeptember hó 2-án.

Adj Uram neki örök nyugo-
dalmat és az örök világosság fényes-
kedjék neki. Amen'

Death notice of the father of
Janos Esterhazy (1905)

Count Janos Esterhazy

Nyitraujlak

Janos Esterhazy in Nyitraujlak, 1929

Janos Esterhazy in 1915

Janos Esterhazy with his sister Louise,
in Nyitraujlak, Summer 1908

Janos Esterhazy in his study

At the Book Fair of Budapest: Dr. Janos
Reinel, Editor of the *Magyar Minerva* of
Pozsony; Janos Esterhazy; Hungarian
Foreign Minister Istvan Csaky, and
Laszlo Mecs, the renowned poet

Janos Esterhazy with his daughter
in Nyitraujlak

Father and daughter in church

Janos Esterhazy with his wife

Janos Esterhazy with his
daughter Alice

Janos Esterhazy at the Komarom bridge at the
time of the Komarom talks of 1938

Janos Esterhazy in traditional
Hungarian dress uniform in
1938

Janos Esterhazy among his
beloved people of the Highlands

Father and daughter with trophies

The young Esterhazys: Antal,
Louise, Pal, Maria and Janos

Janos Esterhazy's son, Janos Jr., in 1948

Tombstone of Janos Esterhazy's wife in Budapest

Copie d'un télégramme adressé le 19 Septembre 1947 à Son Excellence Monsieu Edouard BENES, Président de la République Tchécoslovaque par Mademoiselle Louise ESTERHAZY en faveur de son frère, déporté par les Russes d'une prise tchécoslovaque et condamné "in absentia" par le tribunal de Bratislava, le 16 Septembre 1947.

<u>Texte du télégramme:</u>

à Son Excellence

Monsieur Edouard BENES
Président de la République Tchécoslovaque
P R A G U E

En apprenant la condamnation de mon frère Jean ESTERHAZY par le tribunal de Bratislava, il est de mon devoir de protester contre cette condamnation "in absentia" alors que mon frère était resté à la disposition des autorités tchécoslovaques, mais qu'il a été déporté de la prison tchécoslovaque par des agents d'une grande puissance et empêché de comparaître devant le tribunal tchécoslovaque où il avait cru pouvoir se défendre librement - Stop.

Au nom des exigences de la justice, je vous supplie, Monsieur le Président, de faire renouveler le procès de mon frère et de faire appel à la puissance qui l'a déporté pour que ce citoyen tchécoslovaque soit rendu aux autorités tchécoslovaques, afin qu'il puisse se défendre personnellement devant un tribunal tchécoslovaque - Stop.

J'ai pleine confiance que le sens de la justice de Votre Excellence inspirera les démarches nécessaires pour obtenir ce résultat et que la grande puissance alliée répondra à votre appel avec la générosité dont elle a déjà fait preuve en renvoyant à Bratislava plusieurs personnalités slovaques (1) - Stop.

En espérant une réponse prochaine et favorable, je vous prie, Monsieur le Président, de recevoir l'expression de mon profond respect.

Louise ESTERHAZY
3, Avenue Frédéric Le Play - Paris VIIe

(1) MM. CATLOS, SPISIAK et SOKOL que les Russes déportèrent de Tchécoslovaquie mais rendirent aux autorités tchécoslovaques.

Appeal for clemency, submitted by Louise Esterhazy to President Benes on September 12, 1947.

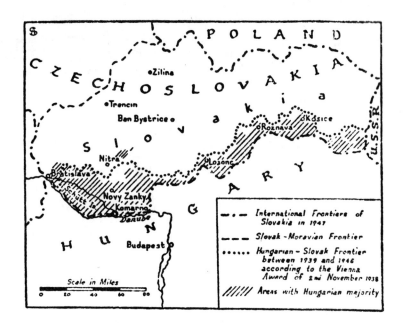

Slovakian name:	Hungarian name
Banska Bystrica	Besztercebanya
Bratislava	Pozsony
Komarno	Komarom
Kosice	Kassa
Nitra	Nyitra
Nove Zamky	Ersekujvar
Roznava	Rozsnyo
Trencin	Trencsen
Zilina	Zsolna

Territorial changes in Slovakia

PREFACE

Dr. Szent-Ivany's book fills a huge gap heretofore overlooked in the historical and political literature that deals with the years from the end of the First World War until the conclusion of World War Two. The work was written about a man who did not play an important role in the politics of Europe during that period, and yet his activity in the narrow field of history presents an ideal model and moral example for leading politicians. Had those who shaped the course of events in those fateful times been guided by such ideals, tragic developments in Europe could have been avoided.

Today it is generally acknowledged that the statesmen who controlled world events during those years acted without a clear vision of the actual problems of Europe. They seem to have been guided more by hostility and selfish interests than by a sincere desire to bring true and just peace to this all-important area of the world. They cannot be excused the tragic consequences of their politics that led to mounting international tension and fear, instead of true peace. Now, as Europe slowly emerges from the adverse results of their misconceived policies, it seems to be opportune to investigate the life of a relatively minor figure of that time, who had nevertheless stood for high moral standards among the leading actors of contemporary history.

Janos Esterhazy was such a leader. He devoted his life to the ill-fated cause of one million Hungarians who had been cut off from their mother community by the dictates of the Treaty of Trianon. For one thousand years, their homeland belonged to the Kingdom of Hungary until this infamous treaty, imposed on them against their will, made them part of the newly created state of Czechoslovakia. Esterhazy was the defender of their basic human and civic rights and fought for their interests.

Following the disintegration of Benes' Czechoslovakia when the Slovaks broke away from their Czech partners, Esterhazy faithful ly continued in that role on behalf of that smaller group of Hungarians who were left behind in Tiso's Slovakia. As a member of the Slovak parliament, true to his Christian statesmanship, Esterhazy single-handedly fought Hitler's order to deport the Jews, as well as other manifestations of the Nazi influence penetrating the small Slovak Republic which came into being under Hitler's sponsorship.

At the end of World War Two, the corrupt political course of the victors made Esterhazy a martyr for his Christian political ideals. He was exiled to the Soviet Union for three years before being handed over to his Czechoslovak political opponents. He died in their prison, faithful to the end to his people and to the ideals by which he served his people all his life.

It is rewarding to read the story of Janos Esterhazy's life, presented here so authoritatively by Dr. Gabor Szent-Ivany.

The Reverend Christopher Hites

Portola Valley, California
October, 1989

xiv

INTRODUCTION

I often visit the Highlands[1] in my dreams. Most of the time I go to the region where I was born, to Besztercebanya (Banska Bystrica), considered one of the most beautiful cities of the Highlands.

Human nature is wonderful. Many of the very first impressions of life, of the world itself, stay with us through our entire lives. Instead of diminishing with time, the intensity of these impressions just keeps increasing. We turn to the memory of these impressions to explain facts and events which could not be explained by the cool, somber logic of the mind.

How does a child who steps out for the first time from the warm environment of his family home become acquainted with the world, with humanity around him? First and above all, through his playmates. Whether he wants it or not, those initial experiences and impressions will stay with him through the rest of his life.

That is how I feel about the very first impressions of my own tender childhood. I couldn't count the number of times my memory has recalled one sharp image after another from that period. I can see myself and my little friends -- mostly young Slovak children -- running around accompanied by our carefree laughter, or chasing the baby ducklings to the water. We express our feelings, our childish thoughts in the Slovak language, no matter how primitive or clumsy that may be. This is not surprising at all. After all, I picked up quite a few words from my mother who spoke the Slovak language fluently for all 92 years of her life. The rest of it I learned from my young playmates.

My mother told me that in her childhood she, too, had Slovak girlfriends. Her name was Maria and the little girls gave her the nickname Marcsulka. She also recalled that the girls would often come to her gate and called out "Maysuyka sisi Bisisi?" These three Slovak words, spoken in baby language, meant "Are you in Beszterce, Marcsulka?" Because it often happened that she had to ride with her

1

parents to the countryside. Her father was chief physician in the hospital and also served as a public health doctor which required frequent trips out of town.

These warm, affectionate relationships accompanied my mother into her adulthood.

My own impressions from my earliest youth have also stayed with me. I can state in good conscience that those impressions have not had the slightest trace of animosity towards the Slovak people. On the contrary, I have the same affection and warm feelings toward them today as I had in my childhood. A child has a very sensitive soul. He registers many things better than an adult would. To be absolutely candid, my first strong resentment arose not against the Slovaks -- I remember it all too well -- but against the Czechs. It occurred in 1919 and 1920 when the events forced us to leave our native land quite suddenly. When the Czech colonel didn't even wait for us to pack our belongings, he was in such a hurry to have his trunks moved into our house. When we didn't even have time to say Good-bye to our Slovak friends. It's not necessary to explain these things to a child. He senses what's wrong. But I was able to separate my resentment towards the Czechs from my friendly feelings towards the Slovaks. I knew that living in boxcars, the entire refugee existence, was not the fault of the Slovaks. The Czech politicians of that fateful period were to blame for it, just as it had been explained to us.

Only much later, in the late 1930s did I learn of the hatred of certain Slovak leaders towards Hungarians. Then, after 1945, came the ruthless persecution of the Hungarians by the Slovaks, which could be compared only to the persecution of the Jews. This was totally inexplicable, completely beyond understanding. We tried with my friends and acquaintances from various regions of the Highlands to discuss the whole issue, searching for an explanation. We agreed that none of us has experienced within his own circle any trace of hatred between Hungarians and Slovaks. We couldn't fully agree about what might have triggered the persecution of the Hungarians. Different people placed the emphasis on various possible causes.

I've always been bothered by this question. I've read a great deal, much has become clear to me, but that great turnaround remains inexplicable. Perhaps because I remain convinced to this day that there has never been any natural basis for hatred between Hungarians and Slovaks. Through centuries of living side-by-side, there developed a certain kinship in the soul of the two nations, a kinship which has undergone a spontaneous, natural growth with the passage of time.

A number of explanations could be found for this phenomenon. Two people, the Hungarians and the Slovaks, have always stood closest to each other in this region of the Carpathian Basin. Neither has been attracted by neighboring nations to the extent as, for example, German and Rumanian minorities have been drawn to nearby Germany and Rumania. Up until the 19th century, the ancestors of today's Slovaks have been drawn to the Czechs more by cultural sympathies than by any political or other attraction. Political attraction became noticeable only in the wake of the Austro-Hungarian Compromise of 1867 and the failure of the negotiations for an Austro-Czech Compromise in 1871. It was also promoted by the success of Hungarian efforts for political reform in the 1840s, making Hungarian the official language, which hurt Slovak sensitivities.

Shared fate has been perhaps the most important factor in nearly 1,000 years of peaceful coexistence. The Carpathian Basin occupies a key position in Europe and its possession is a precondition to the success of any imperial aspirations from all directions. Finding themselves in this key position, the Hungarian and Slovak nations have fought and bled together against great power incursions, whether they came from the East or West. Only thus were they able to survive invasions by the Mongols and the Ottoman Turks, followed by the Austrian oppression and the bloody freedom fights to shake it off. Common fate brought the two peoples ever closer together. We find ample evidence of this in the poetry of both nations.

Peaceful coexistence was also fostered by the natural process of gradual assimilation on both sides. Large numbers of Hungarians became Slovak and, by the same token, many Slovaks became Hungarian. This was an inevitable result of centuries of coexistence.

It is also possible that both nations have been aware in their subconscious that the defeat of Svatopluk's[2] Moravian empire by the conquering Hungarians in the late 10th century assured the survival of the ancestors of today's Slovaks. The population of Prince Pribina's[3] realm, which was ethnically different from Svatopluk's Moravians would not have survived, even though Pribina had been driven away by the Moravians. Today, there would be only a Czech-Moravian tongue, the Slovak language would not exist. This circumstance, too, helped create the conditions which made possible the future development of the Slovak nation.

It is not the purpose of this essay to shed scholarly light on the players who had been motivated exclusively by selfish interests in their efforts to destroy this traditionally good relationship. We might name, first of all, the Hapsburg Dynasty which had been inciting the other nationalities against the Hungarians in order to weaken the Hungarian nation. We might also name the Czechs who knew that they could not realize their imperial ambitions without the Slovaks. Those are the roots of the Czechs' answer to the Slovaks when they demanded the autonomy promised by Masaryk[4] in the Pittsburgh Agreement of 1918. The Czechs refused to carry out this pledge, claiming that autonomy would weaken the Slovaks against the Hungarians who were allegedly anticipating such an opportunity. Under the reign of Benes[5] (1918-1938) the Slovaks were unable to achieve the autonomy promised in the treaty signed by Thomas Masaryk.

The results of the Czech incitement against the Hungarians became increasingly apparent. Eventually the Slovaks, too, learned what the empty promises of Benes's policies were worth and where they were to lead ultimately. The Slovaks, too, found themselves driven onto the same road of bitter disappointments as the Hungarians did, a road which carried them into subjugation by Hitler's Germany or Stalin's Soviet Union. The great powers knew how to skillfully manipulate and take advantage for their own political ends of the burning afflictions which should have been assuaged by the Benes administration -- something that both the Slovak and Hungarian peoples have been awaiting for over twenty years in vain.

Benes' policies were even more unwielding toward the Hungarians who became a national minority in the new state of Czechoslovakia created by the Treaty of Trianon in 1920. He did not show the slightest inclination to negotiate seriously about the just complaints and even the most minimal demands of the Hungarians. Only much later, during his election campaign, did Benes summon Janos Esterhazy, the representative of the Hungarians, to ask for his support. The promises he made in return for that support proved to meaningless once again.

The Hungarian revisionist efforts were cited most frequently as an excuse for the refusal of any rapprochement, even though the Czechs knew very well that all rational Hungarians were looking for a peaceful settlement of their so-called revisionist demands. History might have taken a different turn if instead of refusing to negotiate, the Czech would have made at least an attempt to follow the approach taken by Milan Hodza, an envoy of the Czechoslovak government, during his talks in Budapest in 1918. Benes immediately rejected Hodza's approach because he appeared to be willing to make certain sensible concessions.

We will show how the Hungarians have sought to assuage their grievances with a moderation and patience which repeatedly earned the respect of Western statesmen. We will offer ample documentation in support of this assertion. Unfortunately, this moderate approach failed to secure the support of the Western powers and only the forcible intervention of Germany and the Soviet Union brought about a solution for the grievances. To a certain degree, the Slovaks had a similar experience. And so did other national minorities, such as the Sudeten Germans, Poles and Ruthenians. Twenty years of fighting the political windmills had finally swept these abandoned peoples into the orbit of Nazi Germany.

Hitler had his well defined global political goals and he was not choosy in the methods employed to meet those goals. He took turns in making promises both to the Slovaks and the Hungarians, even though he knew all too well that the promised support was often contrary to the interests of those peoples. He tried to seduce them into various risky ventures, holding up as a reward the hope of helping them fulfill their national aspirations.

We shall see how Hitler kept promising the entire Slovakia to Hungarian statesmen in return for active participation in an armed attack on Czechoslovakia. From the moment the Hungarians refused to go along, the sympathies of Hitler and the entire German leadership turned against Foreign Minister Kalman Kanya and several other Hungarian politicians.

It is also well known that in his talks with the Slovak leaders, Hitler painted a grossly distorted and magnified picture of the Hungarian threat against their state. He reminded Father Joseph Tiso[6] of this alleged threat whenever he wanted to persuade to Slovak leader to do his bidding. The tension created between Hungary and Slovakia by the first Vienna Decision of 1938, which returned parts of Slovakia to Hungary, was a tactical goal of the Germans. By playing off the two countries against each other, Hitler was better able to keep both of them off balance.

Hitler followed the same policy in his relationship with Rumania. It is well known that the second Vienna Decision of 1940, which returned parts of Transylvania to Hungary, was unsatisfactory both for Hungary and Rumania. Hitler took advantage of this situation for the furthering of his plans. He told Hungary that he would defend its territorial growth, he even raised the possibility of further territorial gains. At the same time, he kept encouraging Rumania's hopes for the return of territories lost to the Soviet Union.

Hitler's Rumanian policy became the most obvious at the time when Rumanian Marshal Ion Antonescu was going out of his way to become Hitler's most faithful satellite. Even though that had cost Rumania immense military casualties on the Russian front, it gave Antonescu the opportunity, which he never missed, to keep reminding Hitler of Hungary's less than enthusiastic military participation in the war effort. On March 23, 1944, Hitler informed Antonescu that he no longer considered it necessary to continue guaranteeing the Vienna Decision, in part because of Hungary's disloyal behavior and also because Italy had ended its participation in the war. It is a historical irony that even though Antonescu reassured Hitler at their last meeting on August 5, 1944, that Rumania would be the last to betray him, three weeks later Rumania, too, quit the war.

These times and events, if nothing else, should teach these peoples who are so dependent on each other of the fate they can expect if they allow themselves to become the mere toys of foreign powers. More of that when we discuss the life and work of Janos Esterhazy.

We wish to emphasize that in order to understand the accomplishments of Janos Esterhazy it is absolutely necessary to describe his political activities with total candor and faithfulness. And that makes it necessary to describe some circumstances which may offend Slovak sensitivities. But this cannot be completely avoided, unless we were to paint a distorted picture or render this work totally incomprehensible. It should be clear also that often in many cases there may be sharp differences in opinion. This cautionary note is intended to serve as a credible evidence that our goal is something other than the tearing up of old wounds or the endless repetition of old accusations.

We are firmly convinced that the desired establishment of a Central Europe based on the laws of geopolitics demands that instead of accusations and the rehashing of the undoubtedly many mistakes of the past which would be counterproductive in any event, we should seek out each other's hand and -- most importantly -- attempt a reconciliation in our souls. We must be aware of the fact -- and this can be accomplished only through a conscious educational effort -- that such a reconciliation would serve not **only Hungarian** or **only Slovak** interests which would benefit **one side** or the **other**. **We must understand and we must employ every means at our dispos-**

al to bring this into public consciousness. Reconciliation is in the utmost interest of both peoples because we are dealing with the common destiny of Hungarians and Slovaks and their very survival may depend on it.

Gyula Illyes[7] said of Sandor Petofi[8] in a memorial address on December 30, 1972: "National intolerance, the greatest curse of our century, is becoming increasingly severe. Instead of seeking a common voice, the various language communities try to choke each other. The great creative personalities of the nations have a most important pacifying role in this worldwide quarrel. For their voices transcend boundaries... Sadly, peace among nations and national minorities is just as much at stake today as it was then when Petofi attached his greatest hope to this (the pacifying role of the great creative personalities). Let us have the courage to continue believing in this, to fight for this!"

We can regard Janos Esterhazy as one of those "great creative personalities." His words, valid to this day, illuminate his pacifying role among nations and national minorities across boundaries: "Peaceful coexistence among interdependent nations and nationalities in the Danubian Basin should be established on the basis of equal rights. This is equally in the interest of Hungarians, Germans, Slovaks and Ruthenians who have been living here for centuries."

The validity of these words is eternal. It is only necessary -- to quote Gyula Illyes once again -- that "we have resolute courage to believe in it, to fight for it."

There could be no more fitting tribute to Janos Esterhazy's memory than to work for a lasting and peaceful coexistence with the same faith he possessed and determination he demonstrated.

On the following pages we will attempt to outline the aspirations and struggles of the Hungarian and Slovak peoples in search of their freedom and independence. For centuries these aspirations and struggles of the two peoples followed a parallel track. In the last 200 years, unfortunately they have often gone in opposite directions. But in the final analysis, from their own point of view both peoples had the same goal: the Slovaks wanted to remain Slovak, the Hungarians wanted to remain Hungarian.

As long as the Slovaks' ancestors felt that their aspirations remained secure within the framework of the Hungarian state, the two peoples were headed in the same direction, supporting and complementing each other's aspirations. Dr. Gyula Varsanyi, the outstanding expert in international law who recently passed away referred to

Hungary's "ethnoprotective" role in defending the various elements of the Slovak people against efforts from different directions to assimilate them.

For various reasons and due to various influences, the aspirations of the two peoples became separated in the 19th century. That has led to repeated confrontations between them.

We shall attempt in a new arrangement to describe first the aspirations and struggles of the Slovak people. In Part Two we will sum up the aspirations and struggles of the Hungarians. Both parts include events which were of great importance in the aspirations of both peoples. In general, we will describe those in one part only, with only a reference and, if need be, additional material in the other.

NOTES TO THE INTRODUCTION

(1)Highland (Felvidek) is the Hungarian name of former Northern Hungary, which became Slovakia as part of the Czechoslovak Republic, established in 1920 by the Treaty of Trianon.

(2)Svatopluk, 9th century Moravian prince, believed to be one of the founders of the Moravian empire.

(3)Pribina, Slav prince. According to some Czechoslovak historians, he and princes Mojmir and Rastislav founded a principality along the upper Danube river in 820.

(4)Thomas G. Masaryk, first president of the Czechoslovak republic.

(5)Eduard Benes, one of the chief architects of Czechoslovakia.

(6)Father Joseph Tiso, president of the independent Slovak republic during World War II.

(7)Gyula Illyes, one of the most outstanding Hungarian poets and authors of the 20th century.

(8)Sandor Petofi, a great poet who was killed in 1849, at age 27, in the Hungarian war of independence against Hapsburg rule.

COUNT JANOS ESTERHAZY

PART ONE

The Struggles of the Slovak People for Autonomy and Independence

A. Up to **1918** when the Slovak National Council, meeting in Turocszentmarton (Turciansky Sv.Martin), declared Czechoslovak unity, complete independence and, thus, secession from Hungary.

B. Up to **March 1939** when the Slovaks declared their secession from the Republic of Czechoslovakia and, under the sponsorship of Germany, established an independent Slovakia.

C. Up to **1945**, when Slovakia lost its independence.

D. The period **since 1945**.

E. **Lessons** for the nations of the Danubian Basin from the Slovak efforts for autonomy and independence.

A.

Slovak and Hungarian Historiographers' Views about the Origins of the Slovak People

Even though the focus of our study is the period after 1918, its understanding requires that we look at Slovak and Hungarian historiographers' views about the origins of the Slovak people -- views which have been often in sharp conflict. We will confine ourselves to the discussion of the substance of the two schools of thought without entering into any argument. That would run contrary to our goals outlined in the Introduction. Still, we feel we must acquaint the reader with these opposing views so that he or she may comprehend the numerous references that will be made to them.

According to one Slovak belief, the ancestors of the Slovak people began moving to the South even before the various Slavic tribes became separated. The most popular Slovak view maintains that the Slovak people are heirs to the Great Moravian Empire. What follows is a review of this concept, based largely on the writings of Slovak authors living in the West.

This belief traces the dawn of Slovak history to the Sixth Century, B.C. That is when the ancestors of the Slovak people crossed the Carpathians and established a permanent home along the shores of the central Danube River and its tributaries. Today's Slovakia had been inhabited already in prehistoric times. The Romans fought there with the neighboring Teutons. The sources name several leaders who had ruled over the Slavic tribes. These tribes were the ancestors of today's Slovaks.

To the West lay the Frank Empire of Charlemagne, which united Austria with the Slavs of Bohemia and Moravia. When Charlemagne defeated the Avars in the late Eighth Century, the Slavs along the upper Danube became part of a larger political unit which was founded by Pribina, Mojmir and Rastislav. The first principality

12

was established by Pribina, in 820 A.D., in the territory of todays' Nyitra (Nitra).

Another principality came into being under the rule of Mojmir in the Morava River Valley. Between 833 and 836 Mojmir managed to bring Nyitra under his control, thus laying the groundwork for the Great Moravian Empire. According to historian Pavel Jozef Safarik, in 1843, "Today's Moravia in its entirety, as well as parts of Austria and the Slavic regions of Hungary formed the nucleus of the Moravian Empire..."[9] For about 10 years after 884 it also included the former Roman province, Pannonia, ultimately even Bohemia for some 17 years,[10] but the death of Svatopluk (894), changed the situation. His successors, the two Czech princes, seceded from the Great Moravian Empire and swore allegiance in 895 to Arnulf, ruler of the Eastern Frank Kingdom, becoming his vassals and fighting on his side against the Great Moravian Empire.[11]

The Great Moravian Empire had to defend itself first against the Eastern Frank Kingdom, then beginning in 895, the Hungarian invaders from Asia who defeated Mojmir II in 906. This battle was fought near Pozsony (Bratislava). The Hungarians gradually united under their rule the territories of today's Slovakia, Pannonia and, eventually, Transylvania.

Slovakia remained an administratively separate entity but it was to become more important culturally than politically in Europe. The only exception was in the 14th Century when much of Slovakia came under the rule of Mate Csak, a powerful member of the Hungarian nobility.

According to the prevailing Hungarian thinking, in a nutshell, the Slovak ethnic group came into being in the centuries following the Hungarian conquest as the ancestors of today's Slovaks gradually infiltrated the Northern regions of historic Hungary. This was not a homogenous ethnic group. It was formed from the merger of different Slavic tribes, as noted by Slovak historians, too.

Hungarian historians place the emergence of Slovak nation building into the 17th Century. They reject the proposition that there existed a politically organized state of sorts when the Hungarians arrived on the scene and that this state was destroyed by the conquering Hungarians. The Hungarian view also rejects the Slovak hypothesis of a Great Moravian Empire because, according to this view, there is no scholarly evidence in its support. Even the location of that empire is subject of serious scholarly controversy.[12]

As noted earlier, we have touched upon these questions only for the sake of clarifying future references to the contrasting views about the origins of the Slovak people. In any event, the prevailing Hungarian view holds that it is pointless to debate which people was first in the region. Such debate can only lead to the creation of romantic myths without any scholarly foundation. Such myths, as we have seen, do not help at all in the creation of the conditions needed for peaceful coexistence.

There is one fact that remains beyond any debate in the Hungarian view, namely that following the fall of the Roman Empire only the Hungarians were able to establish in the region a state which survived for over a millennium, despite the greatest adversities.

Hungarian historians regard the Turkish occupation of Hungary as one of the most important milestones in the history of Slovak ethnicity. The greatest burden of the Turkish occupation of more than 150 years was borne by the Hungarians. Their villages were obliterated, their numbers were reduced beyond belief. Northern Hungary, on the other hand, provided refuge for newcomers. The size of its Slavic population was swelled by Slavic refugees from the South, who were fleeing the Turks. The refugees from the Turks were joined by a steady stream of Protestant refugees from Bohemia and Moravia.

We witness the establishment of a very strong Slavic presence in that period in Northern Hungary. The face of countless villages had completely changed with the arrival of new Slavic settlers. These settlers, along with the Slavs who had been already living in Northern Hungary, laid the foundations of a future Slovak nation. The shift in the ratio between the Slovak and Hungarian populations in this period was to determine the ethnic boundaries between the two peoples, establishing two distinct cultural spheres.

At the same time, many Slovaks gradually assimilated into the framework of Hungarian society and economy, reaching high positions and joining the ranks of nobility. According to the Hungarian view, this demonstrated that the settlers, too, regarded Hungary as their home. The fact that they were also able to take the first steps toward establishment of their nationhood only proves the tolerance and understanding of the host country. This stands in contrast with the allegations of certain Slovak authors about a thousand years of Hungarian oppression, something that the Czech propaganda had exploited for the furtherance of its goals by skillfully planting those allegations into European public opinion. A number of Hungarian writers pointed out that if this were true there would not be even today Slovak settlements in the immediate vicinity of the Hungarian capital, where the Slovaks have been able to retain their ethnic identity undisturbed for all these centuries. Those settlements date back to the period following the Turkish occupation when the vacuum left behind by the massacre of the Hungarians was filled by Slovak, rather than Hungarian settlers.

The Awakening and Growth of
Slovak National Consciousness

The awakening of Slovak national consciousness occurred only later, in the 18th Century. Its impact was felt primarily in the use of the language. It was also closely linked to changes in the religious situation of the period. As a result of the religious movements of the 16th and 17th centuries, the Lutheran faith became dominant in Northern Hungary. Refugees streaming in from the Czech regions had brought with them the Czech literary language.

In connection with these events we must mention briefly the role of Peter Pazmany[13] who had a major impact on the subsequent development of the Slovak language and, thereby, of the Slovak culture. In 1553, Miklos Olah who had received a humanistic education in Italy became the Archbishop and Primate of Esztergom. He made Nagyszombat (Trnava) the center of the Counter-Reformation he had launched. Later, when Ferenc Forgacs, Bishop of Nyitra, became Archbishop of Esztergom, he summoned Peter Pazmany from the Jesuit seminary of Vagsellye to be his assistant.

Eventually, Pazmany became Forgacs's successor. He founded in 1635 a University at Nagyszombat (Trnva), and established in Vienna the renowned Pazmaneum where many priests of Slovak origin were trained up to the late 1910's. A printing shop at the University of Nagyszombat was placed at the disposal of the national minorities. In addition to the Hungarian publications, many Slovak and German books were printed there. About half as many publications were in the Slovak language as in Hungarian. Later, when the university was moved to Buda, in 1778, it continued to publish many Slovak books. One of them was *Slavy Dcera*, a strongly anti-Hungarian work by Jan Kollar.

Pazmany issued strict orders to the Slovak-speaking priests to preach to the Slovak population in their mother tongue. This, too, contributed greatly to the development of the Slovak literary language. One of Pazmany's successors arranged the publication of the Slovak edition of the *Cantus Catolicus*. Pazmany's Jesuits published the first books in the Midwestern Slovak dialect, rather than in Czech. The Czech publications (in *biblictina*) were intended to prevent the development of a separate Slovak language.

At this stage we can already see the beginnings of the future Slovak independence movements against the Czechs. The foundations for Anton Bernolak's efforts were laid more than a hundred years earlier by Peter Pazmany's Jesuits, thus greatly influencing the development of Slovak national consciousness.

The Hungarian national consciousness arose earlier than that of the other nationalities. It was manifested above all in the struggles against the oppressive policies of the Hapsburg Dynasty. Vienna had attempted to make German the official language, and in 1784, Joseph II succeeded in doing so. The Hungarian efforts to counter this measure came to fruition 60 years later in 1843-1844, when the renewal of the Hungarian language and literature were accomplished at the Diet of Pozsony and Hungarian was officially recognized as the language of the land. Even though this legislation was not aimed at any of the nationalities, it provoked considerable resentment among them.

Anton Bernolak, a Roman Catholic priest, in the late 1790s contributed to the creation of a unified Slovak literary language. The Slovak people can thank him not only for helping the Slovak literary language prevail over the Czech language but also for the tremendous boost this gave to the development of Slovak national consciousness. He is believed to have been one of the first to use the terms Slovak and Slovensko. It should be noted that Bernolak showed no hostility toward the Hungarian language, he even encouraged the Slovaks to learn Hungarian. He saw the real danger in the Czech language. Later, through the efforts of Ludovit Stur, the unified Slovak literary language emerged.

The ideas of the 18th century philosopher Johann Gottfried Herder had a major influence on Slovak national awakening. The same ideas were also fueling the Panslavic movement.

There commenced a strong incitement against Hungarians among the Slovak students at German universities. This is how Herder saw the future of the Slavs: "The Slavs will be liberated from their ancient dream, they will shed their ancient shackles and rule over their ancient lands from the Danube to the Moldova River."

These ideas prompted a very violent campaign of slander, directed by Vienna, to project a totally distorted image of the Hungarians before the world. Jan Kollar, a Slovak clergyman in Pest (Budapest), paints an even more enthusiastic picture of the glorious future of the Slovaks in his great poem, *Slavy dcera*. A few Slovak leaders, such as Ludovit Stur, Josef Hurban and Milan Hodza, offered their loyal services to Baron Haynau[14] who gave them several assignments. Following the defeat of the Revolution in 1849, they were rewarded by being placed under police surveillance. Stur suffered a nervous breakdown.

Slovak Grievances Against Hungary

The Slovak leaders summed up their grievances and demands in several petitions. The first petition, submitted March 28, 1848, in Liptoszentmiklos, Northern Hungary, contained demands pertaining to the use of language. The second, dated May 10, demanded a national assembly and the drawing of ethnic boundaries. However, the Slovak leaders failed to present this petition to the Hungarian govermnent. Unfortunately, the same fate befell Kossuth's proclamation of November 18, 1848, which the Hungarian authorities failed to publish.

On June 6, 1861, in Turocszentmarton, also in Northern Hungary, the Slovaks demanded establishment of a Slovak ethnic district (Okolie) where Slovak would be the **only** official language. They wanted territorial autonomy, just as they did in 1918 from the Czechs, which the Czechs have never granted to them.

The jealousy of the Czechs toward the Hungarians grew by leaps and bounds after the Austro-Hungarian Compromise of 1867. At the same time, the Slovaks were grieved by the emerging Hungarian nationalism. Thus there followed a natural convergence of Czech and Slovak sentiments.

In 1868, the Hungarian Parliament enacted the Nationalities Act, created by Ferenc Deak and Jozsef Eotvos, which was unparalleled in providing legislative protection of the rights of national minorities. By that time, however, the Slovak leaders no longer demanded the protection of minority rights, they wanted to establish a fully coequal nation within the Hungarian state. Because of their insistence on having all their demands met, the Slovak leaders refused to accept the Nationalities Act of 1868 as a basis for negotiations. Neither side was willing to compromise and this resulted in serious mistakes on both sides.

The Hungarians have stated countless times since then that the forced Magyarization did not serve the cause of good relations between Hungarians and Slovaks. Count Istvan Szechenyi -- hailed as "The Greatest Hungarian" -- said the desire for unity is of greater importance than the question of what language should be spoken. But the Hungarian political leadership of the time did not have historical foresight and subsequently the Hungarian people had to pay dearly for that shortcoming of their leaders. The leaders should have seen that their mistakes played into the hands of the very people, such as Masaryk and Benes, who did not care about Slovak or Hungarian interests, whose only goal was to destroy the Austro-Hungarian Monarchy.

There were plenty of mistakes and shortcomings. To name just a few, the closing of Slovak language secondary schools in Nagyroce, Turocszentmarton and Zniovaralja, or the banning of the Matica Slovenska. Laying the legislative basis of forced Magyarization and the policy of enforced assimilation were serious mistakes. However, even when the Hungarians admitted these mistakes, they always emphasized that the nation's universal system of law and order was equally extended to everybody. Thus, the courts passed judgment in an impartial manner, regardless of anyone's nationality. Hungary had no press censorship. There were no restrictions imposed on the economy. Everybody was free to engage in industry or commerce. That made possible the establishment of banks by the national minorities. Nor was there any discrimination in the social sphere: the burdens were shared equally by Hungarians and by the national minorities.

It should be noted that during the debate over the Nationalities Act and even after its enactment into law, there have been Slovak attempts to bridge over the differences. Here we should mention J.N.Bobula, editor of *Slovenske Noviny*, the Slovak language newspaper in Budapest, who said that instead of establishing ethnic districts (Okolie), as demanded in the 1861 memorandum of Turocszentmarton, the issue could be solved within the framework of county self-government whereby counties with a Slovak majority would come under Slovak administrative rule.[15]

Similarly, the 1895 Congress of National Minorities in Hungary, which produced a political program for the national minorities, also came out in favor of the county system. The Congress called for, in effect, total freedom for the non- Hungarian nationalities. The Slovaks were represented by Pavol Mudron. On the Hungarian side, mainly politicians of the Independence Party sought a compromise solution in 1870.[16]

This period witnessed emerging signs of conflict between the Czechs and Slovaks also. Aside from the struggles, already noted, to establish an independent Slovak literary language, there began economic and even social conflicts, albeit they remained below the surface for the time being. The roots of these conflicts can be traced to the growing strength of the Czech bourgeoisie after 1849. These conflicts became increasingly apparent following the Austro-Hungarian Compromise and, even more so, after 1918 when the Czechs assumed a leading role even in the economic life of the new Slovakia. More of that later.

The Concept of "Czechoslovakism" and the Creation of the Artificial Czechoslovak State

Czech-Hungarian relations have also deteriorated sharply after the failure of the 1871 attempts to reach an Austro-Czech Compromise. This, in turn, had an unfavorable impact on the Slovak-Hungarian relations as well.

It is noteworthy that in the course of the Austro-Czech negotiations no mention was made of any Slovak-Czech union. The Czechs then began spreading the idea of the so-called Czechoslovak concept which was to lead eventually to the notion of "Czechoslovakism." As it became increasingly obvious, this was a fictional notion but it proved to be an extraordinarily effective propaganda move in that fateful period.

Dr. Joseph Kirschbaum, the current Vice President of the Slovak World Congress, expressed this the most aptly: "Since 1918, Slovakia became known in European history as a part of Czechoslovakia... The goal of the Czech political parties, of the government and of exile groups was to dominate Slovakia and to assimilate the Slovak people. Therefore, the Slovak people was portrayed as a branch of the Czech nation, with Slovakia as an underdeveloped country which needs to be ruled by the Czechs."[17] Kirschbaum also quotes Professor Watson Kirkconnell who said: "One cannot emphasize strongly enough that there is no such creation as Czechoslovakia."[18]

Prior to World War I, one of the seemingly most effective arguments put forth by the Czechs was that a Czech-Slovak union would provide the best defense against German expansionism. Later on it became abundantly clear for all to see that this argument was just as empty as the notion of "Czechoslovakism."

In the early 1900s it had not yet occurred to the Czech leaders to destroy the Austro-Hungarian Monarchy. This is clear from a speech delivered by Thomas G. Masaryk in 1902 in Chicago: "The Czechs want a parliament for the Bohemian lands; they would like to

22

be as independent as the Hungarians; that is the goal of our struggle." No mention was made here of the destruction of the Monarchy. Nor did Masaryk say anything about territories that he was to demand 17 years later from Hungary, territories that became part of the new Czechoslovakia.[19]

In the subsequent years Thomas G. Masaryk and his chief collaborator, Eduard Benes, played a decisive role not only in determining the fate of Slovaks, Hungarians and Czechs but in the transformation of Europe as a whole. Ancestrally, Masaryk's father was Slovak, his mother was Czech. Benes was of Czech origin, General Stefanik, one of his chief collaborators, was of Slovak ancestry.

As early as February, 1916, Masaryk was trying to convince French Premier Aristide Briand that both France and England had vital security interests in the creation of an independent Czecho slovakia. He asserted that Pan-Germanism was spreading ever wider in the Austro-Hungarian Monarchy and that it could not be curbed without rearranging Central Europe. Such rearrangement requires the liberation of the oppressed national minorities, such as the Czechs, the Slovaks, the Croats, the Rumanians and the Poles. That would require, of course, the dismemberment of the Austro- Hungarian Monarchy but that would provide the strongest bastion against the Pan-German aspirations. Briand was very much impressed by this argument even though, up to that time, maintenance of the Austro-Hungarian Monarchy had been a cornerstone of French foreign policy.[20]

His success with the French, along with the support he was receiving from England, gave so much encouragement to Masaryk and his colleagues that they began planning their future policies based on a security system that was to be established by the great powers. It was to become apparent for all to see that this policy, built on quicksand, had been doomed to total failure. That, too, **demonstrates the validity of our thesis, stated in the Introduction, that the security of small nations dependent on the goodwill of great powers is illusory at best. The great powers, obeying the dictates of their own interests, will scrap any promised guarantees, even if enshrined into treaties, whenever it is in their interest to do so.**

The National Council of Czech Provinces was soon established. It was headquartered in Paris, with Benes serving as secretary general. A Czech National Army was also formed from prisoners of war and deserters. Later on this army had an important role in the propaganda campaign of Benes and his company.

In 1916-1917 Benes was constantly on the road, visiting London, Rome, Geneva, Zurich, Paris. He was setting up press bureaus everywhere to mold public opinion in support of his goals.

General Stefanik who was a citizen of France, was Benes' chief collaborator in Paris. Stefanik helped him establish a close relationship with journalists on the staff of major papers, such as *Le Temps, Paris Midi, Journal des Debats*. These papers played a major role in Benes' propaganda campaign.

The Slav Press Bureau in New York was also operating under Benes's direction. He credits this Bureau with winning the support of Senator Kenyon of Iowa, with very important consequences. In May 1917, Senator Kenyon introduced a Resolution calling for the establishment of an independent Czechoslovak state.

At the same time, the New York bureau was busy influencing public opinion with glowing accounts of the heroic deeds of the Czech Legion in Russia and its valiant dash through Siberia. General Syrovy who lost one eye in battle became an instant national hero. Some two decades later he was made Prime Minister of Czechoslovakia.

It goes without saying that Masaryk was the other great hero in America. On September 11, 1918, Lloyd George sent a congratulatory message to Masaryk, hailing the heroism of the Czech forces in Siberia. "We shall never forget the services rendered by the Czechoslovak forces in the struggle against despotism," said Lloyd George. Twenty years later, Neville Chamberlain called the Czechs, "a people about which we know nothing."

Franz Joseph, the emperor-king of the Austro-Hungarian Monarchy, died on November 21, 1916. He was succeeded by the well-intentioned Charles IV. France and England called on Austria and Hungary to seek a separate peace. The secret negotiations toward this end were carried out mostly in Switzerland and it is easy to understand that they caused deep concern among those who were moving full speed ahead toward the realization of the Czech political goals. Had the negotiations for a separate peace succeeded, the Czechs, who were striving for full independence, would have been forced to content themselves with some form of autonomy at best. It was the great good fortune of Benes and company that the Central Powers made many strategic mistakes and the peace efforts failed.

In the meantime Benes had lots of troubles with the Czech Army which was causing disturbances in France. The troops were quartered in barracks in a remote location. They were revolting because of the discomfort they had to suffer and, above all, on account of their uncertain legal status. Benes tried to salvage the delicate situation and took strict measures against the revolting troops.

By early 1918, Benes' popularity in Paris was declining. He was hated by many Czech soldiers. Some regarded him a traitor; he even had to deal with assassination attempts. In the end, though, Benes prevailed. The army, as noted before, performed a great service in helping to meet his political goals. Masaryk himself said that nothing would have been gained without the soldiers.

Getting back to the relationship between Czechs and Slovaks... as early as February, 1915, the American Slovak League agreed to a union between Czechs and Slovaks. However, there was no full agreement among the leaders of the Slovak National Party and the Slovak People's Party about the future of the Slovak people. Some wanted autonomy within Hungary, others advocated union with the Czechs. **The leaders of the Slovak People's Party met on October 30, 1918, in Turocszentmarton (Turciansky Sv.Martin), where Father Andrej Hlinka called for union with the Czechs. Thus, a new chapter was reached in the Slovak struggle for autonomy and independence.**

B.

In Defiance of President Wilson's Original Ideas Masaryk and Benes Are Busy Destroying the Austro-Hungarian Monarchy and Establishing Their Brainchild, Czechoslovakia

Prior to this move, on May 20, 1918, Masaryk signed an agreement in Pittsburgh with representives of American Slovak organizations, promising the Slovaks full autonomy in the new Czechoslovak state that was to be established. However, as noted before, the Czechs have never granted this autonomy. Masaryk also talked with American Ruthenian leaders, holding out the same promise of autonomy. Then, in Philadelphia, he made a separate pact about Ruthenian autonomy with Gregorij Zatkovic, leader of the Ruthenian American Council, even though Zatkovic had not been authorized to do so by the Ruthenian population of Subcarpathian Ruthenia. Subsequently, these agreements made by Masaryk were presented as legitimate documents at the Peace Conference.

By declaring Czechoslovak unity and full independence along with secession from Hungary, on October 30, 1918, in Turocszentmarton, the Slovak National Council tied its destiny to the policies of Benes. It is worth noting that one year later when Father Hlinka -- dodging Benes' spies as he arrived in great secrecy at the Paris Peace Conference -- told Stephen Bonsal, a friend of Colonel House, a close associate of President Wilson, that the Czech had doublecrossed the Slovaks into agreeing to the union. More on this later.

Meanwhile, diplomatic events had taken an interesting turn. In September, 1918, Austrian Foreign Minister Burian submitted a peace offer to the governments of the Entente powers. But it was not convincing. Instead of a thorough territorial rearrangement, the proposal only called for administrative reforms. According to these reforms, the empire was to have been divided into four regions:

26

Austria, Hungary, a South Slav region and a Polish region in Galicia.[21] This was too little and too late. The only remaining question was whether Vienna would be able to offer a new and substantially better proposal?

On September 2, 1918, President Wilson issued a declaration recognizing the Slovaks who were represented in the Czechoslovak National Council as *de facto* belligerents. On October 14 the Council became a provisional government. On October 28 the Czechoslovak Republic was proclaimed.

Masaryk who was in America at the time learned on October 6, 1918, of the latest German-Austrian peace offer. He at once began a feverish activity to nail down and make public immediately the Czech political goals.

Masaryk was not yet fully clear about Wilson's position. Wilson had proclaimed his Fourteen Points early in the year, on January 8, and they were based on the retention of the Austro-Hungarian Monarchy. He declared in the tenth point that "The peoples of Austria-Hungary... should be accorded the freest opportunity of autonomous development."

With adroit political skill, Masaryk wanted to make the most of the similarities between Czech political goals and American political traditions. He decided to draft a Czechoslovak Declaration of Independence on the pattern of the American Declaration of Independence. Writing in the newspaper *The Nation*, Masaryk said that the United States cannot accept the so-called Austrianism because that would contradict, even deny, the principles of the Declaration of Independence and the American ideals in general. He was fortunate to have Secretary of State Lansing share these views. Lansing was convinced that the Austro-Hungarian Monarchy must be dismembered and an independent Czech and Slovak state must be established.[22]

Wilson was still undecided about how to respond to peace feelers from Germany and Austria-Hungary. As he was drafting a reply, he summoned Colonel E.M.House, his closest friend and confidential adviser, seeking his counsel. Colonel House found Wilson's draft too moderate. Secretary of State Lansing was drawn into the process and he told the press about the new, jointly drafted reply.

The reply, strangely, did not mention Austria. That made Masaryk uneasy. His discomfort was aggravated by a report in *The New York Times* about the intention of the Austro-Hungarian cabinet to grant autonomy to the national minorities. On October 12, it was reported in the press that a new state would be formed from the

South Slav territories of Austria and that a proclamation was about to be issued granting the right to the various peoples in the empire to determine their own destiny.

Masaryk knew that he had to act immediately. He and his colleagues set out at once to draft the Czech Declaration of Independence. With feverish work, they completed the first draft by October 13. The finished product was ready the next day. Its main thrust was acceptance by the Czechs and Slovaks of the American principles as laid out by President Wilson.

Masaryk declared that the Czechoslovak state will be a republic whose citizens will be given full freedom of conscience, speech, press and assembly. The rights of the national minorities will be preserved and protected. He promised that the new state would participate in the rearrangement of Eastern Europe. He indicated that far reaching social reforms would be forthcoming. He stressed that according to the American principles, government derives its power from the will of the people and that this is in full accord with Czech democratic principles dating back to the time of Jan Huss. It is obvious from the foregoing how anxious Masaryk was to conform the declaration to the American principles.

In the meantime Masaryk learned that President Wilson was working on a reply to a new German note. He was under the impression that the Germans were anxious to end the war as soon as possible. They had given assurances to Wilson of their acceptance of the Fourteen Points, as well as subsequent declarations, even the required evacuation of disputed territories.

Masaryk went to work again. He had to act before Wilson responded to the German note. So on October 13, in addition to the Declaration of Independence, he was also drafting a memorandum pertaining to the new German note. He sent copies of the memorandum to Lansing, to Colonel House and to several diplomats of the allies.

In this memorandum Masaryk expressed his doubts regarding the German intentions and suggested several conditions for inclusion into the reply. But his most significant and perhaps strangest suggestion was that the Fourteen Points be revised. They have become obsolete, he wrote, and new terms of peace were required, foremost among them the recognition of Czechoslovakia.

Wilson's response to the German note was most decisive. He demanded absolute guarantees for the maintenance of the military superiority of the allies. He indicated that he would send a separate note to Austria-Hungary.

All the while, in Paris, Benes was also working feverishly. He called in Philippe Barthelot who was in charge of the political department of the French Foreign Ministry. Barthelot assured Benes that under no circumstances would the allies engage in separate negotiations with Austria-Hungary.

At Barthelot's urging Benes drafted a note regarding the conversion of the Czechoslovak National Council into the Provisional Government of Czechoslovakia.[23] He had the note delivered at once to French Foreign Minister Stephen Pichon. With Masaryk's approval which he had obtained earlier, Benes announced that the head of the new government and its Finance Minister would be Masaryk; Benes would become Foreign Minister, as well as Minister of Home Affairs, while Stefanik would be Minister of War.[24]

Benes' note was delivered in the French Foreign Ministry on October 14. Since the Czechoslovak Declaration of Independence was not yet proclaimed, Benes sent a letter to Masaryk to explain why his action had to be taken without delay.[25]

On October 13, King Charles IV of Hungary (Emperor Charles I of Austria) reached a momentous decision regarding the national minorities of Austria-Hungary. He ordered the drafting of a Manifesto. It was discussed in Crown Council in Vienna on October 15. The ruler wished to emphasize that the Manifesto would be but the first step toward turning Austria into a federated state.[26]

On October 16 U.S. Secretary of State Lansing takes delivery of the Czechoslovak Declaration of Independence. At the same time, Benes' proclamation is being studied in Paris. In Vienna, officials are busy drafting the Manifesto and it is being approved by the Monarch. According to the Manifesto, Austria was to become a federated state, with each nationality establishing its own state in its own territory.[27]

The Manifesto had one crucial shortcoming. It failed to deal with the national minorities in Hungary. Thus, a federal transformation could have been carried out only in the Austrian half of the Empire. Meanwhile in America, the anti-Austrian propaganda campaign was moving full steam ahead. Masaryk received valuable support from his friend Ira E. Bennett, Editor of *The Washington Post*. He and Professor H.A. Miller of Oberlin College, another friend of Masaryk, were instrumental in the propaganda effort.

Masaryk wanted to have the Declaration of Independence published before the proclamation of the Austrian Manifesto lest it be overshadowed by the Austrian document. Eventually, both appeared in the press on the same day, October 18. Ira E. Bennett very skillfully juxtaposed the two documents, accompanied by an editorial entitled Freedom and Forgery. President Wilson's response, dated October 19, appeared in the American press on the next day. It dispelled all hopes for safeguarding the territorial integrity of the Austro-Hungarian Monarchy -- hopes which were based on the tenth of Wilson's Fourteen Points. Wilson explained in his reply that certain events had caused him to change his position, foremost among them the recognition of the Czechoslovak National Council as a *de facto* belligerent.

Lansing, in a private memorandum on September 7 urged that Germany and Austria-Hungary be treated differently. "Let us not give the impression that we intend to destroy the German Empire, and let us give the impression that we intend to end forever the Austro-Hungarian Empire," wrote Lansing.[28]

On October 19 the Czech politicians rejected Charles's Manifesto and declared their full solidarity with the Czech revolutionaries in the West.

The most significant declaration to be issued by the Slovaks was the resolution, noted earlier, which was approved on October 30 in Turocszentmarton, proclaiming Czechoslovak unity and declaring that "The Slovak nation is part of the Czechoslovak nation... therefore we demand for the Czechoslovak nation the absolute right of self-determination, based on full independence."[29]

Hungarian historians have noted repeatedly that this document was not approved by every Slovak leader. Thus, the Slovak National Council at its meeting in Eperjes (Presov) decided not to secede from Hungary and demanded a plebiscite. Furthermore, the Slovak National Assembly in Kassa (Kosice) also called for a solution within a Hungarian framework.

Representatives of the Slovak National Party, the Slovak Peoples Party and the Slovak Social Democratic Party formed a Slovak National Council under the chairmanship of Matus Dula, with Karol A. Medvecky serving as its Secretary.[30]

On October 23, 1918, the Hungarian Parliament met for the last time. On October 31 the Hungarian cabinet resigned and the Hungarian National Council which had been formed some time earlier under the chairmanship of Count Mihaly Karolyi came to power. On November 16 the Hungarian Republic was declared, Parliament was dissolved and Mihaly Karolyi became the chief of state.

A Hungarian government representative traveled to Prague to negotiate with the Czech National Committee about a peaceful solution for the Slovak question so that the territorial integrity of the state may be preserved.[31]

Karolyi himself, in a message to the Slovak National Council, emphasized the Slovaks' right of self-determination but none of his attempts succeeded. The Hungarian churches, too, supported Karolyi's efforts. Archbishop Janos Csernoch of Esztergom, of Slovak descent himself, reminded the Slovak clergy of the dangers the Slovaks would face at hands of the anticlerical Czech leaders. He predicted that the Czechs would force the Slovaks to surrender their ethnic identity. The Archbishop pointed to his own example of a Slovak clergyman having been elevated to the highest ecclesiastical post in Hungary. Lutheran Bishop Sandor Raffay addressed a similar appeal to the Slovak ministers.

Father Hlinka replied to the Archbishop on behalf of the Slovak clergy. He said that they support the decision of the Slovak National Council. Personally, Hlinka added, he endorses the establishment of Czechoslovakia, which he sees as the dawn of the fulfillment of ancient Slovak dreams and a protection against a thousand years of injustice.[32]

There arose military conflicts between the Karolyi government and the Czechoslovaks. The armistice signed with the Austro-Hungarian Monarchy on November 3, 1918 in Padua did not authorize the Czech legions to cross the Hungarian border. The armistice did not touch upon the question of national boundaries and did not give the Czech troops the right to occupy Hungarian territory.

On November 7, 1918, in Belgrade, Mihaly Karolyi reached a military agreement with French General Louis Franchet d'Esperey, the head of the Entente mission. According to this agreement, all Hungarian territories, with the exception of Croatia and Slovenia, were to remain under Hungarian administration.[33] The Prague government did not accept this agreement.

Karolyi requested Franchet d'Esperey to forbid the Czechoslovak government to send troops to Hungarian territory at least until the Peace Conference. Benes, however, did everything in his power to occupy as much land as possible in order to create a *fait accompli* before the Peace Conference. When V. Srobar, a Slovak politician, declared that "He who first puts his hands on Slovakia will get to keep it," he just echoed Benes' oft-voiced opinion that Slovakia must be occupied and a *fait accompli* must be created.[34]

French Prime Minister Clemenceau ignored Karolyi's protestations and sided with Benes. Even though his troops have already crossed the line of demarcation in Slovakia, Benes wanted to lend this move at least an appearance of legitimacy and once again he turned to Paris. Clemenceau agreed to place the Czechoslovak troops in France under the command of Marshal Foch, supreme commander of the French forces, so that -- as requested by Benes -- they may be available "If need be, to maintain order and halt the Bolshevik expansion."[35]

Lieutenant Colonel Vyx, chairman of the Armistice Control Commission in Belgrade, was visiting Budapest on December 3 and sent a note to Karolyi, demanding the immediate withdrawal of his troops from Slovak territory. Karolyi rejected this demand. This was followed by talks between Hungarian Minister of War Albert Bartha and Milan Hodza, Czechoslovak Ambassador in Budapest, about a line of demarcation between the two countries. We will discuss these negotiations in greater detail in Part Two. But it should be noted here that Hodza's position was based largely on the same ethnic principles that were to be agreed upon at the time of the so-called Vienna Decision of 1938.[36]

The peace negotiations at Trianon (Versailles) might have taken a different turn and the subsequent events also might have turned out in radically different fashion if Benes had not repudiated and recalled Hodza. But Benes had already gained the approval of the Western powers for his plan to condemn Hungary at Trianon without giving her a chance to defend herself. The damage so brought was beyond description. In the Hungarian view it matched or exceeded the tragedy of the lost battle of Mohacs in 1526, which led to the country's Turkish occupation

In a legislative act passed on March 19, 1919 Hungary recognized the autonomy of Slovenska Krajina as the Slovak territory was called. This meant, in effect, recognition of an ethnic district, called Okolie, originally demanded back in 1861.[37] Later, in June 1920, the government of Hungarian Prime Minister Karoly Huszar proposed autonomy for Slovakia, with an independent national assembly, with Slovak ministers in the national government and proportional Slovak representation in the Hungarian national assembly.[38]

The Slovaks did not accept these far reaching proposals. In the Hungarian viewpoint, the rejection was due to pressure from the Czech political leaders. As a result of the Czechs' worldwide anti-Hungarian propaganda campaign, the question could no longer be solved within the framework of the Hungarian state. This propaganda campaign destroyed the last opportunity for a mutually agreed upon settlement. And the same shortsighted, selfish policies of Benes were to drive subsequently both the Slovaks and the Hungarians into the embrace of Hitler's Germany.

Returning to the controversy over the line of demarcation, it is worth noting that on March 19, 1919 Franchet d'Esperey instructed General de Lobit to inform the Hungarian government of the February 26 decision of the Peace Conference in this matter. At the same time, he instructed General Gondrecourt to deliver the Entente Powers' *demarche* to Mihaly Karolyi. He also ordered General de Lobit to extend the neutral zone in Galicia to the south to include the city of Munkacs (Mukachevo), even though this move had not been authorized by the Peace Conference.[39] He requested therefore Clemenceau's approval after the fact.[40]

Colonal Yates, the British Military Attache in Belgrade, met Karolyi on March 15. Karolyi registered his protest against the one-sided French instructions to change the line of demarcation in favor of the Czechoslovaks.

On March 20, Lieutenant Colonel Vyx was instructed to deliver a Memorandum from the Entente powers to the Hungarian government and to demand a reply within 48 hours.[41] The Memorandum stated, among others, that the Peace Conference has given Czechoslovakia permission to have a common border with Rumania across Subcarpathian Ruthenia.

The Vyx Memorandum came to be known as the Vyx Ultimatum. The Berinkey government (Karolyi having become President of the Republic in the meantime, replaced by Denes Berinkey as Prime Minister) found the Ultimatum unacceptable, rejected it, and resigned.[42]

On March 21, a Revolutionary Government Council was established under Sandor Garbai. But the real power was in the hands of Foreign Commissar Bela Kun. On March 24 the new government sent a note to the Entente powers, which created a heated debate among them. British Prime Minister Lloyd George was concerned whether Vyx had made it clear that the boundaries of the neutral zone will have no impact on the final borders because it was essential that the defeated countries must not be thrust into the arms of the Bolsheviks. He proposed sending a mission to Budapest, headed by General Ian Smuts. Smuts promised that the new line of demarcation will not influence the drawing of the final borders and that he would suggest that the representatives of Hungary be invited to the Peace Conference.[43]

Meanwhile, General Franchet d'Esperey began organizing Czech and Rumanian troops for an attack against the Hungarian Communist government, even though this was not expressly authorized by the Entente powers. Rumanian, then Czech troops crossed the line of demarcation. Their goal was to overthrow the dictatorship of the proletariat. In May, the Rumanians reached the Tisza river and the Czechs occupied Subcarpathian Ruthenia. In the North, however, the Hungarian forces were advancing.[44]

In Vienna, in the meantime, an Anti-Bolshevik Committee was formed by Count Istvan Bethlen and Count Pal Teleki, and it sought closer ties with the Entente powers.

On May 5, 1919, Count Gyula Karolyi formed a government in Arad, which soon moved on to Szeged where it was reorganized. Dezso Abraham became Prime Miniszter, Count Pal Teleki Foreign Minister and Admiral Miklos Horthy Minister of War.

On June 15, Clemenceau sent an ultimatum to Budapest, outlining the final boundaries and demanding that the Hungarian troops be withdrawn within four days beyond those boundaries. The Communist government accepted the ultimatum and, to the great jubilation of the Czech troops, evacuated the Northern territories.[45]

On June 28, 1919, the Treaty of Versailles with Germany was signed in Paris. Wilson and Lloyd George left Paris, leaving Clemenceau in charge. It was his idea to overthrow the Hungarian dictatorship of the proletariat with Czech, Rumanian and Yugoslav troops. But the French plan was thwarted by the reluctance of the other Entente powers.

The Hungarian government launched one more military attack to liberate the region East of the river Tisza but it was halted by a Rumanian counterattack.[46]

At the end of July, the Peace Conference declared that it will sign a Peace Treaty with Hungary only if the dictatorship of the proletariat is replaced by a government acceptable to the Entente powers. With the Rumanian forces approaching Budapest, the Communist government resigned on August 1 and was replaced by a new government formed by Gyula Peidl.

On August 3, the Rumanian troops entered Budapest. Two days later, in an ultimatum, the Rumanians issued new armistice conditions which were unacceptable because their acceptance would have led to total economic ruin for Hungary. On August 6, the counterrevolutionary group of Istvan Friedrich forced the resignation of the Peidl government. Archduke Joseph Hapsburg who had been named earlier by King Charles IV as *homo regius* assumed the position of Regent and appointed Istvan Friedrich as Prime Minister.

Since the Entente powers were unable to force the Rumanians to leave Hungary, they sent -- under British and American pressure -- Sir George Russell Clerk, a British diplomat, to Bucharest to deliver an ultimatum drafted by Prime Minister Arthur Balfour, ordering a Rumanian withdrawal from Hungary. Clerk was then sent to Budapest to negotiate with the political parties about the formation of a coalition government.[47]

On November 15, the Entente sent another forceful ultimatum to Rumania. One day before the delivery of this ultimatum, on November 14, the Rumanian forces left Budapest. Clerk informed Admiral Horthy that his troops may enter Budapest to maintain order.

On November 22, Karoly Huszar formed a new government which was invited by the Entente powers, on December 1, to send its representatives to the Peace Conference. In January, 1920, Admiral Horthy had several talks in Budapest with British High Commissioner Thomas Hohler and General Reginald Gordon. Hohler's reports to London reflected a very favorable impression of Horthy.

On March 1, 1920, the National Assembly elected Miklos Horthy Regent of Hungary.

The Paris Peace Conference and the Treaty of Trianon

The Hungarian nation faced the Peace Conference with the worst expectations. It did not trust the great powers because it saw how impotent they were in controlling the Rumanian forces which were illegally in Hungary and how difficult it was for them to force the Rumanians to evacuate Budapest.

It was under such circumstances that the Hungarian delegation, led by Count Albert Apponyi left for Paris to receive the draft of the Peace Treaty. The delegation submitted countless notes to the Peace Conference, only to be ignored for the most part. In a major address, Apponyi proposed a plebiscite for the disputed territories so that their inhabitants might determine their own destiny. Czechoslovakia, Rumania and Yugoslavia issued a joint note to reject the Hungarian remarks.

The Hungarian political leadership was trying to gain British support to revise the borders as defined in the draft Peace Treaty before it was signed. At Horthy's request, in a report to Lord Curzon, the Foreign Secretary, Hohler pointed out the injustice of the territorial decisions. Lord Curzon was asked to intervene before signing the Peace Treaty. But the British diplomats found it was too late to carry out any revisions.

Suddenly, France became interested in the fate of Hungary. Premier Millerand and General Secretary Paleologue of the Foreign Ministry were considering a new, rather significant idea. They were thinking about establishing a Central European entity which would have centered on Hungary. The French began negotiating with representatives of the Hungarian government and these negotiations included a serious discussion of revising the borders which had been proposed in the Peace Treaty.

More of this in Part Two. Also in Part Two we will discuss the talks between Horthy and Fouchet, the French envoy, which included

-- in Fouchet's words -- "rectification of the ethnic and economic injustices of the Peace Treaty." But these attempts came too late because, on May 6, 1920, the Supreme Council of the Peace Conference declared the text of the Hungarian Peace Treaty final. Thus, the Hungarian government had no choice but to sign the Peace Treaty, no matter how grievous its conditions were.

The signing took place on June 4, 1920, in the Palais Trianon.[48] There is no question that the conditions of the Peace Treaty were imposed to the benefit of the victors and to the detriment of defeated Hungary which was not allowed to speak up in her own defense at the peace table.

There is a sharp difference between the Czechoslovak and Hungarian interpretations of the Peace Treaty. Czechoslovakia considered the Trianon borders correct and just because they represented the final triumph of its no-holds-barred propaganda campaign for that very end. Benes and his circle whose efforts resulted in the treaty resisted every attempt even for its slightest revision, except for two occasions when revision would have paid off to the benefit of Czechoslovakia. More on that later.

According to Professor Yeshayahu Jelinek, every inch the Slovaks received in Paris as a result of Benes' efforts was considered by them as "sacred patrimony of the Slovak nation, the gift of the Allmighty, land soaked in the blood and sweat of the sons of Slovakia. While the Hungarian patriots were mourning the loss of parts of their bleeding, amputated homeland, the Slovaks were singing odes of joy. No wonder because the territorial growth proved to be most profitable, particularly with the acquisition of the intensively cultivated agricultural land in the South, which provided plenty of food and employment opportunities."[49]

Hungarians, regardless of gender, age, religion or social position, regarded the Treaty of Trianon a peace dictate, rather than a peace treaty and considered it totally unjust and untenable as far as the Hungarian nation was concerned. It is a historical fact that the Peace Treaty became the source of constant bickering. While Czechoslovakia regarded it inviolable and its foreign policy was aimed at maintaining the status quo, the cornerstone of the Hungarian foreign policy was to work for peaceful revision of those provisions of the Peace Treaty which were considered unjust by Hungary. Foremost among these efforts was the negotiated, peaceful return of adjacent territories overwhelmingly inhabited by Hungarians.

It became clear that the drafters of the Peace Treaty paid **no attention to the thought of somehow bridging the differences between Hungary and Czechoslovakia, eliminating the mutual distrust so that a conciliatory atmosphere could be created which would prevent the future development of hostile tensions. The great powers would have been able to accomplish this. It was within their power to exert the required pressure but they applied it only against the vanquished. Unfortunately, political foresight had been pushed aside by the immediate interests of the great powers, especially of France.**

All the Slovaks were able to perceive at the time that the agreements of Pittsburgh and Turocszentmarton have come to fruition. Czechoslovak national unity and self-determination have been accomplished. At the same time, Hungarians were denied the right to determine their own destiny.

It took a while for the Slovaks to realize that, in fact, they have accomplished neither. The only major result of their effort was that, thanks to the policies of Benes, after a thousand years of coexistence they seceded from the Hungarian state.

The Slovaks Begin Their Efforts for Autonomy

The Czech political leaders have never regarded the Slovaks as their equals. They even denied the existence of a distinct Slovak nation. As early as 1921, Masaryk declared, "There is no Slovak nation; it has been invented by Hungarian propaganda."[50]

Some of the Slovaks have started to realize that the Czechs are not going to honor the agreements of Pittsburgh and Turocszentmarton.[51] This realization led to disintegration of Slovak unity. Some Slovaks approved the Czech policies of political integration. Others were demanding Slovak national autonomy within Czechoslovakia as provided in the agreements of Pittsburgh and Turocszentmarton. Andrej Hlinka, a Roman Catholic clergyman, was the foremost among those urging autonomy right from the beginning. Later on he was to demand full national independence.

A diary entry by an outsider -- Stephen Bonsal, confidant of President Wilson and Colonel House -- sheds the sharpest light on the treatment that Father Hlinka, this highly respected Slovak leader, received at the hands of Benes.

After a three-month-long difficult journey, dodging Benes' intelligence agents, Father Hlinka and his entourage reached Paris in September, 1919. Even though the Pittsburgh Agreement had promised the Slovaks that they could attend the Peace Conference alongside the Czechs, Father Hlinka and his entourage had to travel surreptitiously to Paris where they hid in a monastery. In great secrecy, they called on Stephen Bonsal, carrying a letter of introduction from General Stefanik of the Czech Legion. Stefanik requested that Father Hlinka be received either by President Wilson or his adviser, Colonel House. Bonsal briefed Colonel House who then authorized Bonsal to talk with Father Hlinka.

Bonsal assured Father Hlinka that he would listen carefully to what he had to say and relay it to Colonel House but, he said, it is doubtful that anything could be done because the terms of the Peace

Treaty had been settled already. Father Hlinka replied that this is exactly what he had been afraid would happen and this is why Benes was trying to keep him away from Paris. He came, he said, to protest Benes' misrepresentations at the Peace Conference.

Referring to the assassination of General Stefanik, Father Hlinka said that if the general had not been silenced, everybody would have paid attention to him because the general had fought in Siberia and on the Italian front not only for his own people but for the Entente powers as well. Father Hlinka noted that General Stefanik was allegedly killed in an airplane crash. But this was not true, he said, because the plane from Italy had reached its destination and landed safely. As General Stefanik emerged from the plane, he was shot to death by soldiers waiting for him. According to Father Hlinka, it was Benes' diabolic idea to send the assassins to the airport.

On a later occasion Bonsal confronted Father Hlinka with the fact that he and Stefanik had been advocating a union with Prague. A contrite Father Hlinka admitted that he had done so because the Czechs pretended to be understanding. They had fought together in war, they wanted to remain together in peace as well. He compared the situtaion to a trial marriage. The Czechs had promised, he said, that if the union would fail both parties could go on their separate paths. But in three months -- in fact after three weeks -- he said, the Czechs showed their true colors. **In this short time, Father Hlinka added, the Slovaks had suffered more at the hands of the aggressive Czechs than they had under a thousand years of Hungarian rule.**

Father Hlinka declared that he now really understood the old Hungarian saying that "There is no life outside Hungary." He called Benes an ambitious scoundrel who wants to incorporate even Cesky Tesin. Bonsal remarked at this point that a union with the Hungarians would run counter to the then popular concept of ethnic solidarity. Father Hlinka's response was that the Slovaks cannot and would not want to mix with the Hungarians but from an economic and especially from a religious point of view, they would rather go with the Hungarians than with the irreligious and free-thinking Czechs who, as it has become clear, fear neither God nor man.

"The Slovaks," Father Hlinka continued, **had lived side-by-side with the Hungarians for a thousand years and the traditional links have been reinforced by the close proximity of the two nations. All the Slovak rivers flow toward the Hungarian Great Plains and all the roads go to Budapest. On the other hand, he**

40

added, the Carpathian mountains separate the Slovaks from Prague."[52]

Father Hlinka then reminded Bonsal that in the Pittsburgh Agreement Masaryk had guaranteed Slovakia autonomy and promised that the Slovaks would be represented at the Peace Conference. He also noted that Slovakia had become a colony and the Czechs treat the Slovaks as if they were African natives.

Some time later Bonsal learned that -- apparently acting on reports from informers -- the Parisian police picked up Father Hlinka and his entourage and took them to a railroad station where they were put on a train headed for the East.

Bonsal also recorded in his memoirs that in 1938, Czechoslovak troops took Father Hlinka from his home, threw him into jail where he was cruelly mistreated. Not long afterward he died from the injuries received in captivity. (It is difficult at this point not to be reminded of the similar fate that befell Janos Esterhazy.)

Shortly before his death, Father Hlinka was given by American Slovaks the original copy of the Pittsburgh Agreement. **According to Bonsal, Father Hlinka was accurate when he said that the Agreement had promised the Slovaks autonomy and a seat at the Peace Conference.** Even in his final words, the dying Father Hlinka was demanding that those promises be honored.[53]

The example of Father Hlinka demonstrates most clearly that it was not the ethnic affinity, nor the romanticized notion of common past and ancestry that had brought together the Czechs and Slovaks in 1918. Rather, both were driven by their separate interests as leaders of the two peoples perceived those interests.

The Czechs would not have been able to establish a significant state without the Slovaks because they were surrounded by much stronger nations. At the same time, the Slovaks, too, needed the support of the Czechs because they could not have become an independent state on their own. And it had never occured to the Slovaks who wanted full equality with the Czechs that their seeking assistance from the Czechs would stimulate in the Czechs an increased sense of superiority which would become more and more evident with the passage of time.

The Czechoslovak government began early on to assert its authority in Slovakia by establishing various state agencies. Their eagerness in the endeavor led to serious mistakes which only served to sharpen the conflict with the Slovaks. The Prague government instructed Vavro Srobar on November 4, 1919, to form the first Slovak government. Meanwhile, however, Srobar joined the Prague government as Minister for Slovak Affairs. Srobar first bypassed then dissolved the Slovak National Council and established a new body which became fully subordinated to the Prague government.[54]

There is no doubt that the moves of the Prague government were inspired by the goal of assimilating the Slovak people through the artificial concept of Czechoslovak national unity. In this respect, Joseph M. Kirschbaum quotes the British historian C.A.Macartney who wrote: "The fact remains that the (Czechoslovak) government has been obliged more often than not to rule Slovakia against the wishes of most of its inhabitants, maintaining itself only by the expediency of restricting the powers of the self-governing bodies to within the narrowest possible limits, of filling the seats designated for 'experts' with its own nominees, utilizing freely weapons of censorship and police supervision."[55]

The economic and social policies of the Prague government were also in conflict with Slovak interests. About one-third of Slovak industrial enterprises were shut down. Heavy industry and the textile industry were the hardest hit. This led to a massive emigration of the unemployed.

Between 1919 and 1938, some 220,000 people out of a population of 3,300,000 emigrated. In addition, every year another 220,000 Slovak seasonal workers sought employment abroad. During the same period, 200,000 Czechs moved into Slovakia to occupy the most important and highest-paying positions.[56]

In 1927, all the banks and savings associations were placed under state control. The Prague government placed its own people in charge of the financial institutions.

The taxation policies of the Czechoslovak government also had a severe impact on Slovakia. Slovakia contributed 15% of all tax revenues but its share of the national budget amounted to a mere 6%. In addition to that, many taxes that had been abolished in the Czech part of the country, remained in effect in Slovakia.

Consumer statistics show that the annual per capita ratio in Slovakia amounted to 15 kilograms of meat, 2 kilograms of lard, 14 kilograms of sugar and 89 Czech Crown's worth of tobacco. The Czech population received twice as much in consumer goods while the people in Subcarpathian Ruthenia were even worse off than the Slovaks.[57]

The Czech oppressive policies were equally felt in the areas of politics and culture as well. The concept of so-called

"Czechoslovakism" served these policies very well. Invoking the slogan of "one nation," Czech officeholders kept squeezing the Slovaks out of government offices. The same held true in other white-collar fields. Even the armed forces did not escape discrimination. In 1930, the Czechoslovak Army had 140 Czech generals and one general of Slovak descent.

Neglect of the Slovak language was another means of maintaining Czech superiority. As author Hans Keller notes, "In the institutes of higher learning, it occurred to none of the many Czech teachers to consider the Slovak language of equal rank with the Czech, even though it is regarded by many otstanding Slav linguists as one of the most beautiful and clearest dialects. One need not be a linguist," Keller adds, "to recognize that Slovak is a much more musical language, softer and more pleasant to listen to than the hard-to-pronounce Czech with its crowding of countless consonants.[58]

An article in the Slovak Communist newspaper *Dav* launched a sharp attack on Czech cultural imperialism for refusing to recognize the existence of an independent Slovak culture. The author condemned "Czechoslovakism" in all its manifestations, not the least its advocates who counseled Slovak authors that instead of writing in the Slovak language, they should represent Czech literature and Czech culture before world opinion. The *Dav* article also stated that the ideology of forced unification harms the Czechs as much as the Slovaks.[59]

The growing influx of Czech workers into Slovakia made the situation increasingly worse. **The Slovaks were seeking political means to remedy their grievances. A number of groups came into being** because the Slovaks were unable to present a united front. A small faction was willing to accept the policy of centralization and go along with Prague. But this was rejected by the vast majority which went on to form several political parties.

The Slovak Peoples Party, under the leadership of Father Hlinka, was the largest. It embraced some 80 percent of the Slovak people. The party was first organized on December 18, 1918, at Father Hlinka's parish in Rozsahegy (Ruzomberok). Many Roman Catholic priests participated in this movement. Ultimately, the Slovak Peoples Party became the rallying point of the efforts for self-rule.

Another group met earlier, on October 18, 1918, in Eperjes (Presov) to form the Slovak National Council. Later this group met in Kassa (Kosice) to declare Slovakia's independence.

Yet another group met in Krakow, Poland, on May 26, 1921, to form a Slovak Revolutionary Government under the leadership of Francis Jehlicka. Members of this group were forced into exile and settled in Geneva. Jehlicka was anti-Czech but understood the feelings of the Hungarians. Later he went to the United States where he cooperated with Slovak organizations working for Slovak self-rule.

The Slovak Peoples Party was continuously bombarding Prague with its demands for self-rule. Representative Vojtech Tuka introduced a bill to this effect in the Czechoslovak legislature but it was defeated.

After a while, the Czechoslovak government changed its tactics in an effort to calm the sharpening conflict. It invited several Slovak and Sudeten German activists to join the government. Prague disarmed the Slovaks by granting a measure of self-government at the local level, as well as two seats in the national government. As a result, things went fairly smoothly from 1927 to 1929. But after two years, the cooperation fell apart and the Slovak Peoples Party left the central government.

This move was triggered by an article, entitled "Vacuum Juris," by Slovak Peoples Party Representative Vojtech Tuka in the newspaper *Slovak*, on January 1, 1928. He explained that the cooperation between Czechs and Slovaks, which was called for by the Turocszentmarton Declaration of October 30, 1918, had come to nothing after ten years, therefore the Slovaks had every right to freely determine their destiny. The Prague government found the article offensive, it had Tuka's parliamentary immunity suspended, the author was tried and received a 15 year jail sentence. With Tuka's imprisonment, the Slovak independence movement was silenced for ten years.

The Prague government resorted to increasingly violent means to suppress the opposition which was becoming more vocal every day. In total defiance of the democratic principles it enacted new laws, such as the 1923 and 1933 acts for the defense of the republic, which made it impossible to give voice to the grievances of the nationalities. Censorship was introduced, opposition newspapers were banned. The *Slovak, Narodny Noviny, Rude Pravo* and the Hungarian-language *Pragai Magyar Hirlap* were among those most frequently silenced. The government obtained legislative authorization to dissolve political parties it deemed as dangerous. Even the threat of sending in the army was employed to intimidate the opposition.

The Prague government accomplished only one result with these openly antidemocratic measures. **It pushed the Slovaks ever closer to the other oppressed and embittered minorities. Instead of pursuing more conciliatory policies which might have prevented the disintegration of the republic, Prague's brutal, provocative acts inevitably led to the collapse of Czechoslovakia.**[60]

There was at least one flagrant incident where the machinations of the Prague government backfired. On August 15, 1933, a celebration at Nyitra (Nitra) marked the 1,100th anniversary of the first Christian church established by Pribina. The government was also represented at the ceremonies.

Although the celebration was intended to demonstrate Czechoslovak solidarity, Father Hlinka was not invited. However, he surreptitiously joined the crowd and received a warm ovation when recognized by the people. Hodza, who was also present, had the good political sense to demand that Father Hlinka be allowed to speak. He even reached out his arms to help the aged priest to the rostrum. At this point, the government's representatives disappeared from the scene. This gesture, however, helped Hodza regain his reputation as a Slovak patriot.[61]

The Struggle of National Minorities in Czechoslovakia for Their Rights

The Sudeten Germans were the first national minority to take a stand against the Prague government. Their sheer numbers lent the Sudeten Germans sufficient weight to be heard. According to the official statistics of 1921, the so-called "united Czechoslovak nation" constituted 65.5 percent of the total population. Next came the Germans with 23.5 percent, then the Hungarians with 5.7 percent.

There were two reasons why the clout of the Germans and Hungarians exceeded that of the other nationalities. They lived in contiguous blocks and in close proximity to their mother countries. This proximity to the mother country gave an immense clout to the Sudeten Germans, especially with the rapidly growing power of Germany, accompanied by its interest in the fate of the Sudeten German people.

The Sudeten Germans fielded five parties in the 1920 parliamentary elections and emerged with great strength. Of the 281 seats in Parliament, the Sudeten Germans won 72 and they numbered 37 in the 142 member Senate. At the very first session, the German legislators declared that Czechoslovakia was created against their will and they would not relinquish their right of self-determination. The Slovak Peoples Party followed suit by a similar statement and subsequently the Hungarian opposition parties also declared that the Hungarians in Czechoslovakia were separated from Hungary against their will.[62]

In 1925, the Sudeten Germans declared once again that they do not recognize the peace treaties signed in Versailles, Saint-Germain and Trianon. On April 30, 1930, 80 Sudeten German, Hungarian, Ruthenian and Polish members of the Czechoslovak Parliament signed a petition demanding the establishment of a parliamentary committee to study the problems of national minorities and make recommendations for their solution. The Czech parties opposed this measure and it was not even considered. **Benes dismissed every opportunity for** a serious consideration of the problem of the minorities and for seeking a negotiated solution. He showed willingness to do so only when he felt his very existence threatened.

In 1935, Konrad Henlein united the Sudeten German parties. The new, unified party was named Sudeten German Party. The new party made an outstanding showing in the 1935 elections. Henlein was invited to London to explain his program. It demanded the granting of rights guaranteed by the Czechoslovak constitution and it condemned Pangermanism which the program called just as dangerous as Panslavism. The program stated that the Sudeten Germans want to remain loyal to a Czechoslovak state which allows them to exercise their constitutional rights.

Soon, the Czechs came to realize that the Sudeten German problem was fraught with great dangers. A local Czech organization, in Reichenberg (Liberec), passed a resolution in 1937, calling for the dissolution of the Sudeten German Party. Meanwhile, the Sudeten Germans sought to establish ever closer ties with the other oppressed nationalities, such as the Slovaks, Hungarians, Poles and Ruthenians. In September, 1938, this rapprochement resulted in the formation of a united front against the Czechs.

Earlier, on November 10, 1936, Prime Minister Milan Hodza declared that he wanted to find a solution for the problems of national minorities, as demanded by the so-called activist ministers who were representing minority groups in the government. On February 18, 1937, Hodza signed an agreement with the ministers. The Czech press hailed the agreement as a major accomplishment. The agreement dealt with cultural questions and contained various promises for the future but it did nothing to improve the condition of the Sudeten Germans, the Slovaks, or any of the other nationalities.

Henlein, in a speech delivered in Aussig (Usti), reiterated the basic demands of the Sudeten Germans:

Transformation of Czechoslovakia into a state where the rights of the national minorities are guaranteed.

Autonomy which is not in conflict with the unity of the state.

Recognition of the several nationality groups and providing for their free development within the state.

Protection of the rights of the national minorities and rectifying the grievances suffered by the Sudeten Germans since 1918.[63]

Hodza asked for a year's delay so that he might prepare a detailed response to the Sudeten German demands.

Benes, in his Christmas message of 1937, also promised to rectify the grievances but that, too, remained an empty promise. Barely had Benes delivered his Christmas message when Minister of Justice Ivan Derer, a pro-Czech Slovak member of the government, called Father Hlinka and his friends rascals.[64] In his reply to Derer, Father Hlinka voiced shock over hearing such insults from the mouth of the Minister of Justice. There were demands that the minister be hailed to court.

The Slovak demands were summed up in 33 points and submitted to Hodza who, at the end of February, 1938, invited Father Hlinka, as he had also invited German, Hungarian and Polish leaders. In keeping with his familiar tactics, Hodza gave more promises. He offered the Slovaks two more seats in the Prague goverment, those of Minister of Postal Affairs and Minister without Portfolio. Father Hlinka said in an interview that his conditions for joining the government included the demand to incorporate into the constitution the autonomy of Slovakia, as promised in the Pittsburgh Agreement.[65]

The year 1938 started on a sour note for Benes. Rudolf Beran, president of the Czech Agrarian Party, created quite a stir by proposing in the New Year's Day edition of the newspaper *Venkov* that both the Sudeten German Party and the Slovak Peoples Party should be invited to participate in the Prague government.[66] The paper also carried on the same day an interview with Henlein who said that looking back over the last 20 years, one will find a very large number of dissatisfied German, Slovak, Hungarian and Polish people living in Czechoslovakia. It is within the power of the Czechs, Henlein said, to make serious proposals which would lead to mutual understanding.

The Prague government's response was another strong attack against the advocates of Sudeten German, Slovak and Ruthenian autonomy and against the Hungarian and Polish national minorities.

The Sudeten German Party sent a delegation to Father Hlinka at Rozsahegy (Ruzomberek) to make plans for cooperation and to designate liaisons between the two parties.[67]

The delegation then traveled to Budapest to talk about cooperation with the United Hungarian Party in Slovakia. (More on that in Part Two.) The talks included plans for a joint Slovak-Hungarian-German demonstration in Pozsony (Bratislava) on the twentieth anniversary of the Pittsburgh Agreement.

On March 15, 1938, President Benes met Father Tiso, leader of the Slovak Peoples Party. **Benes refused to recognize the Pittsburgh Agreement.**

Janos Esterhazy was also engaged in talks with the Slovak Peoples Party. And Father Tiso, who visited Budapest in late May to attend the Eucharistic Congress, met Undersecretary Tibor Pataky in the Hungarian Prime Minister's office. Contemporary sources termed Father Tiso's behavior as "reserved."[68]

The leaders of the national minorities were astonished by the Prague government's failure to take their grievances and demands seriously. The promises made to the so-called activists, which were made in response to a miniscule part of their demands, remained largely just that one year later. In February, 1938, Karol Sidor, a leading politician of the Slovak Peoples Party, held a meeting with Janos Esterhazy of the United Hungarian Party, Konrad Henlein, of the Sudeten German Party and Pjescak of the Ruthenian Autonomist Agrarian Party. On the twentieth anniversary of the Pittsburgh Agreement, the three parties were demanding autonomy for the nationalities they were representing. Esterhazy, in his statement, recalled that the Slovaks and Hungarians had been sharing the same goals and destiny for a thousand years.[69]

On April 8, 1938, the official newspaper of the Hungarian opposition summed up the Hungarian demands (for a detailed account, see Part Two). Once again, the report emphasized the promise of autonomy for the Slovaks and Ruthenians.[70]

Esterhazy was negotiating with Polish Foreign Minister Jozef Beck, also. He outlined the Hungarian government's promises for Slovak self-rule within the Hungarian state, with a Slovak governor, parliament and army. Sidor of the Slovak Peoples Party was in Warsaw when he learned of these plans and expressed the desire to negotiate with Esterhazy instead of the Hungarian government.[71]

On June 17, 1938, Esterhazy, acting on behalf of the Hungarian government, once again made an offer of autonomy in the event the circumstances should be changed. This autonomy would be along the lines of the Croatian model as it existed in the Austro-Hungarian Monarchy, with separate parliament, army and administration. Esterhazy emphasized that under no circumstances would Hungary offer less than Czechoslovakia.[72]

Meanwhile a delegation of Slovak-Americans arrived in Slovakia to meet Father Hlinka. They had brought along the original document of the Pittsburgh Agreement. The delegation also visited

Prague where it had talks with President Benes and Foreign Minister Kamill Krofta. From Prague it traveled to Pozsony (Bratislava) to attend the Congress of the Slovak Peoples Party on June 4-5, 1938.

The Congress speakers were demanding autonomy for Slovakia.[73] An estimated 100,000 people demonstrated in support of self-rule. Esterhazy sent a telegram expressing his good wishes to the Slovaks in their struggle for autonomy. Hodza was also present at the Congress and, in response to questions by the leader of the Slovak-American delegation, he threw cold water on the Slovak hopes.

The Western Powers Become Involved in the Problem of Czechoslovakia's National Minorities

The British and French governments had been watching with growing concern the increasing rigidity of Prague's attitude, despite several diplomatic attempts to urge Benes to moderate his position, as the European situation was becoming extremely delicate. The total rigidity of Benes's policies had the inevitable effect of pushing Henlein and the advocates of Slovak autonomy into the arms of Hitler's Germany.[74]

The British government decided to send Lord Runciman to serve as an impartial mediator. He arrived in Prague on August 3, 1938. His chief assignment was to find a solution to the Sudeten German problem. The other nationalities, too, wanted to be heard by Lord Runciman. He was briefed by Slovak, Hungarian, Polish and Ruthenian leaders about the situation of their respective nationalities.

K.H. Frank, a Sudeten German representative in the Prague Parliament, assured one of the Hungarian political leaders that the Sudeten Germans "will only accept an agreement which automatically includes the Hungarians, Slovaks and Poles."[75]

In the meantime, **the *Little Entente*[76] met in Bled, Yugoslavia, on August 21-22.** Hungary, even though not a member of the *Little Entente*, was also represented at the conference which agreed to full parity in armaments between Hungary, Rumania and Yugoslavia. The three states also agreed about the problems of their national minorities. However, the armament and nationalities disputes between Hungary and Czechoslovakia were not settled.[77]

The Bled conference coincided with **Admiral Horthy's state visit to Germany.** The Hungarian chief of state accepted the German invitation back in April, 1938. He was accompanied by the Prime Minister and the ministers of Defense and Foreign Affairs.

The Germans took umbrage at Hungary's participation in the Bled conference, which interfered with Hitler's plans to invade Czechoslovakia. **The Germans tried to persuade the Hungarians to march into Slovakia at the same time the German army was to invade Czechoslovakia and to participate in the liquidation of Czechoslovakia. The Hungarians refused to go along, even though Hitler told them that they could have all the Czechoslovak territory they wanted if they would participate in the invasion.**[78 79 80]

The Hungarian leaders lost Hitler's sympathies with their reluctance to go along with his demands. Later on, this had a very noticeable effect.

The Prague government pursued delaying tactics in its negotiations with Lord Runciman. It presented one plan after another. One plan, based on the Swiss model, proposed a cantonal program to organize the Sudeten German territories into four administrative districts. The Sudeten German Party rejected the plan. Yet another plan was rejected by the advocates of Slovak autonomy. This plan would have divided Slovakia, too, into administrative districts.

On August 29, 1938, the situation further deteriorated with a Prague demonstration against Lord Runciman.[81]

Hungary displayed a rather passive attitude in these troubled times. The tone of the Hungarian press was much more moderate, compared with the German *Volkischer Beobachter*, for example.[82]

On September 8, 1938, the leaders of the German, Hungarian, Slovak and Polish minorities held a joint meeting. The Sudeten Germans raised the question of whether the other national minorities would be willing to join the struggle for the fulfillment of their, the Germans', demands. Father Tiso was the first to reply, saying that the Slovaks are even more radical because since 1920, they had been demanding the transformation of Czechoslovakia into a federated state. It is only natural, he said, that the Slovaks want to march side-by-side with the other nationalities. After comments by leaders of the Hungarian and Polish minorities, **the meeting unanimously approved the demand for the reorganization of the Czechoslovak state as soon as possible.**[83]

Leaders of the Slovak Peoples Party requested an appointment with Lord Runciman to brief him about the Slovak problems. The appointment was not granted on the grounds that he had been requested by the Czechoslovak government and the Sudeten German Party only to help solve their disputes. Therefore, Lord Runciman was not willing to mediate between the Czechs and Slovaks without Prague's approval.

The Slovak Peoples Party felt that if the Sudeten Germans are entitled to autonomy, the Slovaks have the same right to demand it. **In a 13-page memorandum, Father Tiso called the concept of the "Czechoslovak Nation" fiction. There is no such thing, he said, just as there is no such thing as a Czech-Polish nation.**

Leaders of the Ruthenian parties turned to Hodza with a similar request on September 1, also demanding autonomy for the Ruthenian people.[84]

In Prague, the autonomists established a common front. The Sudeten German Party, the Slovak Peoples Party, the United Hungarian Party and the Polish Union Committe held a joint session under the chairmanship of K.H. Frank.

Benes, in a speech on September 10, called for moderation and understanding.

An article entitled "Our Patience, Too, Has Reached Its End" in the September 11 edition of *Slovak*, official organ of the Slovak Peoples Party, reminded Benes that in 1935, when he ran for President, he received the Party's vote. As loyal citizens, the Slovaks did everything in their power to persuade the Czechoslovak leaders to take the necessary steps for changing the Constitution. The article noted that the time has come to do so. It said that **the Slovaks are demanding their rights and their freedoms, employment opportunities, in one word, their future.** They no longer believed in promises. The patience that has lasted 20 years has reached the outermost limits of human endurance.[85]

The Czechoslovak government declared a state of emergency in 14 counties. The Sudeten German Party was dissolved, its offices were seized by the police, its documents were confiscated. The government initiated judicial proceedings against Henlein.[86] The party was dissolved because, on September 15, Henlein demanded that the Sudeten German territories be transferred to Germany. Ninety-five percent of the Sudeten Germans were in favor of that move and Henlein was unable to persuade them to remain in Czechoslovakia. Henlein met Lord Runciman and told him that the events of the last days had removed any basis for further negotiations. **Lord Runciman returned to England.**[87]

On September 15, 1938, before Lord Runciman's departure was announced, an article entitled "Letter to Runciman" appeared in the *Popolo d'Italia*, probably by Mussolini. The article pointed out that in addition to the Sudeten German problem, there is also a Hungarian, Slovak and Polish problem in Czechoslovakia. The Peace Treaty of Versailles did not restore historic Bohemia. Instead, it created an artificial state which carried the seeds of its disintegration from the moment of its birth. The author of the article expressed the hope that Lord Runciman would suggest to Benes to hold a plebiscite, not only for the Sudeten Germans but for all nationalities which request it.[88]

At about that period, an article in the French weekly, *Gringoire*, stated that there is no such thing as a Czechoslovak nation and Czechoslovakia is nothing but a political artifact.[89]

Mussolini made several speeches about the Czechoslovak problem in Trieste, Treviso, Padua and Verona.

The Meetings at Berchtesgaden and Godesberg
as Preludes to the Munich Conference

Events began moving at a faster pace. **The British Prime Minister met Hitler in Berchtesgaden.**[90] There was intense diplomatic activity everywhere. The British and French governments were engaged in consultations. The British Minister in Prague told Esterhazy that the Hungarians will receive far fewer concessions than the Poles.[91] Hungarian Prime Minister Bela Imredy, in a speech at Kaposvar, spoke of the problems of the Hungarian minority in Czechoslovakia. Meanwhile, the Czechoslovak government declared another state of emergency.

Marshal Herman Goring, the German Prime Minister, stressed before the Hungarian Minister in Berlin that "the right of self-determination for the Hungarian minority in Czechoslovakia should be demanded most forcefully and emphatically." He said, the Hungarians should "provoke armed incidents, strikes; should disobey military induction orders, because only incidents of this magnitude would draw the Western powers's attention to the Hungarian demands." Goring also suggested that the Hungarians should "persuade the Slovaks to act likewise and demand autonomy." The Hungarian Minister reported that "Goring has apparently detected a measure of reluctance in our attitude so far."[92]

The two-faced attitude of the Germans was amply demonstrated by a report received by the Hungarian Foreign Ministry from confidential sources. According to this report, Goring who had constantly been inciting the Hungarians had told the Rumanian minister in Berlin that Germany does not wish to see Hungary become too strong, nor would it help Hungary toward that end. Germany, said Goring, is willing to give every assurance to Rumania and Yugoslavia against any and all Hungarian designs on them, but only if they remain neutral when or if Hungary attacks Czechoslovakia, their partner in the *Little Entente*.[93]

The Hungarian Minister in Prague delivered a note to the Foreign Ministry, relaying the Hungarian government's demand that at the negotiating table the Hungarians in Czechoslovakia be treated the same way as the Sudeten Germans. The Polish Minister in London told of a similar demand by his government to the Czechoslovak government.[94]

The British government promised in a note that at the appropriate time, it will duly consider the Hungarian position and noted that it is aware of the condition of the Hungarian minority in Czechoslovakia.[95]

Prior to the **Hitler-Chamberlain meeting in Godesberg** on September 15, Hungarian Prime Minister Imredy and Foreign Minister Kanya visited Hitler. Hitler brought up the Hungarians' indecisive attitude in the current critical times. He stressed that he will not bring up the Hungarian claims for Slovak and Ruthenian territories, unless the Hungarian government undertakes to play an active role in the dismemberment of Czechoslovakia.[96]

Imredy and Kanya requested 14 days to think it over. Hitler, in an aggressive manner, forced the Hungarian statesmen to follow and act only according to Hitler's timetable which served only his interests. The Hungarians, with their hesitation and their failure to send troops to the Hungarian-inhabited territories of Slovakia, as the Poles had done in Teschen, forfeited their claims for Slovakia and Ruthenia as a whole and also lost Hitler's sympathy.[97]

At the second Godesberg meeting, on September 23, Hitler endorsed the right of self-determination for the Hungarian and Polish minorities. Prague ordered general mobilization. The Hodza government resigned. The United Hungarian Party, in a message to the Hungarian population of Czechoslovakia, called for calm.[98] Benes did likewise in a radio address. But he added, "We shall fight if we must."[99]

On September 23, Father Tiso went to Prague to meet Benes. The Slovaks had clearly two different attitudes toward the Hungarians. While Sidor was giving pro-Czech statements, Father Tiso summed up in three points the Slovak demands in the event Slovakia was to be returned to Hungary. These were: central executive authority and the official use of the Slovak language in Slovakia; separate legislative authority, and proportionate share of revenues and expenditures. Foreign Minister Kanya informed Father Tiso that the Hungarian government was willing to accede to the Slovak demands. This had reassured him and he asked Kanya not to consider his call on Benes a sign of distrust.[100]

Benes and General Syrovy, his new Prime Minister, tried to prevent the transfer of the Sudeten German territories to Germany, even at the cost of a European war. But the French and British assistance failed to materialize, as has any help from the Soviet Union and Benes' castles in the sand collapsed.

The Munich Four Power Conference
and Its Consequences

The threatening European situation led to the convening of the Four Power Conference of Munich on September 29, 1938. The four powers -- Britain, France, Germany and Italy -- were represented by their chiefs of state. As a result of the Conference, the Sudeten German territories were transferred to Germany. In the Hungarian and Polish questions, the Conference decided to convene again if the governments involved could not solve their disputes within three months.[101]

After the conclusion of the Munich conference, Poland did not wait until Prague would be ready to meet its demands. It sent an ultimatum to Prague with a 14 hour deadline to transfer Teschen to Poland. The ultimatum served its purpose and the Polish troops occupied Teschen. Thus both Germany and Poland resorted to the threat of force to acquire the Sudeten German territories and Teschen, respectively.

Hungary did not follow these two examples in the hope that its claims, which it considered just, would be satisfied in a peaceful manner. Hungary asked for self-determination and a plebiscite from the Western democracies. The West had given Hungary credit for this tolerant behavior (more on this in Part Two) but little else. Thus Hungary was being pushed more and more into the arms of the totalitarian powers.

The Hungarian government launched a feverish diplomatic activity. On October 3, it sent a sharply worded note to the Czechoslovak Foreign Minister and proposed that representatives of the two governments begin negotiations on October 6. On the eve of the negotiations, the Hungarian Minister in London sent a message to Foreign Minister Kanya. He said, among others, "It goes without saying that Britain does not, as it can not, doubt the moral justification of our demands, but in the course of the current direct talks between Hungary and Czechoslovakia, Britain will be, at most, a sympathetic mediator, but it will not exert any pressure."[102]

On October 5, Czechoslovak Prime Minister Syrovy announced on the radio that **President Benes has resigned. Three weeks later, in great secrecy, Benes fled to London by way of Rumania.**

On October 6, the Slovak Peoples Party invited the other Slovak and Ruthenian parties to **a conference at Zsolna (Zilina, Sillen).** The conference **reached an important decision: it declared Slovakia's autonomy.** On November 22, in Prague, this decision was incorporated into the Czechoslovak Constitution.

Hungarian-Czechoslovak Negotiations in Komarom (Komarno)

Meanwhile, the Hungarian-Czechoslovak direct talks began on October 9, 1938, in Komarom (Komarno). The Hungarian delegation included Foreign Minister Kalman Kanya, Count Pal Teleki, Minister of Religious Affairs and Public Education, undersecretaries Tibor Pechy and Tibor Pataky, and Janos Wettstein, the Hungarian Minister in Prague. The Czechoslovak government was represented by Father Jozef Tiso, Prime Minister of Slovakia, Dr. Ferdinand Durcansky, Justice Minister of Slovakia, and Ambassador Dr. Ivan Krno.

Foreign Minister Kanya raised the question, whether the delegation on the other side of the table represented the Czechoslovak government in Prague or the autonomous government of Slovakia? The Hungarian delegation remarked repeatedly that the Czechoslovak side kept postponing the conference. Kanya wanted to know whether these postponements had anything to do with the report broadcast by Radio Pozsony (Bratislava) that Durcansky had flown to visit Hitler? Father Tiso replied that he was not aware of Durcansky's trip.

Father Tiso and his colleagues must have been familiar with Hitler's latest plans to turn Slovakia into a satellite state. That would explain their rigid attitude and refusal to accept more than 10 percent of the Hungarian territorial demands. Therefore, four days later, on October 13, the Hungarian delegation declared the conference terminated and requested the four Munich powers to settle Hungary's territorial claims against Czechoslovakia. Hungarian diplomatic representatives in Berlin, Rome and London were immediately informed of this decision.

During the Hungarian-Czechoslovak conference, Editor Franz Karmasin of the German newspaper *Grenzbote*, who was also leader of the *Karpatendeutsche Partei* and later of the *Deutsche Partei*,

60

was present in Komarom as an observer. Some thought he was a Nazi spy. Through Seyss-Inquart, the German governor of Vienna, Karmasin arranged a meeting between Goring and Durcansky. Durcansky briefed Goring of the Slovak political goals and the Hungarian demands.[103] Czechoslovak Foreign Minister Chvalkovsky visited Berlin on October 13. His and Durcansky's visits had undoubtedly influenced the attitude of the Czechoslovak delegation in Komarom.

On October 10, Janos Esterhazy declared that it would be a grave mistake to incorporate Slovakia into Hungary. Next day, in an interview, Esterhazy emphasized that even though the territories with an overwhelmingly Hungarian population should be immediately and unconditionally transferred to Hungary, the Hungarian nation has the warmest sympathy toward the Slovak and Carpatho-Ukrainian efforts for autonomy.[104]

Several representatives of the United Hungarian Party, including Janos Esterhazy, were in Komarom during the conference to assist the Hungarian delegation. Prior to the termination of the conference, the Hungarian National Council in Slovakia sent a memorandum to Father Tiso, Kanya and the Ruthenian leaders, demanding a seat at the conference table. It was signed, among others by Dr. Bela Szilassy, member of the Czechoslovak Senate, Janos Esterhazy, and Andor Jaross, leader of the United Hungarian Party.[105]

The Hungarian demands represented 14,150 square kilometers of land and an overwhelmingly Hungarian population of 1,090,000. The territory included 12 of the 13 towns and 812 of the 830 villages which were given to Czechoslovakia in 1918, where 77.9 percent of the population was Hungarian.[106]

After the termination of the Komarom conference, both sides began a diplomatic competition for the favors of the great powers. Following his talks with Goring, Durcansky met the Italian consul in Pozsony (Bratislava), asking him to arrange for Father Tiso and himself a meeting in Rome to outline the Slovak attitude towards Hungary. However, the Italian government did not wish to receive the two men because such a meeting would have only delayed the settlement of the Hungarian demands.[107]

Hitler and his Foreign Minister Ribbentrop received Czechoslovak Foreign Minister Chvalkovsky. Hitler urged a prompt solution for the Hungarian problem. Diplomatic observers in Berlin had the impression that the German pressure on Chvalkovsky was not very forceful. The Czechoslovak Foreign Minister assured Berlin that his government would pay closer attention to the wishes of Germany.[108]

Father Tiso sent emissaries to Warsaw and Zagreb to secure Polish and Yugoslav support for the Slovak position.[109]

The Hungarian government sent former Prime Minister Kalman Daranyi to Berlin and Istvan Csaky, a high official of the Foreign Ministry, to Rome. The reason Daranyi was chosen for the Berlin mission was that following the Bled conference of the *Little Entente* powers which Hungary also attended, Prime Minister Imredy and Foreign Minister Kanya lost the confidence of Hitler. Daranyi announced that Hungary would hew more closely to the German line, would leave the League of Nations and would join the Anti-Comintern Pact.[110]

A map Daranyi had with him showed the territories claimed by Hungary. The essence of those claims was that areas with a pure Hungarian population would be transferred to Hungary. The areas with mixed population would be grouped into districts, with each district deciding by plebiscite under British supervision about its destiny.

Daranyi reported Imredy by telephone that Ribbentrop had prepared a rough sketch, which came to be known as the Ribbentrop Line, and presented it to the Czechoslovak Foreign Minister. Daranyi also reported that he had been told to drop the idea of another Four Power Conference and resume direct talks with the Czechoslovak government.

Csaky flew to Rome to inform Mussolini and Foreign Minister Ciano of the Hungarian demands. He hinted that the Germans were favoring Czechoslovakia, therefore Hungary would like to bring the issue before the Four Power Conference. Ciano was agreeable but, out of deference to the Germans, the proposal had to be dropped.[111] Subsequently, Hungary requested Italian-German arbitration in Western Slovakia and Italian-German-Polish arbitration in Eastern Slovakia.[112]

Ribbentrop telephoned Ciano to tell him that he was opposed to the Four Power Conference as requested by Daranyi.[113] A few days later, however, the Germans reversed their position and recommended a Four Power Conference. According to Ciano, Ribbentrop was reluctant to go along with the arbitration because it would have revealed his anti-Hungarian position.[114]

There ensued exchanges of notes between Budapest and Prague and various proposals were made. Finally, when it became clear that they could not reach an agreement, both governments agreed to accept German-Italian arbitration.[115]

The Hungarian Foreign Minister instructed the Hungarian Minister in Rome to persuade Ciano to agree to arbitration. In the event the German or the Italian government were to refuse to agree to arbitration, the Hungarian government was prepared to turn to the four great powers.[116]

The French government was reluctant to interfere in Central European affairs. When the question of German-Italian arbitration arose, nobody charged that the Western powers were intentionally excluded.[117] According to Ciano, the British Ambassador stated that "even though his government would not object to a Four Power Conference, it would much prefer arbitration by the Axis Powers."[118]

Ribbentrop went to Rome ostensibly to discuss the territorial issues with Ciano. However, his main goal was to persuade Mussolini to agree to a German-Italian-Japanese tripartite military pact. Should the *Duce* agree to the tripartite pact, the Germans would relax their rigid attitude toward a proposed common border between Poland and Hungary in Subcarpathian Ruthenia.[119] The Germans regarded the idea of a common Polish-Hungarian border as a plot against Germany. This feeling was fueled by the French press which, to the annoyance of the Germans, promoted this notion.

Even though Ciano managed to persuade Ribbentrop to drop the so-called Ribbentrop Line and to transfer the disputed towns to Hungary, Ribbentrop's hostility towards the Hungarians was quite obvious to the Italian Foreign Minister.[120]

A delegation from the United Hungarian Party, led by Janos Esterhazy, also went to Rome to brief Ciano about the problems. Esterhazy demanded cultural and religious rights for the Hungarians who were to remain in Slovakia after the arbitration.[121]

Czechoslovak Minister Jan Masaryk met Foreign Office Undersecretary Lord Halifax on October 26 in London and reported subsequently that the Undersecratary did not object to the German-Italian arbitration.[122]

Lacroix, the French Minister in Prague, told Foreign Minister Chvalkovsky that his government does not intend to take part in the arbitration.[123] It was largely the lack of interest displayed by the Western powers that led Chvalkovsky to steer his government toward calling for German-Italian arbitration.

On October 30, German Foreign Ministry Undersecretary Weizsacker outlined before the French and Polish ministers and the

British Charge d'Affaires the plan for German-Italian arbitration. Neither the British nor the French government objected.[124]

Ciano, citing the British agreement, among others, demanded most forcefully that Ribbentrop agree to arbitration.[125]

The Hungarian government notified the Czechoslovak government in a note that it has requested the great powers to arbitrate, and it called upon the Czechoslovak government to do likewise within 24 hours.[126]

The Hungarian delegation was satisfied with the overall outcome. Foreign Minister Kanya thanked Esterhazy and his colleagues for their great efforts on behalf of the Hungarian minority in Czechoslovakia. Prime Minister Imredy spoke on the radio, thanking the Axis Powers for their great contribution. He emphasized that the Vienna Decision had provided the conditions necessary for a peaceful coexistence between Hungary and Czechoslovakia.

On November 12, 1938, the Hungarian Parliament enacted the Vienna Decision into law.

In Part Two, we will take a closer look at the Hungarian views of the Vienna Decision.

Slovakia Declares Its Independence

In the months that followed, the tension increased between Pozsony (Bratislava) and Prague. Hitler wanted to take advantage of this situation by arranging a coup d'etat which would force the Slovaks to ask for his help, thus giving him a pretext to send the German Army to Slovakia. Weizsacker writes in his memoirs that Father Tiso knew all too well that once the Germans are invited to enter the country, they would never leave.[144]

Hitler summoned Father Tiso to Berlin. While in Hitler's presence, Ribbentrop handed him a Slovak Declaration of Independence and asked Father Tiso to read it on the radio. Father Tiso declined on the ground that such a move would be in violation of his country's constitutional requirements.

Before long Father Tiso realized, however, that Slovakia was in danger of being split up and divided among its neighbors or incorporated as a protectorate into Germany. **The Slovak leaders therefore decided to secede from Czechoslovakia and establish an independent Slovak state.**[145] **This was unanimously approved by the Slovak Parliament on March 14, 1939.**[146]

Berlin offered military assistance to the new Slovak state but this was declined by Pozsony (Bratislava) because the situation in the country was quiet. The Slovak leaders also felt reassured when **on March 15 Hungary and Poland recognized Slovakia's independence.**

A few days later, accompanied by Ribbentrop and General Keitel, Hitler went to Vienna. Father Tiso and Durcansky were also in Vienna. They were initially received by Ribbentrop and Keitel only. **Father Tiso** was ready to depart when Keitel started making military demands on him. Eventually, he was **persuaded by Hitler to agree to a treaty of mutual defense with Germany**.

After the Slovak Parliament took note of the guarantees offered by Hitler, Father Tiso signed the treaty on March 18. In a

secret protocol accompanying the treaty, Hitler managed to secure
certain privileges for the German armed forces, greatly confining
Slovak sovereignty. Later on, these privileges opened the way for all
kinds of abuse.[147]

C.

Bohemia Becomes A German Protectorate

In the meantime, the Germans marched into Prague. In order to give this move a veneer of legitimacy, Emil Hacha, who became Benes's successor in the presidency, and Chvalkovsky were summoned to Berlin. In a meeting attended by Goring, Ribbentrop and Keitel, Hitler told Hacha that because nothing had changed since the January 22, 1939, meeting with Chvalkovsky, he, Hitler, was going to occupy Czechoslovakia. He called on Hacha to sign a proclamation requesting the establishment of a German protectorate.

Hacha wanted to obtain his government's approval first. Goring and Ribbentrop began threatening Hacha. Goring said that he would turn Prague into rubble unless Hacha puts his signature on the request.[148]

Hacha became ill from the excitement and a doctor was called. Finally, around four in the morning, **Hacha and Chvalkovsky signed the declaration which placed the Czech people under the protection of the German Empire.**[149]

Hitler's promise of protection proved to be worthless. Hungarian troops which occupied Subcarpathian Ruthenia on March 14, marched into Eastern Slovakia on March 23. These events taught the Slovaks the worthlessness of their mutual defense treaty with Germany.

Within a short period, Slovakia was recognized by 27 governments, including its neighboring states and the Vatican

Later on when Berlin demanded that Slovakia join in the war on Poland and hinted at the return of territories in Northern Slovakia, which were annexed by Poland in 1938, the Slovak government was unable to refuse.[150]

Certain Slovak authors talk about two political lines that had developed under the growing German pressure in the coming months.

One was represented by Father Tiso, the chief of state, the other by Dr. Vojtech Tuka, the Prime Minister. According to this view, Father Tiso tried to maintain a distance between Slovak politics and Nazi ideology. Dr. Tuka, on the other hand, was very much aware of Slovakia's dependence on Germany, therefore he was not in favor of taking any stand against the Germans.

Dr. Durcansky and Dr. Kirschbaum, Secretary General of the Slovak Hlinka Peoples Party, were Father Tiso's closest collaborators. The Germans did not trust Father Tiso and his circle. In 1940, they summoned him to Salzburg and told him that he must get rid of Durcansky and Kirschbaum.

Dr. Kirschbaum was sent to Rome. Later he was placed in charge of the Slovak legation in Berne. He and Dr. Arved Grebert, his press attache, were trying to persuade the Western powers that when it comes to the postwar political rearrangement of Europe they should be aware of the fact that the idea of a Czechoslovak nation is nothing but fiction and should keep in mind the needs of the independent Slovak nation. However, Benes's emigre organization kept thwarting these efforts.[151]

Let us turn now to the political machinations of Benes, particularly the period after his resignation on October 5, 1938 and his escape to England. He was replaced by General Jan Syrovy as provisional president. Chvalkovsky, whose ties to the Axis powers were well known, became Foreign Minister. On November 30, Syrovy convened the National Assembly to elect a new President. Emil Hacha, president of the Supreme Administrative Court, was chosen chief of state for a seven year term. Agrarian Party leader Rudolf Beran formed the new government, with Karel Sidor, a politician of Slovak origin, as his deputy

On March 14, 1939, Czechoslovakia split into two parts, with Bohemia and Moravia becoming German protectorates.

Further Political Machinations of Benes

In London, Chamberlain gave Benes a cool reception. This atmosphere did not change until the outbreak of World War Two and, above all, the fall of Chamberlain. Following the collapse of France, Winston Churchill, the new Prime Minister, gave his recognition on July 23, 1940, to the Czechoslovak Provisional Government in London. Once again, **the British press portrayed Czechoslovakia as the model of European democracy. At the same time, it was not mentioned in the papers that after a twenty-year struggle the Slovak people, long proclaimed by Benes as a "sister nation," took the very first opportunity to declare its independence from the Czechs.**

As soon as the atmosphere turned in his favor, the exiled Benes started plotting again. He came up with the idea of a Polish-Czech confederation which was to play a pivotal role in postwar Central Europe. There were many obstacles in the path of this idea, not the least being the traditional animosity between the Poles and the Russians, or the problem of Teschen.

Following the outbreak of the German-Soviet war, in June 1941, the Soviet Union recognized the Czechoslovak Provisional Government in London and signed with it a treaty of mutual assistance against Germany. The Soviet Union also recognized Czechoslovakia's borders as they existed before the Munich Pact. On August 5, 1942, British Foreign Minister Anthony Eden declared that his government no longer considered itself bound by the Munich Pact. Also in London, a Czechoslovak Council of State was formed and it declared Benes's presidency still valid, despite the election of a new president in 1938.

In the United States, Benes faced a more difficult situation. The American Slovaks regarded Hodza, who had broken with Benes, as the leader. And President Roosevelt was coming under increasing Soviet influence.

In 1942, Benes attempted to win the support of the American government with a major article in the journal, *Foreign Affairs*, entitled "The Organization of Postwar Europe." Presenting himself as "one of the foremost authorities" in this question, Benes outlined the basic principles -- as he saw them -- for the postwar organization of Central Europe. Foremost among these were the restoration of twenty-year-old Czechoslovakia and the status quo as it existed before Munich. **Subsequently, Benes turned more and more to the Soviet Union. He went to Moscow and, on December 12, 1943, signed an agreement of friendship and mutual assistance.**[152] The notes of Jaromyr Smutny, Benes's presidential chief of staff, provide a clear picture of the Moscow talks. They show that Benes had indeed offered his services to Stalin in a fashion that gave Stalin license to interfere in Czechoslovakia's domestic affairs. Benes, in fact, wanted to use the Soviets to intimidate Slovaks who had taken an anti-Soviet stand. In Moscow, **he met General Secretary Klement Gottwald of the Czechoslovak Communist Party. They agreed on a solution to the question of national minorities. The solution was to expel the German and the Hungarian minorities and thus create a new national state.**[153]

Benes was opposed to any cooperation among the small nations. Thus, he opposed the so-called Hodza Plan which had envisioned a Czech, Slovak and Polish federation. He also opposed Churchill's idea of a South German Federation which would have included Bavaria, Austria, Wurttemberg and Hungary (the latter was opposed by Stalin, too). The only plan which, for various reasons, Benes did not oppose was Sikorsky's proposal for a Polish-Czechoslovak Confederation. However, that plan was rejected by Stalin.

Instead of promoting cooperation among the small nations, Benes was advocating the greatest possible Soviet involvement in European affairs. He conducted an intense propaganda campaign for that end, trying to convince everybody that the Soviet Union was becoming increasingly democratic and would respect the independence of the small nations.

"The Slovak National Uprising"
Benes Returns under the Protection of the Soviet Army

According to Slovak authors, Benes joined forces with a handful of third-rate Slovak politicians, living in Slovakia or abroad, in order to achieve his political goals. **With Moscow's support, in August 1944, they organized the so-called Slovak National Uprising. Benes intent for the uprising was to demonstrate the Slovaks' desire to be reunited with the Czechs.**

Only a few Slovaks, mainly Communists or members of the old Agrarian and Social Democratic parties took part in the uprising, according to the Slovak authors. Large numbers of Soviet partizans were parachuted into Slovakia to support the uprising. False rumors were spread to mislead the Slovaks into believing that Tiso had been killed and the German Army has invaded Slovakia.

The main purpose of this move was to open the way for the Red Army and to incite the Slovak population against the Germans. The "uprising" began with the killing of a German general and his entourage of 27, including women and children, who were traveling by private train from Bucharest to Berlin.

Some 30,000 Slovaks fell victim to the massacre. They had belonged to various political fractions. The "rebels" claimed the victims were "reactionaries," "liberals," and so on.

The "uprising" prepared the ground for the Soviet occupation. **The Slovak authors consider the "uprising" neither national, nor Slovak**. It was thought to have been the best means to provoke German intervention.[154]

These events, with the unspoken consent of the Western powers, prepared the return of Benes and Gottwald, the future Communist Prime Minister. They also resulted in the loss of Slovakia's independence which was won in 1939.

The *Kosice Government Program*, proclaimed in April 1945, in Kassa (Kosice), became the basic law of the new order in postwar Czechoslovakia. Its provisions deprived the Slovaks of any hope for an independent, democratic state. We will discuss in Part Two its extraordinarily cruel measures against the Hungarians.

The "National Uprising" not only paved the way for Benes's return to Prague but also his reelection as President on May 19, 1946. A merciless fate awaited the functionaries of the erstwhile independent Slovakia. **Thousands of Slovaks were deported to the Soviet Union and many of them were executed.** A simple denunciation provided sufficient grounds for arrest. The Catholics were particularly hard hit, with hundreds of them taken away on grounds of alleged "conspiracy against the state and the people's democracy."

According to some statistics, 362 people were executed, 420 received life sentences and 13,548 were given jail terms of varying length.[155]

Father Tiso, the President of Slovakia, was sentenced to death by the People's Court of Pozsony (Bratislava) on April 18, 1947. There was widespread hope that Benes would exercise his prerogative to set aside the death sentence. However, in order to get rid of his rival, **Benes refused to grant clemency**.

Ultimately, **Benes'** fall was brought about by the same Soviet Union which had restored him to power. **On February 25, 1948, he was removed from office and on June 7, 1948, he resigned from the presidency -- for the second time. Four month later, he died on his estate at Sezimovo Usti.**

Reportedly, the chief cause of Benes' fall was his refusal to agree to the new constitution. His death marked the departure of the most important symbol of twenty years of anti-Hungarian and anti-Slovak chauvinistic policies. **Undoubtedly, Benes was the chief obstacle to the development of a sound, harmonious relationship among the nations of the Carpathian basin.** The denial of the rights of the Hungarian minority in Czechoslovakia also came to an end more or less at the same time with Benes' disappearance from the scene.

D.

The Constitutions of 1948, 1960 and 1968

The new Constitution was approved on May 9, 1948. It is characteristic that it was based on the concept of the "national state," the same as the Kassa (Kosice) Program. "Our liberated nation will be a national state... free of hostile elements," says the first document. "The Czechoslovak Republic is the unified state of two Slavic nations, the Czechs and the Slovaks, who share equal rights," says the second document. Neither has any provisions to protect the rights of the national minorities.

Twelve years later, on July 11, 1960, a new constitution was adopted. In 1968, Alexander Dubcek attempted to introduce "Socialism with a human face." His attempt was crushed by military intervention by the Warsaw Pact nations, led by the Soviet Union. According to Slovak authors, **the next constitutional law, approved on October 27, 1968**, pays only lip service to the so-called federalization because all political power is concentrated in the hands of the Czechoslovak Community Party.

As we noted earlier, we will discuss in Part Two the various measures taken in this period to deprive the Hungarian minority of its rights. We will also discuss in Part Two the provisions of the Paris Peace Treaty of February 10, 1947. At this point we only wish to note that in addition to giving back to Czechoslovakia the territories returned by the 1938 Vienna Award to Hungary, the Paris Peace Treaty gave three more Hungarian villages -- Horvatjarfalu, Oroszvar and Dunacsuny -- to Czechoslovakia. The Czechoslovak government had demanded five villages on the South bank of the Danube, facing Pozsony (Bratislava) in order to broaden its "bridgehead" there. Following rejection of this demand by the United States and Britain, a compromise was reached, resulting in the transfer of three villages. These three villages were inhabited by Hungarians and Croats, with no Czechs or Slovaks living there. Clearly, strategic considerations were allowed to prevail over ethnic principles.

E.

Lessons for the Nations of the Danubian Basin from the Slovak Efforts for Autonomy and Independence

We have surveyed the struggles of the Slovak people for autonomy and independence. As the subtitle of this work also indicates, it deals with the "lessons to be drawn from the events of a stormy period in European history, to facilitate the efforts for the achievement of a lasting and peaceful cooperation among the peoples of the Danubian basin." And, as we noted in the Introduction, our goal is not the "tearing up of old wounds or the endless repetition of old accusations."

With that in mind, let us see what lessons can be drawn from the Slovak efforts for autonomy and independence, as discussed earlier. These lessons are first of all for the Slovaks but could be applied just as much to the Hungarians, Germans and Ruthenians living in the Danubian basin.

We believe, the Slovaks are the most competent to carry out this task. Therefore, we look at Slovak publications for the most appropriate answers. Such as the publication, *The Slovaks: Past, Present, Future*, which attempts to bring together in a nutshell all these questions and the lessons that can be drawn from them. Here is what it says:

Slovakia typifies the tragic problem of small nations which within the present international community are still being handled like cattle. From a satellite of Germany, it, as part of Czecho-Slovakia, has become one of the Soviet Union. Thus, the international feudalism attaching the small nations to the wheels of a bigger power continues with impunity to destroy them. Within this system the small nations, deprived of their international identity and dignity, are not subjects of law and justice. They are peons of bigger powers.

In historical retrospect, the experience of the Slovaks during their over 60-year long life in one state with the Czechs has been a deception. There has been no regime in Prague that has not abused the Slovaks.[156] Since 1918 Slovakia has appeared in European history as part of Czechoslovakia. It remained the lesser known or completely unknown part, of course, because the Czech policy at home as well as abroad was not interested in making the world acquainted with the Slovak problem. It has been the aim of all Czech political parties, government and exile groups to dominate Slovakia and to assimilate the Slovak people. Therefore, they presented the Slovaks as a branch of the Czech or Czechoslovak people and Slovakia as a backward country that needed the Czech rule.[157] Czech discrimination had been equally detrimental to Slovakia under the rule of T.G.Masaryk and E. Benes as it is under Communism. Not only has Slovakia been exploited economically and socially, but the Czechs have been doing everything possible to prevent Slovakia from culturally progressing at a normal pace...

   The entire Central-European area should be recognized on the principle of equality applicable to all nations of the area. The realization of such a situation is the aspiration of the Slovaks in Slovakia as well as those in the free world.[158]

   As we have seen here and will see again in Part Two, the two neighboring nations had wasted too much energy for things of no benefit to them, but rather to the benefit of the great power which has promised some kind a solution, or help toward the solution, of the various problems. Much more could have been accomplished if we had had more patience, more goodwill, more mutual understanding, greater willingness for compromise to solve our own problems ourselves. That is one of the most important lessons.

   How well a state takes care of its minorities is one measure of how far democracy has come in that state. The state that has been unable for twenty years to secure the loyalty of its national minorities should not expect those minorities to come to the rescue in time of international crisis. It is too transparent to try to blame those minorities, as demonstrated by the mistaken policies of Benes over twenty years. That is another very important lesson. Unfortunately, in some places there is still some confusion over this question.

   The source of the problems has not been the decision of the Western powers to buy peace by handing the Czechoslovakia of Benes to the Germans. The error began much earlier than that, thanks to the same Benes who has been lamented by so many. It began when the vanquished small nations were deprived of the right of self-determination and were forced into such an intolerable situation that they became desperate in their search for a remedy by peaceful means. The great powers,

however, were concerned only with the interests of those who created the intolerable situation in the first place.

The drafters of the Paris peace treaties should have looked into the future, guided by the principle of reconciliation, instead of barring even the hope for reconciliation by creating rigid categories of victorious and vanquished states. Such a regime had its days numbered from the very beginning. **Had Benes not denied the autonomy the Slovaks were promised in 1918, he could have counted on the their loyalty against the Germans when the great crisis came. This was equally the mistake of Benes and the great powers which had been trying to keep a nonviable political system alive to the very end. These, too, are important lessons.**

The conclusion reached by the Slovak essay we have quoted is in full accord with the concepts outlined in the Introduction. **The reorganization of Central Europe must be based exclusively on the principle of equal rights. That can be the only determining principle,** as Janos Esterhazy declared in 1942. There is and there can be no other way.

In order to accomplish this between Hungarians and Slovaks, both sides face a great and difficult task ahead of them. As we have stated, the spiritual reconciliation must be the first step. And that can be accomplished only by setting our sights on the goal of reconciliation and cooperation and implanting it firmly into our consciousness.

The question is, do these two peoples, Hungarians and Slovaks, understand that the time has come and are they aware of their historic destiny? All is in vain if they do not. The proclaimed words, no matter how noble they may be, the brilliant intellectual exercises, no matter how deeply felt and sincere they may be, will go nowhere just by themselves. **But if these nations are able to climb to the summit their Creator set before them, then and only then, there is no manmade obstacle they could not overcome.**

NOTES TO PART ONE

(9)Safarik, Pavel Joseph, *Slawische Althertumer.* II.9.496

(10)Bohm, Jaroslav, et.al, *La Grande Moravie.* Prague: Czechoslovak Academy of Science, 1963, p.31.

(11)Dvornik, Francis, *The Making of Central and Eastern Europe.* London: Polish Research Center, 1919. p.293.

(12)Thus, for example, at a 1980 conference on ancient history, arranged by the Hungarian Academy of Science in Budapest, as well as at other forums, Dr. Peter Puspoki-Nagy has sharply criticized the Czechoslovak statements regarding Svatopluk's empire. He presented his theory, supported by scholarly documentation, which refuted the various views about Svatopluk's empire and the theories of Great Moravian-Slovak continuity.

See also: Puspoki-Nagy, Peter, *On The Location Of Great Moravia; A Reassessment.* Pittsburgh, Pa.: Duquesne University, Department of History, 1982, and by the same author: *A tenyek erejevel.* New York: Puski, 1985.

(13)Archbishop Peter Pazmany, founder of the University of Nagyszombat (Trnava), leader of the Jesuit Counter-Reformation in Hungary.

(14)General Joseph Haynau was commanding general of the Austrian Third Army which was sent to Hungary to bring her under martial rule in 1849. Subsequently the Austrian government appointed him military governor of Hungary. His military courts prosecuted the Hungarian and Austrian officers who took part in the Hungarian uprising against the Austrian rule. The punishment meted out by Haynau's courts was so cruel that England, France and even Russia exerted pressure on Austria to moderate the policy of reprisal.

(15)Borsody, Istvan, *Magyar-szlovak kiegyezes.* Budapest: Officina (1945?), p.44.

(16)idem pp. 44-45.

(17)Kirschbaum, Joseph M., *An Outline Of Slovakia's Struggle For Independence*. Toronto: Canadian Slovak League, 1964.

(18)Kirkconnell, Watson, *Canada, Europe and Hitler*. Oxford University Press: 1939. p.43.

(19)Masaryk, Thomas G., *The Lectures of T.G. Masaryk At The University Of Chicago, Summer 1902*. London.

(20)Lias, Godfrey, *Benes of Czechoslovakia*. London: George Allen & Unwin Ltd. (1940) pp.73-74.

(21)Rumpler, Helmut, *Das Volkermanifest Kaiser Karls vom 16. Oktober 1918: letzter Versuch zur Rettung des Habsburgerreiches*. Wien: Verlag fur Geschichte and Politik, 1966. p.96.

(22)House, Colonel Edward Mandell, *Papers, 1891-1938*. Yale University Library.
Recent research results show that until the end of May, 1918, President Wilson not only declined to support the independence movements of the various nationalities and the dismemberment of the Austro-Hungarian Monarchy, but he was in fact leaning toward the recommendations of a Commission of Inquiry he had appointed. His Fourteen Points were drafted with the assistance of this Commission, but without any participation of the Department of State. Plans for the federalization of Austria-Hungary, proposed by Charles Seymour, a member of the U.S. peace delegation, reflected Wilson's conceptions.

Seymour's plan called for a federation of six constituent states: Austria, Hungary (including a self-governing Slovakia), Bohemia, Transylvania, Yugoslavia and Poland-Ruthenia (Subcarpathian Ruthenia). A map accompanying this plan, along with an explanatory note, were signed by Seymour on May 25, 1918.

Recent research also shows that Wilson ignored the agreement reached at a conference in Rome in March 1918 by representatives of the "oppressed nations" within the Austro-Hungarian Monarchy. According to Benes, "There was no longer any doubt that Wilson was not in favor of the dissolution of the Monarchy; that his plan for the liberation of the peoples of the Austro-Hungarian Monarchy did not call for the establishment of independent states. Rather, he was in favor of self government or some sort of a confederation."

Austro-Hungarian Emperor/King Charles' secret correspondence with Prince Sixtus of Parma, disclosed by Clemenceau in May 1918, showed that the monarch was ready to conclude a separate peace with the Entente powers.

Disclosure of the secret correspondence put an end to negotiations with the

United States. Secretary of State Lansing who was in favor of the dismemberment of the Monarchy swung into action. "I have hesitated thus far to raise the question of Czech, Ruthenian and South Slav independence because the President wanted to maintain the inviolability of dual Monarchy. I believe, however, that the President must abandon this principle," Lansing wrote.

The decision by England and France in favor of the dismemberment, pressure by Clemenceau and Lloyd George, as well as U.S.domestic politics finally persuaded Wilson to change his position and agree to a whole series of concessions in Paris. (Adam, Magda, "Egy amerikai terv Kozep-Europarol, 1918". *Historia*, IX. évf. 4. sz. 1987.)

(23)Kovtun, George J., *The Czechoslovak Declaration Of Independence. A History Of The Document.* Washington, D.C.: Library of Congress, 1985. p.21.

(24)ibid

(25)ibid

(26)Novak, Karl, *The Collapse of Central Europe.* Westport, Conn.: Greenwood Press (1970) p.62.

(27)Rumpler op.cit. pp.348-349.

(28)Lansing, Robert, *Papers, 1890-1933.* Washington, D.C.: Library of Congress, Manuscript Division.

(29)Medvecky, Karol A., *Slovensky prevrat.* III. Trnava: 1930-1931. p.347.

(30)Dukes, Frantisek, *Dejiny Slovenska a Slovakov.* Bratislava, 1946. p.39.

(31)ibid pp.368-369.

(32)ibid

(33)Bogdan, Kriaman, "The Belgrade Armistice Of November 1918." *Slavonic And East European Review.* LXVIII. No.110, 1970. pp.67-87.

(34)Perman, Dagmar, *The Shaping Of The Czechoslovak State.* Leiden: Brill, 1962. p.78.

(35)Kramar, Karel, *Reci a projery.* Prague: 1935. pp. 22-26.

(36)Hodza, Milan, *Federation In Central Europe*. London, 1942.

(37)Orszagos Torvenytar. 1919. Budapest. p.175.

(38)Durcansky, Ferdinand, *Pohl'ad na slovensku politicku minulost*. Bratislava, 1943. p. 266, cited in Borsody, Istvan, *Magyar-Szlovak kiegyezes. A csehszlovak-magyar viszony utolso szaz eve*. Budapest: Officina (1945?).

(39)Franchet d'Esperey to Clemenceau and Foch, March 10, 1919. Ministere des Affaires Etrangeres. *Correspondence des Affaires Politiques, Roumanie*.

(40)Franchet d'Esperey to Barthelot, March 19, 1919. Ministere de la Guerre, Etat Major de l'Armee. Archives historiques. Campagne Contre Allemagne (1914-1918) 27 N 89.

(41)*Papers Relating To The Foreign Relations Of The United States, Paris Peace Conference, 1919*. (Washington, D.C.: 1942-1947) (Hereafter *FRUS PPC*) XII. 411-416.

(42)ibid

(43)Deak, Ferenc, *Hungary At The Paris Peace Conference; The Diplomatic History Of The Treaty Of Trianon*. New York: 1942. pp. 409-410.

(44)*FRUS PPC* 6:284ff 351-52, 399, 411-16.

(45)ibid 4:811.

(46)ibid 9:872-84.

(47)*Documents On British Foreign Policy 1919-1939* (Hereafter *DBFP*) Series III. London, 1949-1952. 7:284, 384, 387-89.

(48)*FRUS PPC* 3:105-6. See additional citations in Part II.

(49)Jelinek, Yeshayau, "The Treaty of Trianon and Czechoslovakia: Reflections." *War and Society in East Central Europe*. v. VI. New York: Columbia University Press, 1982. p. 442.

(50)Durcansky op.cit.p.148.

(51)Thomson, S. Harrison, *Czechoslovakia In European History*. 2nd ed. Princeton: 1953. pp. 313-15.

(52)Cited in Bonsal, Stephen, *Suitors And Supplicants. The Little Nations At Versailles.* Port Washington, N.Y.: Kennikat Press, Inc., 1946

(53)ibid

(54)Arato, Endre, *Tanulmanyok a szlovakiai magyarok eletebol, 1918-1975.* Budapest: Magveto Konyvkiado, 1977. p. 23.

(55)Kirschbaum, Joseph M., op.cit. p. 7.

(56)Arato, Endre, *A magyar-csehszlovak viszony otven eve. Torteneti attekintes.* Budapest: Kossuth Konyvkiado, 1969. pp. 35-36.

(57)idem

(58)Keller, Hans, "Die kurze Jahren der Slowakischen Republik, 1939-1945." *Geschichte,* historisches Magazin (St.Gallen, Schweiz) Marz/April 1985, No..69.

(59)Arato, Endre, *A magyar-csehszlovak viszony.* op.cit. p. 42.

(60)Wojatsek, Charles, *From Trianon To The First Vienna Arbitral Award.* Montreal: Institute of Comparative Civilizations, 1980. pp. 59-62.

(61)Baumgarten, Vladimir, "Federalism Vs. The Policies Of Opportunism; The Career of Milan Hodza". *The Central European Forum,* Astor, Florida: Danubian Press, Inc. v. 1, no.1, Spring 1988.

(62)Hoensch, Jorg, *Der Ungarische Revisionismus und die Zerschlagen der Tschechoslovakei.* Tubingen: J.C.R.Mohr, 1967. p.19.

(63)Szvatko, Pal, "A csehszlovak-szudetanemet kiegyezes kiserlete." *Magyar Szemle* III. May 1937, No.71.

(64)*Pragai Magyar Hirlap.* January 10, 1938.

(65)*Prager Montagsblatt.* February 25, 1938.

(66)*Venkov.* January 1, 1938.

(67)*Documents Of German Foreign Policy, 1918-1945.* (Hereafter *DGFP*)

Series D, II. 124-125.

(68)Hoensch op.cit. p.63.

(69)*Slovak*. February 27, 1938

(70)*Pragai Magyar Hirlap*. April 8, 1938.

(71)*Affari Esteri*. No.3193R and 2813R.

(72)Roos, Hans, "Polen und Europa. Studien zur Polnische Aussenpolitik, 1931-1939." *Tubinger Studien zu Geschichte*. Tubingen, 1957.

(73)Public Record Office, Foreign Office (Hereafter PRO FO), 371/21578.

(74)PRO FO, 341/21426. 194

(75)*Pragai Magyar Hirlap*. August 6, 10, 1938.

(76)Little Entente, a post-World War One political and military alliance between Czechoslovakia, Rumania and Yugoslavia.

(77)Adam, Magda, "A muncheni egyezmeny letrejotte es Magyarorszag kulpolitikaja, 1936-1938." *Diplomaciai iratok Magyarorszag kulpolitikajahoz, 1936-1945*. II. Budapest: Akademiai Kiado, 1965. No.275, 288a, 294, 298, 301a, 301b, 305.

(78)Pritz, Paul, "A kieli talalkozo; forraskritikai tanulmany." *Szazadok*. 1974, p.650.

(79)Kallay, Nicholas, *Hungarian Premier. A personal account of a nation's struggle in the Second World War*. New York: 1954. p.53.

(80)Horthy, Nicholas von, *Ein Leben fur Ungarn*. Bonn: 1953. pp.162-163.

(81)*Affari Esteri*. No. 12332/8.

(82)Hoensch op.cit. p.181.

(83)Adam, Magda, op.cit. No.318.

(84)PRO FO, 800/306, 58.

(85)*Slovak*. September 11, 1938

(86)*Pragai Magyar Hirlap*. September 18, 1938.

(87)PRO FO, 341/21438, 186 and 341/21482, 115, 240.

(88)*Akten zur Deutschen Auswartigen Politik, 1914-1945* (Hereafter *ADAP*). Serie D. II.448 and *Popolo d'Italia*. September 15, 1938.

(89)As quoted in the Polish newspaper, *Gazetta Polska*. September 23, 1938.

(90)*Pragai Magyar Hirlap*. September 17, 1938.

(91)Adam, Magda op.cit. No.309

(92)ibid No.361; *ADAP*. II. 506; *Allianz Hitler-Horthy-Mussolini*. ed. Lajos Kerekes, Budapest: 1965. p.34.

(93)Adam, Magda op.cit. No.425.

(94)ibid No.378, 379.

(95)ibid No.306, 373, 375; *ADAP*. II. 554, 555; *ADAP*. V. 272.

(96)Adam, Magda op.cit. No.368, 373, 375; *ADAP*. II. 554, 555

(97)Hoensch op.cit. p.91.

(98)*Pragai Magyar Hirlap*. September 23, 1938.

(99)ibid September 29, 1938.

(100)Adam, Magda op.cit. No.388, 403.

(101)ibid No.460.

(102)*DGFP*. D. II. 1016.

(103)Durcansky, Ferdinand, "Mit Tiso bei Hitler." *Politischen Studien*. 7, 1956, No. 80, p.2, and Hoensch op.cit. p.136.

(104)Hoensch op.cit. p.138

(105)*Pragai Magyar Hirlap*. October 15, 1938.

(106)Chaszar, Edward, *Decision in Vienna, The Czechoslovak-Hungarian Border Dispute*. Astor, Florida: Danubian Press, 1978. p.39.

(107)*Affari Esteri*. No.5519 October 16, 1938.

(108)*ADAP*. IV. 65.

(109)ibid IV. S.63.Anm.2.

(110)*ADAP*. IV. 72.

(111)*Ciano Diary*. October 14, 1938.

(112)*Affari Esteri*. No.12332/PR/C, October 21, 1938.

(113)ibid October 22, 1938.

(114)*Ciano Diary*. October 22, 1938.

(115)Adam, Magda, op.cit. No.585.

(116)ibid No.586 and 589.

(117)ibid No.592.

(118)ibid No. 598 and 604.

(119)*Affari Esteri*. No. 5519, October 28, 1938.

(120)Hoensch op.cit. p.176.

(121)*Ciano Diary*. October 28, 1938.

(122)ibid

(123)Hoensch op.cit. p.173.

(124)ibid

(125)*ADAP*. IV. 98 and *DBFP*. III. 240.

(126)Adam, Magda op.cit. No. 598.

(127)ibid No.609.

(128)ibid No. 607.

(129)Hoensch op.cit. p.186.

(130)*Slovak*. October 31, 1938.

(131)Hoensch op.cit. p.181.

(132)ibid

(133)ibid p.182, quoting from the notes of Paul Otto, an interpreter at the meeting.

(134)*ADAP*. IV. 99.

(135)Hoensch op.cit. p.184.

(136)Wojatsek, Charles, op.cit. p.165.

(137)*ADAP*. IV, 99, III.

(138)Ciano, Galeazzo, *Tagebucher*. Hamburg. November 3, 1938.

(139)Hoensch, op.cit. p.186.

(140)*Slovak*. November 4, 1938.

(141)ibid

(142)Chaszar, Edward op.cit. p.55.

(143)Wojatsek, Charles op.cit. p.165.

(144)Weizsacker, Ernst von, *Erinnerungen*. München. 1950.

(145)For details on the Hitler-Tiso meeting, see *ADAP*. Serie D. Bd.IV. 202, 212-214.

(146)Keller, Hans op.cit.

(147)Keller, Hans op.cit.

(148)Hajek, Milos, *Od Mnichova k Breznu*. Praha. 1959. p.151.

(149)*ADAP*. Serie D. Bd.IV. 229, 2351.

(150)Keller, Hans op.cit.

(151)Grebert, Arved, *Dr. Jozef Kirschbaum, Politik a Diplomat*. Köln. 1984.

(152)Smutny, Jaromyr, "Vyvoj vztahu ceskoslovensko-sovetskych" (The Development of Czechoslovak-Soviet Relations). v.1. In *Smutny Papers*. Arch. of Russian and East European History and Culture. Columbia University.

(153)Taborsky, Edward, *President Benes between East and West, 1938-1948*. Stanford, California: Hoover Institution Press, 1981.

(154)Keller, Hans, op.cit.
For different views on the "national uprising," see the following:
The Czech view: Lettrich, Josef, *History of Modern Slovakia*. New York, 1955.
The views of the Slovaks who were demanding autonomy and independence: Kirschbaum, Jozef, *Slovakia: Nation at the Crossroads of Europe*. New York, 1950.
The Communist view: Butvin, Jozef et.al., *Dejiny Slovenska slovom i obrazom*. II. Bratislava, 1981. 264-283.
A look at the background and history of the "uprising" from various points of view: Baumgarten, Vladimir, "Slovakia's 1944 Uprising Reexamined." In *Central European Forum*. Astor, Florida: Danubian Press, Inc. V.1, No.2, Fall 1988.

(155)Mikus, Joseph A., *Slovakia, A Political History, 1918-1950*. Marquette Univ. Press, 1964 and Zubek, T.J., *The Church of Silence in Slovakia*. Whitting, Ind., 1956. Also, Wojatsek, Charles, op.cit. p.181.

(156)Mikus, Joseph A., *A Misunderstood History*. Stoney Creek, Ont.: The Battlefield Press, 1979.

(157)Kirschbaum, Joseph M., *Slovakia's Struggle for Independence*. Hamilton, Ont., 1979.

(158)Mikus, Joseph A., op.cit.

PART TWO

The Struggles of the Hungarians in Slovakia to Enforce Their Right of Self-Determination, to Secure Their National Minority Rights and for the Peaceful Revision of the Inequities of the Peace Treaties of Trianon and Paris

A. The origins of Count Janos Esterhazy and the beginnings of his political career.

B. From the period of 1918-1920 to March 1939.

C. From the declaration of Slovakia's independence to the restoration of the Republic of Czechoslovakia in 1945.

D. The period since 1945.

A.

The Origins of Count Janos Esterhazy and the Beginnings of His Political Career

Much of this Part will be focused on Janos Esterhazy, it is in order therefore to begin with a discussion of his origins and his first appearance in public life.

Janos Esterhazy was the scion of one of the most prominent Hungarian families, the Esterhazys of Galanta, which has produced many outstanding men of nationwide, indeed, Europe-wide fame.

It is not the purpose of this study to look at the history of the entire family. It would require a separate volume to examine all branches of the Esterhazy family. Still, to obtain a clear image of the character and persona of Janos Esterhazy, it is necessary to have at least a sketchy look at the origins of the family before we take a closer look at its Csesznek branch where he came from.

The Esterhazy family traces its origins to Mokud (Mocud), a military hero of the Salamon clan, who was also a landowner in the Csallokoz region of Western Hungary, and a *Pristaldus*, a judicial functionary in the court of King Bela III (1148-1196).

Ancient records show that in 1239 the family owned an estate at Alsohidja in the Csallokoz, in 1242 at Vatta and Salamonfalva, and in 1248 at Salamon.

The name Esterhazy was first used by Benedek Esterhazy. He also assumed the title of Galanta after the dowry of his wife, Ilona Bessenyei. His son, Ferenc, married Ilona Illeshazy and was elected chief executive of Pozsony County in 1580. The highly respected and wealthy Ferenc Esterhazy saw to it that his four sons received the best education. Daniel established the Csesznek branch of the family, Pal became the founder of the Zolyom branch and Miklos of the Frakno branch.

Count Pal Esterhazy (1635-1712) of the Frakno branch was elevated by Austrian Emperor Leopold I to be a Prince of the Empire on December 7, 1687, when Leopold's son, Joseph I, was crowned King of Hungary in Pozsony (Bratislava). The title was passed on from generation to generation to the first-born son. Then, on July 11, 1783, King Joseph II extended it to all male and female descendants of Prince Miklos-Jozsef Esterhazy.

Ferenc (1641-1683), the youngest son of Count Pal who was named the first Prince Esterhazy, founded the Frakno branch of the Count Esterhazys. Following the death in 1758 of Chief Treasurer Ferenc Esterhazy, his branch of the family split into two, headed by his sons, Ferenc and Miklos (1711-1785), the latter a Custodian of St.Stephen's Crown and Minister to St.Petersburg, and the one who started the Cseklesz branch of the family.

The Csesznek branch split once again with the two sons of Janos and his wife Erzsebet Berenyi. The older branch was headed by General Imre Esterhazy, the younger, or Transylvanian branch, by Daniel Esterhazy.

The title *Csesznek* came from the fortress Csesznek in the Bakony Mountains which was given with the surrounding estate to Daniel Esterhazy by Austrian Emperor Ferdinand II in 1636. The fortress was built by the Csak family and then came into the possession of the Garay family. During the Turkish occupation of Hungary it occupied a key strategic position in the Bakony Mountains. The Turkish pashas of Simontornya and Buda kept taking turns plundering Csesznek and the surrounding estates.

Field Marshal Mihaly Esterhazy (1640-1686) died a martyr's death at the siege of Buda. Previously, he fought in the battle of Szentgotthard and the siege of Zerinvar fortress. In the battle of Vezekeny, on August 16, 1652, seven members of the Esterhazy family lost their lives, including Gaspar, son a Daniel Esterhazy of the Csesznek branch.

General Janos Esterhazy of Gyor and his son were captains-in-chief of Csesznek for life. A contemporary record refers to Csesznek as a *kuruc*[159] garrison. Later on, the fortress fell into *labanc* hands.

Mihaly Esterhazy's son, Daniel, followed his father's footsteps and chose a military career. In 1691 he became a Colonel and in 1703 he joined the *kuruc* army of Ferenc Rakoczi. In 1704, he shared with Sandor Karolyi the command of the Transdanubian Army under very difficult circumstances. He reported on April 4 that, having been betrayed by Istvan Torok and Istvan Fekete, his cavalry suffered a severe defeat, with some of his troops forced into a swamp. General Bercsenyi reported that Esterhazy had fought very bravely against the overwhelming imperial forces until he was captured and imprisoned in Sopron.

Mihaly Esterhazy (born in 1783), son of Janos Esterhazy, Governor of Veszprem County and Agnes Banffy -- who became great-grandfather of Janos Esterhazy, chairman of the Hungarian Party in Slovakia -- was a devoted follower of Lajos Kossuth, leader of the 1848-1849 Hungarian War of Independence against Hapsburg rule. Mihaly Esterhazy became a member of the Revolutionary Committee in 1848 and was subsequently imprisoned for five years by the Hapsburgs.

Istvan Esterhazy, grandfather of Janos Esterhazy, served as a Captain of the Hussars in the Hungarian revolutionary *Honved* army in 1848-1849. He, too, became a prisoner of the Hapsburgs, but following the restoration of the Hungarian Constitution, Istvan Esterhazy was named Governor of the city and county of Pozsony. He was a military hero and a great patriot ready for any sacrifice who had inherited his father's loyalty to the Hungarian nation. In the *Honved* army he served as aide-de-camp to commander-in-chief Arthur Gorgey, always fearless in the thickest of every battle.

It became Istvan Esterhazy's sad duty, along with Count Gergely Bethlen and Captain of the Hussars, Count Kalman Schmideg, to deliver Gorgey's message of surrender to Count Rudiger, commander-in-chief of the Russian Imperial Army which had come to the rescue of the Hapsburg forces as they were about to be defeated by the Hungarians.

Following the surrender came a period of persecution and humiliation. Istvan Esterhazy was forced to serve as a private in the Hapsburg imperial army. Ultimately, he married Baroness Gizella Jeszenak, daughter of Janos Jeszenak, a martyr of the War of Independence, whose wife was well-known for her charity work. Baron Janos Jeszenak, born in 1800 in Pozsony, was Governor of Nyitra County. Following the defeat of the War of Independence, he was imprisoned in the fortress Kufstein. On October 10, 1849, the Austrian General Haynau had him shot to death.

Istvan Esterhazy had two sons. Janos, born in 1864, who was to become the father of Janos Esterhazy, chose a military career. As Captain of the Hussars, he became aide-de-camp to Archduke Otto. He married Erzsebet Tarnowski, daughter of Count Sanislo Tarnowski, Ph.D., a privy councilor and president of the Krakow Academy of Science. The patriotic officer bequeathed loyalty to the Hungarian nation to his children. He died in 1905 in Nyitraujlak.

Gyula, the second son of Istvan Esterhazy, was born in 1868. He fought in several World War One battles in Bukovina. He died in 1918 of injuries suffered in the battle of Dobronoutz.

Captain Janos Esterhazy had three children. Lujza, born in 1899, was to play a very active role in helping to maintain Hungarian national consciousness in Slovakia. His only son, Janos Esterhazy, was born in 1901 and a second daughter, Maria Zsofia, in 1904.

Count Janos Esterhazy was born on March 19, 1901 in Nyitraujlak. He married Livia Serenyi who died on October 5, 1961 in Budapest. Their children, Janos and Alice, live with their families in Australia and Italy, respectively.[160]

Janos Esterhazy lost his father very early, at age four. He recalled in a speech that he had been summoned to the deathbed of his father's whose final words to the young boy were, "Always be a faithful Hungarian!" "I could not have understood my father's parting words to me, had it not been for my mother whom I wish to thank second only after God. She helped me understand my father's last utterances. Even though she was not a native Hungarian, she had become so deeply Hungarian that her every heartbeat belongs to the Hungarian cause."[161]

The parting words of his father left an indelible mark in Janos Esterhazy's heart. No wonder that he decided early in his youth that after completion of his studies he would enter politics in order to serve the Hungarian cause.

The period of 1918-1920 which had brought so much suffering to his nation left an impact beyond description on the young man. Overnight, his native land came under foreign rule. His grief over the loss of his homeland brought the 19-year-old young man into trouble with the Pozsony police. In December, 1919, he was arrested and locked up for eight hours for singing patriotic songs in the Baross Cafe.

Much of Esterhazy's Nyitra estates was taken away by the Czechoslovak land reform of 1926. He had to struggle very hard to retain what was left of the land because the retroactive taxation had brought him to the brink of financial ruin. He had to spend much of his time negotiating with finanacial institutions in Pozsony and Prague. That gave him an opportunity to become acquainted with the leaders of the Hungarian minority.

Esterhazy's activities on behalf of National Christian Socialist Party, along with his outstanding talents and his willingness to sacrifice, earned him the undivided gratitude of the party. As a result, on December 14, 1932, at the Otatrafured meeting of the national party leaders, he was elected to the chairmanship.

The young man, not yet 31, enjoyed great popularity in all circles. He even earned the sympathy of the Slovak Peoples Party because he supported that party's efforts to gain Slovakia autonomy. He often told his Slovak friends about King St.Stephen, the founder of the Hungarian state. Esterhazy told them that it was St.Stephen who 900 years ago introduced the concept of administrative pluralism among various groups speaking different languages. He said repeatedly that the Hungarian government was prepared, on the same basis, to grant the Slovaks territorial autonomy.

B.

From the Period of 1918-1920 to March 1939

Hungarian Views on the Peace Treaty of Trianon

Before going into greater detail about this highly significant event in the life of Janos Esterhazy, it is necessary to take a sketchy look at conditions in Hungary at the time. That will make it easier to understand the extraordinary driving force behind Esterhazy's unrelenting devotion to the Hungarian cause. In this Part, we will examine the events and problems from the Hungarian perspective.

We noted in Part One that there are sharp differences between the Czechoslovak and Hungarian views with regard to the Peace Treaty of Trianon. Czechoslovakia has approved the decisions of the peace treaty and found them just and fair. The political line espoused by Benes who had been a kind of godfather to the Treaty of Trianon has been to resist by tooth and nail even the most modest revision of the treaty.

The Hungarian view, on the other hand, has been that the peace treaty was, in fact, a peace dictate, with the victors dictating to the vanquished without even permitting them to be present at the peace negotiations. This, notwithstanding the fact that in a June 7, 1919 note to the Hungarian Revolutionary Governing Council, the participants at the peace conference declared: "It is the intent of the Allied Powers to **invite representatives of the Hungarian Government to appear before the peace conference so that they may be informed of the principles regarding the just borders of Hungary.**"[162]

This invitation turned out to be just a tactical maneuver because, despite the promises to the contrary, this crucial question of Hungary's borders was settled without a hearing given to Hungary's representatives, but with the full partipation of Czechoslovakia.

The peace dictate of Trianon completely ignored the right of self-determination, totally distorting historic and demographic facts and without asking the people involved, indeed, contrary to their wishes, transferred 1,070,772 Hungarians to the newly created Czechoslovakia. It is little wonder then that the Hungarian people in their entirety, regardless of age, gender, religion, social status or political standing, unanimously condemned this unfairly created and unjust peace dictate. This is how the world-famous Hungarian author Gyula Illyes, who has never been regarded a political "rightist," summed it all up: "More than three million Hungarians have been detached from Hungary without asking about their desires; that is, without a plebiscite, by a dictate and not by a lawful peace treaty."[163]

Even more bitterness was generated by reports leaked from the peace negotiations to the effect that Benes was permitted to present his demands before the "Council of Ten" without any objection. It had not occurred to anyone that the task was not to increase controversy and tension but to find a long range solution for the future. Even if such a solution would not have been the answer to every single problem, it would have created a more conciliatory atmosphere between Hungary and Czechoslovakia. As we have noted earlier, this could have been accomplished easily by the great powers because they had possessed the ability to exert pressure. Unfortunately, pressure was applied only on the vanquished. This total lack of political foresight was to pave the way for the nations of the region into adventures with dire and long-lasting consequences.

It also came to light that Benes had demanded a corridor between Czechoslovakia and Yugoslavia. This question also came up during the Prague talks between President Masaryk and British General J. C. Smuts. The Yugoslavs themselves were rather cool to this idea. Smuts himself was opposed to it. Moreover, he condemned the Czech demands for territories inhabited by Hungarians. Masaryk, at that time, was prepared to revise the Czech position regarding the Csallokoz region with its Hungarian population. On other occasions, too, he had repeatedly hinted at the possibility of revising the border between Hungary and Czechoslovakia. But all suggestions of revision were opposed by the Czechs, especially by Benes.[164]

Thus, the excessive demands against Hungary were apparently instigated by Benes ignoring the principles advocated by the more humanistic Masaryk. It was Benes who wanted to deport the national minorities in order to transform Czechoslovakia into a Slavic national state, instead of working for reconciliation in Central Europe.

According to the Hungarian view, the very fact that the new Czechoslovakia included both the Slovaks and the Sudeten Germans was an internal contradiction. As political scientist Istvan Bibo wrote: "The historical and geographical factors that have been invoked to claim that the Germans living within the cradle of the Carpathian mountains continue to belong to historic Bohemia, could have been invoked with just as much justification by the Hungarians to claim that the Slovak people living within the cradle of the Carpathian mountains should remain within the framework of historic Hungary. The Czechs who should have chosen between historic Bohemia or a Slavic state of Czechoslovakia wanted to have both. As a result, both the Sudeten Germans and the Slovaks became hostile or indifferent toward a political union with the Czech people."

Bibo, one of the greatest thinkers with the best-honed mind in recent Hungarian history, had this to say of the critical events of Munich: **"In Munich, the Czechs had to experience all at once not only the geopolitical consequences of the Munich Pact but, more importantly, the hatred of the Sudeten Germans, the malicious glee of the Hungarians and the Poles and, what may have been the hardest to take, the indifference of the Slovaks."**[165]

Instead of working for reconciliation, the policies of Benes were aimed from the beginning at the creation of an alliance which would include only the victorious successor states of the former Austro-Hungarian Monarchy. This alliance was intended to take the place of the Monarchy and, at the same time, completely isolate Hungary.

In those early postwar years, neither Germany nor Italy would have been an obstacle to the evolution of more natural links among the Danubian states. But that was not the goal of Benes' policies. On the contrary, he tried to crush any Western initiative to promote integration in the Danubian Basin.

Of the various proposals that had been advanced, perhaps the Millerand-Paleologue plan would have been the most important as far as Hungary was concerned. The plan would have brought Hungary under French influence, giving her a key economic position in the Danubian Basin. The plan's provisions included protection of the national minorities, as well as certain revisions of the borders established by the Treaty of Trianon.

French Plans for the Danubian Basin:
Economic Union Followed by Confederation

After French Premier Clemenceau's death in January 1920, Millerand, who became his successor, and Secretary General Paleologue suddenly realized that the policies of Benes were in conflict with the interests of France. By dividing the Danubian Basin between victors and vanquished and perpetuating this situation with a political and military alliance, sooner or later the vanquished nations would be inevitably pushed into the orbit of Germany. Recognition of this danger led to the development of the concept that instead of replacing the former Monarchy with an alliance of the victorious small powers, an economic union should be established under French influence. Ultimately, this union would evolve into a political confederation. As envisioned by the French politicians, this plan would have been centered on Hungary.

There were secret talks held between Hungary and France in early 1920 and, as we have noted earlier, in addition to the question of economic aid, there were indications that the Trianon borders might be revised.[166] However, news of these confidential talks was leaked prematurely by the supporters of Benes and the talks were broken off. Subsequently, Yugoslavia and Czechoslovakia signed a treaty of alliance in August 1920.

Following the fall of Paleologue, the French government began to support the policies of Benes once again. The attempt by King Charles IV to return to Hungary prompted Rumania to join the Czechoslovak-Yugoslav alliance. Thus, with French support, the *Little Entente* came into being.

As a result of Benes' politics, the nations of the Danubian Basin had lost all the opportunities which would have made rapprochement possible in the 1920s. Later, in the 1930s, the strengthening of the Axis Powers diminished these opportunities because they no longer had unrestriced freedom of action.

The member nations of the *Little Entente* became willing to alter their exclusionary policies only after they realized the bankruptcy of the foundations of those policies by the mid-1930s. The security system built solely on the the *Little Entente* and Western Powers collapsed like a house of cards when the first crisis arose.

By that time the *Little Entente* was willing the negotiate with Hungary. However, it was too late. Central Europe had come under the control of the Axis Powers and nothing could be accomplished without their approval. Consequently, the Bled agreement which was signed after 18 months of negotiations between Hungary and the *Little Entente*, could no longer enter into force.

Some Revisionist Notions of Masaryk and Benes

While discussing the possibility of revising the borders established by the Treaty of Trianon we have mentioned the Millerand-Paleologue plan in early 1920, regarding a French scheme for revision. Similarly, we have referred several statements by Masaryk in this regard. We should also note the negotiations in Bruck and Marienbad in 1921, where certain revisionist notions were also put forward, surprisingly, by Benes.

As a result of talks between members of the Czechoslovak government and Count Szapary, unofficial representative of the Hungarian government, Castle Harrach, near Bruck, was chosen as the site for negotiations between the two governments. According to Hungarian notes taken during the negotiations on March 14-15, 1921, both parties were considering alternate solutions before the ratification of the Treaty of Trianon. This could account for Benes' proposal that in exchange for the establishment of autonomous linguistic enclaves in Hungary, Czechoslovakia would be willing to transfer certain territories with a Hungarian population in order to establish a numerical parity between the two national minorities. (Benes' proposal was based on the presence of 300,000 Slovaks in Hungary and 521,000 Hungarians in Czechoslovakia.)[167]

The Bruck meeting appointed four task forces. The work of the four task forces was evaluated on June 23-24 in Marienbad. The task forces were scheduled to meet again in early October, thus nothing was done until the Brno meeting between Hungarian Foreign Minister Banffy and Benes. The matter of settling the question of national minorities came to a standstill in the fall of 1921. The draft treaties prepared up to that time by both parties were focussed largely on education issues.

The Czechoslovak willingness to return certain territories inhabited by Hungarians, as proposed by Benes in Bruck and mentioned repeatedly by Masaryk, was brought up only by the Hungarians at the commercial and trade negotiations about the implementation of the Treaty of Trianon.[168]

It is clear from the foregoing that both Masaryk and Benes did not seem to be opposed, at least in principle, to a certain revision of the borders, on several occasions they suggested it themselves. Still, it appears that they used these initiatives as negotiating tools toward the accomplishment of some of their goals.

Seen from the Hungarian point of view, the mere fact that the main instigators of the Treaty of Trianon, **Masaryk and Benes were not always in opposition to revision, at least in principle, is very significant because it demolishes the frequently stated opinion that the very mention of revision is a criminal offense against the inviolability of the supposedly sacrosanct borders.**[169] The Hungarians spoke only of peaceful revision.

As far as the Hungarians living in Slovakia were concerned, protection of their minority rights was their second most important concern, next to the peaceful revision, based on mutual agreement, of the border which, in their opinion, had been drawn unjustly.

Protection of Minority Rights
and Their Systematic Violation

The treaty to regulate the rights of national minorities in Czechoslovakia was signed by Czechoslovakia and the *Entente* Powers on September 10, 1919, in Saint-Germain-en-Laye. More than three million Germans represented the largest group of these minorities, followed by the Hungarians of Slovakia and the Subcarphatian Ruthenia, whose number was set by the 1910 census at more than a million. 272,000 Slovaks remained in post-Trianon Hungary but the 1920 census counted only 142,000.

According to the Czechoslovak Memorandum Number 5 which had been submitted to the Paris Peace Conference, 860,000 Hungarians lived in the territories claimed by Czechoslovakia, while it estimated the number of Slovaks south of the proposed border at 630,000.[170]

The main significance of these statistics is that Benes and his followers justified the transfer of contiguous territories inhabited by Hungarians to Czechoslovakia mainly by claiming that the size of each other's national minorities would be about the same. In reality, as the figures just cited show, this was not true. This misleading interpretation of population statistics has been one of the consistent cornerstones of Benes' policies. It was not difficult to mislead the great powers which were not familiar with the situation and refused to permit knowledgeable Hungarian experts to present the true facts.

One of the weakest elements of the system established to protect the rights of national minorities was the privilege granted Czechoslovakia to review grievances submitted by the minorities to the Council of the League of Nations and forward the complaints with its own comments attached to them. This procedure provided Czechoslovakia with a measure of judicial authority because it was able to declare the grievances unfounded. In fact, this is what happened.[171]

The treaty signed on September 10, 1919, obligated Czechoslovakia not to enact laws in violation of the rights of national minorities guaranteed by that treaty. The treaty guaranteed these rights "for every inhabitant of the country." However, the Peace Treaty of Trianon made the exercise of such rights in some cases contingent on citizenship which could be granted only by the assent of the republic. That resulted in a significant reduction of the number of inhabitants entitled to their minority rights. Moreover this system gave the government significant discretionary rights. This discrimination extended to several aspects of national minority rights.

The discriminatory nature of these measures was not only seen but also felt by the Hungarians of Slovakia. They were being deprived of their rights virtually from the moment the new Czechoslovak state came into being. Large masses of Hungarians were **made stateless** by Decree No. 4397/1919, dated August 2, 1919. Initially, some 26,000 were affected but by 1930, this number rose to more than 90,000 in Slovakia and Subcarpathian Ruthenia.[172] Very large numbers of people lost their jobs, including the civil servants who also lost their pension rights. There was nothing else left but to leave Slovakia and flee to Hungary.[173] Some 101,907 Hungarians were expelled between 1918-1921, although this number is believed by many to have been much higher.

The authorities suspended the **autonomous governing authorities** that had been previously established; dissolving the district, county and municipal legislative bodies. They were replaced by commissaries and unelected legislative councils, appointed from among members of the governing coalition parties.

The same situation prevailed in the **churches**. The estates of the Catholic Church were placed under government control, the autonomy of the Protestant churches was restricted and government functionaries were put in charge.

The same fate was shared by the **chambers of commerce, trade associations** and **bar associations**.

A 1922 decree reduced the **self-governing cities and towns** to the rank of a large village. Since many Hungarians were city dwellers, they were the most affected by this measure.

The establishment of **parliamentary electoral districts** was also guided by a definite anti-Hungarian bias. A Hungarian candidate needed 40 percent more votes to be elected than candidates in the Slovak districts.

The Hungarians were hurt particularly grievously in the field of **education**. Hungarian lectures were immediately halted at the University of Pozsony (Bratislava). The Prague government consistently neglected the Hungarian schools but, at the same time, countless Slovak schools were established through the *Slovenska Liga*.

In 1921-1922 there were 727 Hungarian language elementary schools in Slovakia, with 101,268 students. Total Hungarian attendance in elementary schools was something over 120,000 at the time. That means that some 20,000 Hungarian children were enrolled in Slovak elementary schools. The *Slovenska Liga* made a conscious effort to turn the Hungarian children into Slovaks.

Slovak schools were established in villages with a vast Hungarian majority. In Eberhard, for example, whose population in 1921 consisted of 891 Hungarians and 14 Czechoslovaks, two years later a Slovak school was opened. In Machaza, with 159 Hungarian and 10 Czechoslovak inhabitants, Slovak was introduced as the school language. And so on.[174]

Based on its numerical ratio, the Hungarian minority in Slovakia would have been entitled to 87 junior **high schools**, but they had only 11. The number of students in the Czech and Slovak language junior and senior high schools was more than 50 times greater than the student body of the Hungarian language schools of the same kind, even though, according to the 1921 Czechoslovak census, the Czechoslovak population was nine times larger than the Hungarian.

Three important **senior high schools** (gymnasium) were closed after 1918 in Leva, Rozsnyo and Ungvar, towns with a largely Hungarian population. In 1931, of the republic's 274 senior high schools only eight -- 2.9 percent -- were Hungarian even though the Hungarians were entitled to 14 such schools. The number of teachers of Hungarian nationality decreased by 600 in a nine year period.

Law Number 122, passed on February 29, 1920, regulated the **right of language usage**. This law was wide open to abuse through the skillful manipulation of the so-called 20 percent ratio. The language act decreed that in those counties and municipalities where the minority population is at least 20 percent, members of the national minorities may use their native tongue, both in writing and orally, when dealing with the courts and government agencies. But the authorities did all they could to keep the ratio under 20 percent by various pressure tactics, resettlement, or through the rearrangement of county and municipal boundaries.

The 1919 law of **land reform** provided the framework for acts of lawlessness against the Hungarian and German minorities. Under the terms of this law, more than four million hectares of agricultural land, 29 percent of the total, were appropriated. Some 325,000 hectares of arable land were taken in the territories inhabited by Hungarians.

The **colonization** program led to the establishment of Czech, as well as Slovak, settlements in Hungarian regions. The harmful effect of this program was felt by the Slovak peasants, too. The settlements were established mainly in those parts of Slovakia which were inhabited by Hungarians, with the obvious goal of breaking up the contiguous Hungarian regions. That is why the largest Czech and Slovak settlements were established in the purely Hungarian Csallokoz and Tiszahat regions and a whole chain of settlements came into being from Ersekujvar through Ogyalla, all the way to the Danube River. In Csallokoz alone, 22 new villages were set up. The settlers had a military and police function, as well. And, with the help of the *Slovenska Liga*, new schools were built with the goal of depriving the Hungarian youth of their national identity.[175]

Nothing demonstrates more the **political purpose of the settlement policy** than the fact that it was carried out largely in the Csallokoz region whose purely Hungarian character has been acknowledged by both Slovak and Czech scholars. Alois Sembera did so in 1876, Emil Stodola in 1919 and Anton Granatier in 1930. It is characteristic that while there were no Slovaks in the Csallokoz in 1880, the Slovak islands -- results of a carefully executed settlement program -- were clearly visible on the Czechoslovak ethnographical maps of 1930.

These anti-Hungarian measures were attacked even by the Hungarian-language Communist newspapers. For example, we can read in volume I, number 8 of the paper *Ut*: "Each of the settlements is wedged into national minority regions. In regions where 80-90 percent of the inhabitants is Hungarian, we can find a total of 73 settlements, each the size of a village.[176] The so-called "remnant land" which had been appropriated but not distributed was given to persons loyal to the Czechoslovak state, thereby preventing Hungarian applicants from receiving land.

As a result of endless official measures the standard of living of the Hungarians continued to decline. Massive inflation made their money worthless. Inheritance taxes imposed a heavy burden on those who had inherited real estate. Railroad freight charges on goods from the Highlands were set higher than in the western parts of the country. Farmers were forced to pay higher workers' insurance premiums because, unlike the Czech and Moravian farmers, they had to pay for accident insurance, as well. This had greatly increased the production costs of the Hungarian farmers.[177]

The list is endless, we could continue forever. Still, this superhuman struggle fought by the Hungarians of Slovakia for their very survival, had a highly positive result: the burdens equally shared by all had brought them much closer together. The walls separating social classes had disappeared and there developed an exemplary solidarity among them. The unconditional acceptance of the common fate became the driving force of this new spirit. And this spirit manifested itself in all aspects of minority life.

In 1920, the Czechoslovak government called parliamentary elections. The Hungarians remaining in Slovakia immediately recognized the vital importance of participating in the elections so that they might give voice to their positions in Parliament.

The Formation of Hungarian Minority Parties in Czechoslovakia

The intense Hungarian political activity led to the formation of two major parties. Both parties emerged from previously existing organizations.

The forerunner of the National Christian Socialist Party was founded by Sandor Giesswein in 1907. In the eastern parts of the country, Lajos Kormendy-Ekes, Barna Tost, Gyula Fleischmann and Geza Grosschmid were among its founders. In the west, the founders included Jeno Lelley, Janos Jabloniczky and Denes Bitto. At its first Congress, on March 23, 1920, Jeno Lelley was chosen the party's national chairman. Much emphasis was laid in the platform on Slovakia's autonomy. Later, in July 1920, the National Christian Socialist Party established its workers' organization.

The other major party was a successor to the National '48 Independent Farmer's Party,[178] founded by Istvan Nagyatadi Szabo. It was renamed National Hungarian Smallholders Party. The party had two centers. One was in Komarom, established on February 17, 1920, by Kalman Fussy and Janos Mohacsi. The center at Rimaszombat was permitted only after the parliamentary elections. Jozsef Szent-Ivany and Jozsef Torkoly organized some 20,000 farmers in the Farmers' Association of Gomor-Nograd which had been banned for a short period. On Whitsunday, 1920, the Smallholders Party held its organizing Congress in Leva and elected Jozsef Szent-Ivany its national chairman. The Smallholders Party opened its ranks to craftsmen and agricultural workers, as well.

In order to promote harmonious cooperation, the two parties established a joint Steering Committee and opened a Central Bureau. Their leaders were well prepared to fight for the destiny of their people and saw to it that the outside world be also kept informed of their problems. Their review on minority rights, *Minorite Hongroise*, published in Lugos, jointly with Hungarian minority leaders in

Transylvania, played a very important role in safeguarding Hungarian national interests. There was also a task force about the joint problems of the Highland and Transylvania. Its members, Geza Szullo, Elemer Jakabffy, Jozsef Szent-Ivany, Jozsef Willer and Erno Flachbart, did similar yeoman's work.

As early as June 2, 1920, the Hungarian parties issued a Declaration which was read by Lajos Kormendy-Ekes in the Prague legislature. It stated the only reason the Hungarian parties had decided to participate in the parliament of the new republic: "This is how they believe they will be able to secure the opportunity to raise a resounding voice of protest against the unprecedented, severe international injustice and the systematic deprivation of basic rights inflicted on them." The Declaration stressed that the Hungarians of the Highlands were transferred to Czechoslovakia without anybody asking for their consent. And it concluded with this firm and dramatic statement: "We will never, under any circumstances, give up our right to self-determination; we insist on this right and we demand this right."

On September 24, 1920, speaking in the budget debate, Jozsef Szent-Ivany, a newly elected member of the National Assembly, made this important declaration: "The Hungarians of the Highland will never recognize the right of mutilated Hungary's rump National Assembly to ratify (the Treaty of Trianon) on its own. We have never consented to this peace treaty and we will never give up our right to shape our own destiny." In a speech in Leva, Szent-Ivany said, among others: "Our position is that the peace treaties proved to be the shame of humanity, treating us like a herd, throwing us at the mercy of foreign powers, granting us minority rights of a dubious value, effectively depriving us of our human rights."

The Allied Opposition Parties of the Highlands also attempted to remedy their grievances before an international forum. In 1923, they addressed a memorandum to the League of Nations, called *"La Situation des minorites en Slovaquie et en Russie-Subcarpathique" Memoire a la Societe des Nations, 1923.* But it was of no avail.[179]

Count Janos Esterhazy emerged out of this group of tireless men who were well prepared and ready for any sacrifice. We have noted earlier that as young man he was active in the Hungarian Christian Socialist Party. His speech at the June, 1932 Congress on National Minorities in Vienna may have been the first major event where he became exposed to the international spotlight.

Esterhazy delivered highly effective speeches on November 18, at the Pozsony meeting of the Hungarian Association of the League of Nations and, on November 26, at the Parkany district meeting of his party. The *Pragai Magyar Hirlap*, the newspaper of the Hungarians in Slovakia, editorially hailed him as "someone in whom we proudly see every promise of the new generation of the Hungarian minority, his tough resilience against every trial of fate, readiness to work, wide European vision and unbending Hungarian courage."[180]

Janos Esterhazy, the New National Chairman
of the Hungarian Christian Socialist Party

It is not at all surprising that at the Ersekujvar party conference on December 28, 1932, it was obvious that in the months since illness had forced Dr. Geza Szullo to resign the national chairmanship of the party, the party became enthusiastically united behind the person of Janos Esterhazy.

On December 14, 1932, the party conference at Otatrafured named Janos Esterhazy, by acclamation, national chairman of the Hungarian Christian Socialist Party.

It is worth to report in some detail about the meeting because it was a very important day in the life of Janos Esterhazy.

Deputy Dr. Janos Jabloniczky presided over the meeting, substituting for Senator Dr. Geza Grosschmid who was ill. The delegates included Dr. Geza Szullo, the previous national chairman. The credentials committee determined that of the 180-member party leadership 169 voting members were present. In the course of the debate preceding the election, Dr. Szullo moved that in addition to naming Janos Esterhazy to the party chairmanship, Canon Dr. Lajos Francisky of Nyitra be elected honorary chairman. His move was received with general approval. At that point, Deputy Janos Esterhazy and Dr. Lajos Francisky were named national chairman and honorary chairman, respectively, by acclamation. The conference also elected two national vice chairmen and members of the executive committee.

Janos Esterhazy thanked the party for its confidence and delivered his acceptance speech in which he also outlined his platform. He emphasized, first of all, that "we look for help in improving our lot and for the victory of our just cause to the One who gave the world our Savior." He stressed that "our opposition politics is not based on childish defiance. Rather, it is a deliberate, brave struggle for our ultimate goal, the establishment of autonomy."

112

"Thus far, we had fought for the equal rights of the nations which have been living on this land since ancient times, above all for the securing of the rights of the Hungarian minority, because our dearly beloved Hungarian nation has been the target of the worst attacks. We want to get rid of the humiliating adjective of a 'minority' nation. Let there be no dominant or minority nations here, let everyone have completely equal rights."

Esterhazy outlined the party's moral, economic, social and cultural platform. He called on the Hungarians to be "caring and compassionate toward all our brethren who have shared our land since ancient times and let us join forces so that each individual may pursue his happiness... Let everyone be entitled to his due as determined by their talents, knowledge, skills, education and honesty. When that happens, there will not be 10,000 chosen ones, like today, while in the shadow of the greatest waste and luxury, hundreds of thousands live unemployed, without any income, in abject misery."

The conference was concluded with a banquet where numerous toasts were offered.[181]

On December 29, 1932, Dr. Gyula Fleischmann, a member of the provincial legislature, discussed in an article the election of Janos Esterhazy. The article was entitled "What Is the Meaning of the Election of A Chairman in the Politics of the Christian Socialist Party?" He pointed out that Dr. Geza Szullo, in his capacity as chairman of the joint parliamentary club, would continue to guide the party's activities in Parliament.

Dr. Fleischmann noted that Janos Esterhazy, the new national chairman, was confronted with considerable prejudice. Some were objecting his aristocratic background. However, he overcame this objection, according to Fleischmann, with his forthright manner, his simplicity and his democratic thinking which was free of any aristocratic exclusivity.

Others, especially some of the older generations, were upset by Esterhazy's youth. But this objection was even less valid because the new times demanded new, energetic young men, not just in the ranks but in leadership positions, as well.

Fleischmann concluded by quoting Esterhazy's keynote, "to follow the old path toward new goals." It met a favorable response everywhere and helped forge unity within the entire Christian Socialist Party, he wrote.[182]

Janos Esterhazy was greeted with great enthusiasm on the occasion of his election by the Hungarian population of Slovakia and

Subcarpathian Ruthenia, by various branches of his own party, as well as the Hungarian National Party.[183]

The new national chairman spent much of the first half of 1933 on the road, giving speeches all over the country. On January 20, he attended the funeral of Rezso Bohm, eulogizing the late senator of his party. On January 21, he was given an enthusiastic reception in Rozsnyo and in Eastern Slovakia. On January 27, he spoke in Bodrogkoz, on the 30th in Munkacs, Nagyszollos, Beregszasz and Huszt. On February 15, in Pozsony, he gave a report about his travels around the country. On February 27, Esterhazy spoke in Kassa, on March 6 in Ersekujvar and on March 18 in Ipolysag where he declared war on the new educational act which was very harmful for the Hungarians. On May 17, he spoke in Zsigard.

On June 28, Esterhazy presented his platform at the Otatra-fured conference of the National Christian Socialist Party. He said: "The party's policies had been correct and the uncompromising opposition politics continues to present the only ray of hope for improving the lot of Slovakia and its original inhabitants. The Hungarians were the hardest hit by the peace treaties because they were transferred to other countries without asking for their consent. The same treaty that provided the successor states with their territory also obligated them to respect the rights of national minorities, guarantee their cultural development and, in general, treat them in the same fashion as those belonging to the national majority are treated.

"Thanks to decades of propaganda efforts, at the end of World War One, the Slovak population of Hungary was led to believe that it would have an independent national existence. The Slavic propagandists did a good job and won many supporters among the Slovak people by promising them complete freedom and, what's more, full autonomy. I can understand that the Slovak people came to believe in those promises and put their trust in them. But the fact is that the promises of autonomy remained just that -- promises.

"For telling the truth and for demanding for everyone their due, the Christian Socialist Party is being ridiculously accused with of being irredentist. We demand our right of self-determination under existing laws, along with full autonomy for Slovakia and Subcarpathian Ruthenia, so that we may secure our national, religious and cultural development... We cannot trust anyone but ourselves because we have been left alone. We will only have what we we have fought for."[184]

In early July, 1933, the party's Slovak and German adherents gave Esterhazy an enthusiastic reception as he traveled through the

Nyitra valley. On July 14 he joined Hungarian leaders from Subcarpathian Ruthenia in briefing the Minister of Interior about flood damage. Next day, he launched a nationwide campaign on behalf of the flood victims of Tiszaujlak and Subcarpathian Ruthenia.[185]

On September 27, 1933, Esterhazy attended party rallies in Szogyen and Kemend. In early October, he spoke at the Pozsony assembly of the Hungarian Association of the League of Nations in the Republic of Czechoslovakia, where he declared once again: "We will always remain on the path of legality but we demand that others, too, follow the same path."[186]

In his Christmas article on December 24, 1933, Esterhazy noted that on his visit to Slovakia, Foreign Minister Benes had thrown "morsels of recognition" to the Hungarians. "Fourteen years had to pass," Esterhazy wrote, "before a bit of recognition was accorded the Hungarians. However, whatever is given by one hand may be quickly taken away by the other.

"In Ersekujvar, Mr. Benes spoke of the nation building ability of the Hungarians which, he said, has been manifested ever since St. Stephen converted the Hungarian people to Christianity. But in the December 17 edition of the *Prager Presse* we read that 'The constructive, nation building ability of the Hungarians has fallen apart before history's seat of judgment.'"[187]

In his Christmas statement to the newspaper *Hirado*, Esterhazy recalled the time when he was greeted by farmers in a village, who told him, "We won't hurt anyone, but nobody should hurt us, either!" "I believe," Esterhazy added," this expresses the wishes of the Hungarians." He emphasized again that "Hungarians respect the law, Hungarians pay their taxes, whether in blood or other currency. Hungarians meet their obligations to the state. But, naturally, Hungarians also demand everything that is their due from the state and the government."[188]

On March 16, 1934, Esterhazy pledged in an editorial solidarity with the Hungarian and German Catholics of Pozsony in their struggle for self-government. On May 5, he and Jabloniczky participated in rallies at Bos and Balonya.[189]

At the May 22 meeting of the national party leadership, Esterhazy outlined his views on every major question in domestic politics. In the same address, he referred once again to the recently heard seductive siren songs of Benes who paid tribute to Hungary's heroic role in the defense of the West. But Esterhazy added: "I'll mention just one thing to illuminate Benes' two-faced, or rather many-faced politics. The other day, speaking in Subcarpathian Ruthenia, Benes excused the delay in granting the region its autonomy by saying that if Subcarpathian Ruthenia had been given autonomy any sooner, the Hungarians and the Jews would have prevailed."

Referring to the oft-discussed role of the so-called Catholic Block in Parliament, Esterhazy declared that "whether we are Catholics or Protestants, we will never permit our religious faith and convictions to be degraded to become political tools of dubious value."[190]

On June 19, 1934, Esterhazy spoke in Parkany, on June 27 in Leker, on July 10 in Benye and Nagyolved, on October 3 in Ipolysag and Szalatnya. Everywhere he was received with the greatest enthusiasm and affection.[191]

On October 20, at the Ersekujvar meeting of district chairmen and secretaries, Esterhazy declared: "Regardless of national, social, professional and any other differences, the National Christian Socialist Party wishes to secure the original inhabitants' basic conditions of existence."[192]

On October 24, 1934, Esterhazy visited the party organization in Subcarpathian Ruthenia.[193]

In the December 25, 1934 Christmas edition of the newspaper *Hirado*, Janos Esterhazy answered a question about his views regarding the destiny of Czechoslovakia's Hungarian population in the immediate future in anticipation of various elections that were expected to take place in 1935. "Our conduct," he said, "must be guided by nothing else but the efforts to secure the existence, happiness and development of the Hungarian people in this land. All Hungarians who live here must participate in this endeavor," Esterhazy added.[194]

With the coming of the new year of 1935, Janos Esterhazy continued his tireless travels around the country, informing the people and keeping their hopes alive. Thus, between February 9 and 11, he visited Gomor and Nograd counties, as well as Losonc, Bussa and Fulek; on February 26, Tardoskedd; on March 5, Galanta; on March 12, the Szepes district, the Golnic valley and Bodrogkoz. On April 3, accompanied by Dr. Geza Szullo, he went to Leva and Zseliz; on April 16, to Ipolysag and the Ipoly and Nyitra valleys, to Csallokoz and the industrial plant of Mecenzef. Everywhere Esterhazy went, he was greeted by enthusiastic crowds.[195]

Prior to the elections of May 19, 1935, Esterhazy delivered a major address to the April 26 party conference at Otatrafured. As he had told in an earlier interview with the *Hirado* newspaper, "The great virtue of the Hungarian people is that when the fateful hour arrives, they always find themselves." Once again he stressed that "we will be able to wage a successful struggle only if all those who have the interests of the original inhabitants on their hearts will share a joint platform and work for the common goal with total selflessness and one-hundred-percent loyalty to each other. This alone," he said, "is sufficient reason to enter a joint slate with the Hungarian National Party in the parliamentary and provincial elections.

"It is not enough just to maintain and protect what we have accomplished, we must continue to build on it. That is the only way we can assure that our role in the opposition may turn into a constructive effort on behalf of the original inhabitants. That is how we can build the foundations and work for a better future which is our God-given right," Esterhazy said, his speech repeatedly interrupted by enthusiastic applause.[196]

Janos Esterhazy had every reason to be satisfied with the outcome of the election. He analyzed it in some detail on November 30, at the Zsolna meeting of the national party leadership, which we will discuss a little later.

Esterhazy' delivered his **first address to Parliament** on June 25. It had a stormy impact. Members in the governing party benches kept trying to interrupt his speech, frequently forcing Speaker Onderco to gavel them to order.

"As I make my first speech here today," Esterhazy began, "I will try to remain objective and speak objectively. The Hungarian people have had grievances for 16 years. The various coalition governments of the day have never remedied these grievances as they should have according to the peace treaties which have guaranteed such remedies for us Hungarians, who are living here.

"We have not been transferred without out consent to the Czechoslovak Republic just to allow the Czechoslovak governments of the day not to honor one-hundred percent our rights as a minority, our cultural, linguistic and economic rights. The economic condition and the poverty of Slovakia and Subcarpathian Ruthenia can be understood only by those who live there and are familiar with the circumstances. I know that in Eastern Slovakia there is no bread, I know that in Vrchovina there is no bread and that the chief causes of the misery are the very same political parties in the coalition government, which have set aside their social concepts and voted for every law that would let them stay near the pork barrel.

"There is another question, to the greater glory of democracy: Even today, after 17 years, there are still some 30,000 citizenship applications, sitting in various offices, waiting to be acted on, still unresolved simply because the applicants are good Hungarians.

"The Prime Minister also spoke of friendship with our neighboring countries. Deputy Teplansky, who belongs to his party, said that Hungary must give up every revisionist effort. Speaking of revision, it is the Czechoslovak government above all which ought to revise its policies in the treatment of us, Hungarians.

"Speaking of myself, all I can say is that there is incredibly great misery in Slovakia and Subcarpathian Ruthenia, the economy and industry are on the verge of bankruptcy, the cold chimneys of the factories throughout Slovakia speak of the terribly great number of unemployed -- something that the government has not done anything to remedy up until now.

"Public works contracts are given to firms in Prague or to the Slovak branches of Czech and Moravian companies whose taxes enrich the treasuries of Bohemia and Moravia. As we can see, the condition of Slovakia and Subcarpathian Rutenia, and above all of their Hungarian population keeps deteriorating through the years. Very soon, no citizen of Slovakia or Subcarpathian Ruthenia will be able to find employment in the public sector. We demand, therefore, autonomy for Slovakia."[197]

On September 28, in an urgent request to the government, Janos Esterhazy urged settlement of the question of county retirees' pensions. On November 1, speaking in the Agriculture Committee, he relayed the demands of the farmers of Slovakia and Subcarpathian Ruthenia. Likewise, on November 28, in a Slovak language speech delivered before the Agriculture Committee, he spoke in great detail about conditions on the state-owned estates.

The state-owned estates, according to Esterhazy, were equally distributed between Bohemia, Slovakia and Subcarpathian Ruthenia. But if we were to look at the distribution of their net income in the three provinces, he said, we would find that the state-owned estates in Bohemia had an income of 30 million Crowns, those in Subcarpathian Ruthenia 8 million and those in Slovakia 21 million. At the same time, government employees working on the state-owned estates earned 41 million Crowns, while those in Slovakia made only 14 million and in Subcarpathian Ruthenia, 9 million Crowns.[198]

The party's national leadership conference in Zsolna was opened by a major speech by Janos Esterhazy, on November 29. He reviewed the previous three years, describing the difficult conditions under which the party began its activities in early 1932. "The conditions were increasingly worsening but our work did not slacken," he said.

"The elections called for the spring of 1935 did not find us unprepared," Esterhazy continued. "We can state with hindsight that we had to fight the election campaign under the most adverse circumstances, yet we can be satisfied with the outcome because we have held our own and kept all our seats. Our main weapon is our spiritual and moral strength, resting on a legal foundation. We use that weapon to fight for our due."

Esterhazy then noted that the government has a new head, a Slovak. That, however "does not affect our previous positions because Prime Minister Hodza is new only to his office but we have never heard him say or do anything which would lead us to believe that he intends to introduce new methods or new procedures in government or in dealing with the problem of the national minorities," Esterhazy said.[199]

Let us take a look now at the important diplomatic developments that took place during this period and had a major impact on the policies of the Czechoslovak government.

The Sudeten German Party Comes to the Fore

The Sudeten Germans, under the leadership of Konrad Henlein, won an overwhelming victory in the May elections and, with their 55 parliamentary deputies, became the largest party of Czechoslovakia. This development did not go unnoticed on the international diplomatic scene. It caught the attention, first of all, of the British government. Henlein was invited by the Royal Institute of International Affairs to visit London.

In his London speech, Henlein emphasized that the Sudeten Germans are demanding only their rights, otherwise they abide by the Czechoslovak constitution. Their movement came into being only because their wishes went unfulfilled. Their goal is to secure the peaceful development of the German people, Henlein said.[200]

In addition to the British, Henlein sought and established contact with French circles and with diplomats of other nations, too, at the League of Nations in Geneva. Everywhere he went, he informed his contacts about the Czechoslovak goverment's repressive policies against its national minorities.

Janos Esterhazy Meets Benes

Another important event, as far as the Hungarians were concerned, occurred toward the end of the year when Benes invited Esterhazy to Prague. With the declining health of Masaryk, presidential elections were on the horizon, with Benes being Masaryk's chosen successor. This prompted Benes to begin talks with leaders of the political parties. Esterhazy was one of the first political leaders he saw and Benes admitted that many injustices have been inflicted on the Hungarians. He promised to put an end to to the injustices in return for Esterhazy's support in the presidential election.

Esterhazy suggested that Jaross be included in the talks. Not long afterwards, a Hungarian delegation went to see Benes and he made all kinds of promises. The delegation wanted to have the promises in writing but Benes was reluctant to do so. Finally, they compromised, with Benes agreeing to confirm his promises in writing in response to a written document containing the Hungarian demands. But he never kept his promise. Nor did Benes keep his campaign promises after he was elected to the presidency.[201]

Returning to Janos Esterhazy's parliamentary activities, he gave the first speech following Prime Minister Hodza's long address on December 5, 1935, in the House of Deputies debate over the 1936 budget. Hodza had said that Czechoslovakia must cooperate, first of all, with its immediate neighbors, Austria and Hungary. He analyzed in some detail the country's foreign trade with Austria and Hungary. Then he outlined his conceptions of Central Europe. And he emphasized that it is a natural task for the government to settle the question of national minorities.

Janos Esterhazy was the first to speak in the debate. He started off by saying that the mistakes which had been cited so many times already, have not been rectified by the new budget. "May I be permitted therefore to address first of all the question of Hungarian schools, Hungarian culture," Esterhazy began. Quoting verbatim Paragraph 9 of the peace treaty of St.Germain, he said, "The national minorities must be assured an appropriate share of the enjoyment and use of the funds which are spent from the public treasury in the state or municipal budgets for educational, religious or welfare purposes." We look in vain in the budget for any item which would show what percentage is being allocated for Hungarian causes, Hungarian schools, Hungarian education, he said.

"Even if I were to take the 1930 census as the baseline -- which I cannot accept as completely reliable," Esterhazy said, "Hungarians represent 4.8 percent of the nationwide population. That means that Hungarians should be allocated the same percentage of the budget. But this is not the case," he said and presented data in support of his argument.

The same situation prevails with the junior high schools, Esterhazy continued. "There are only 18 junior high schools in Slovakia, well below the national average. There is no mention in the budget of funds for the one and only Hungarian teacher's college, even though it was included in last year's budget. Regarding institutions of high education, the situation, as far as Hungarians are concerned, is outright catastrophic. There is not a single Hungarian chair and the authorities have no intention to establish one.

"It is often said that the Hungarians have their share of minority schools. Often, however, what is meant by minority schools is Czechoslovak schools built in areas with homogeneous Hungarian population. These are the schools that Foreign Minister Benes likes to refer to before foreign audiences as proof of loyalty toward the national minorities. Thus, for example, in the village of Vaga the official census shows a population of 93% Hungarian and only 4.3% Slovak. Despite these official figures, the *Slovenska League* has demanded construction of a Czechoslovak school in Vaga. The matter has been considered by several authorities and now the national government is about to decide whether the Hungarians who represent 93% of the population need to have a Czechoslovak school. Similar conditions prevail in Budahaza, Csecs, Makranc, Korosmezo, Beregszasz, Gyorke, Guta, Tiszaujlak... and so on and on. The Hungarian high school in Pozsony shares a building with the local prison. During the break, the students mingle in the corridors with gypsy women waiting for court hearings."

Regarding the *Slovenska League*, Esterhazy registered his objection to the fact that the organization's goal, supported by governmental subsidies, is to encroach on the rights of another national minority. He discussed in some detail a scandalous situation in Eperjes where officially sanctioned posters were used to incite the population against the Hungarians.

"We have never demanded anything to which we are not entitled, we only want what is our just due under the terms of the peace treaty and the constitution. However, if the Hungarian population must pay taxes and those taxes are used to maintain the state without granting the Hungarians their constitutional rights, I cannot agree to this budget," Esterhazy concluded.[202]

Prime Minister Hodza spoke of his conception which became known as the Hodza Plan. He wanted to persuade five Danubian nations -- Czechoslovakia, Rumania, Yugoslavia, Austria and Hungary -- to cooperate economically which would lead to increased political cooperation. Remembering the failure of earlier plans, Hodza sought certain compromises with Germany. He also sought the approval of London and Paris, as well.

The British and the French looked upon the Hodza Plan favorably but failed to give it any meaningful support. This ambivalent attitude was adopted by the Danubian nations, too. Yugoslavia and Hungary did not support the Hodza Plan, while Rumania and Austria looked at it more positively. Hitler, naturally, was opposed to it because, as eventually it became apparent, he had in mind a totally different role for this region in his expansionist plans.

Some sources ascribe the failure of the plan, at least in part, to domestic politics because the foreign policy conceptions of Hodza and his supporters ran counter to Benes' French orientation and, especially, his leaning toward the Soviet Union. The elections resulted in victory for Benes and that sealed the fate of the Hodza Plan. Nevertheless, Hodza managed to secure the posts of Prime Minister and Foreign Minister, allegedly as a reward for lining up support within the Agrarian Party to Benes's election to the presidency.[203]

Following the failure of the Hodza Plan, at the end of February, 1936, Hodza resigned from his post as Foreign Minister. He was succeeded on February 29 by Dr. Kamill Krofta, a historian, who espoused the foreign policy line of Benes.

The Occupation of the Rhineland

The next month saw a highly significant event whose consequences soon became apparent. On March 7, 1936, in defiance of the Treaty of Saint Germain and the Locarno Agreement, German forces occupied the Rhineland. What made this move so significant was that Hitler was able to carry it out without any opposition on the part of the Western powers. The League of Nations and the Locarno powers lodged a protest but nothing else happened beyond that.

The Western powers, particularly Great Britain were eager to end or at least reduce tensions among the the Danubian powers. Prompted by the substantial shift in the balance of power, the British were advocating normalization of the relationship between the *Little Entente* and Hungary. The *Little Entente* states themselves came to recognize by this time the illusory nature of making themselves dependent solely on the Western powers and began to seek a rapprochement with Hungary. But it came too late.

A significant improvement in relations between the two parties was not in the interest of Germany and Italy because they had based their Central European strategy on the skillful manipulation of the existing conflict. Germany wanted Hungary to make revisionist demands on Czechoslovakia and, at the same time, to try to settle its differences with Yugoslavia. Even though the Italian interests at the time were not in full accord with those of the Germans, as a result of the newly-formed Berlin-Rome Axis, Italy's interests had to be put on the backburner.

It fully became apparent by this time how many opportunities have been missed by the *Little Entente* powers over 17 years without ever attempting a serious rapprochement with Hungary. The efforts by Esterhazy and other leaders of the Hungarian minority to persuade the Prague government to meet their just demands were in vain. As long as Prague felt it had the support of the Western powers, it had no intention of taking the Hungarian grievances seriously.

For a thousand years, until the establishment of Czechoslovakia, Hungary and Poland had a peaceful and secure common border. This was of vital interest for both countries. Consequently, in April 1936, Polish Prime Minister Koschialkowski led a delegation to Budapest to discuss the Czechoslovak issue, as well as the question of the common Hungarian-Polish border. The Polish delegates declared that the views of the Polish and Hungarian governments were identical in this matter. This declaration indicated a change in the Polish government's position regarding the so-called Pilsudsky Plan. This plan has called for the establishment of a federated state consisting of Poland, Galicia, the Soviet Ukraine, Bukovina and Carpatho-Ukraine (Subcarpathian Ruthenia).[204]

Meanwhile, on April 3, the Austrian government arbitrarily set aside the military restrictions imposed by the Peace Treaty of Saint Germain and announced that it would re-introduce universal military service.[205] This move stirred quite an alarm among the *Little Entente* powers.

The leaders of the Sudeten German Party wanted to send a delegation to Budapest to explore the possibility of establishing links with the leaders of the Hungarian minority. They contacted the Hungarian government in April, seeking an appointment with the Prime Minister. However, the Hungarian government was unable to grant the request, partly on account of the Prime Minister's illness and also because of the visit by the Polish delegation.[206] The cancellation of the visit did not create a problem because, in the meantime, Benes and Hodza invited the Sudeten German leaders to negotiate.

While these diplomatic efforts were going on, the Prime Minister of Yugoslavia requested Goring to help promote better relations between Yugoslavia and Hungary. Goring received a favorable reply from Hungarian Foreign Minister Kanya.[207]

On May 16, Czechoslovakia and the Soviet Union signed an agreement of mutual assistance. According to diplomatic reports, Czechoslovakia had lost its faith in the Western powers and, driven by its fear of Germany, was drawing closer to the Russians. Overcome by a war psychosis, the Czechoslovak leaders were talking about imminent war.[208]

Turning once again to the Hungarians in Czechoslovakia, as we have already noted, overcoming all their difficulties, the two Hngarian parties emerged stronger than ever from the previous year's elections, gaining several thousand new votes. It is fitting here to pay our respects to the men who had represented the two Hungarian parties in the Czechoslovak parliament and were in the forefront of the Hungarians' poltical struggles prior to the first Vienna Decision. The representives included Count Janos Esterhazy, Janos Holota, Andor Jaross, Endre Korlath, Andor Nietzsch (the leader of the German population of Szepes), Agoston Petrasek, Geza Porubszky, Jozsef Szent-Ivany, Geza Szullo. In the Senate: Kalman Fussy, Karoly Hokky, Miklos Pajor, Jozsef Torkoly (who was succeeded upon his death in 1937 by Bela Szilassy) and Imre Turchanyi.

We have also noted that following Masaryk's resignation from the presidency, the two Hungarian parties trusted Benes's promises and voted for his candidacy. However, Benes never fulfilled his promises, demonstrating that the Hungarians could not trust even the chief of state to honor his word.

Under the pressure of events, the two Hungarian parties decided to carry out their long-planned fusion. Initially, political necessity required to organize two separate parties. Various efforts to drive a wedge between them made it crucially important that they unite. This was clear in the National Christian Socialist Party's response, signed by Geza Szullo and Janos Esterhazy, to the Hungarian National Party's call for a merger. Accordingly, preparations got underway.[209]

Meanwhile in a parliamentary debate on February 19, Esterhazy delivered a sharp criticism of the deficit of 6,000 million accumulated over a five-year period.[210]

On February 28, Esterhazy delivered a major address, criticizing the Uhlir Act to regulate private schools. He noted, among others, that 12,400 Hungarian children are forced to attend non-Hungarian schools. Part of this speech was delivered in Slovak.[211]

On March 25, 1936, Janos Esterhazy urged the government to restore the right to use the Hungarian language at the city hall of Kassa (Kosice). This had been requested three years earlier but no action has been taken about it.[212] On April 22, Esterhazy sharply rejected the government's proposal to dissolve the political parties. "We demand full democratic rights for our people," he said.[213]

At a May 4 political rally in Kassa (Kosice), Esterhazy declared, "The security of the state depends, above all, on the satisfaction of its citizens."[214]

The Merger of the Two Hungarian Parties

Meanwhile, preparations were rapidly progressing for the merger of the two parties. A Congress was called for June 21, 1936, in Ersekujvar. The resolution declaring the merger of the two parties and the establishment of the "United National Christian Socialist and Hungarian National Party" gave voice to the will of the entire Hungarian population of Czechoslovakia.

The Congress was a festive occasion. Following three opening worship services, a crowd of 7,000 assembled in a decorated sports field. In addition to girls dressed in Hungarian folk costume and farmers wearing their traditional attire, some 500 Slovaks, wearing their national costume, from the Privigye and Tapolcsany region, also attended.

Dr. Geza Szullo opened the Congress. "All we need to survive is God's grace and our insistence on our rights," he began. "The survival of our race is not due to happenstance, it is the result of Divine wisdom. Let us follow our own direction and remain loyal to the laws based on the constitution. Let us insist on the fulfillment of our constitutional guarantees and let us not relinquish any of our rights. Our insistence on our rights makes us the protectors, rather than the destroyers of the state," said Dr. Geza Szullo.

Dr. Janos Holota greeted the Congress on behalf of the Hungarians of Ersekujvar. He read a letter from Jozsef Szent-Ivany, head of the former Hungarian National Party, whose illness prevented him from attending the Congress. Szent-Ivany expressed the desire for "an understanding among all Hungarians united in service of the national aspirations, eliminating every conflict between Hungarian and Hungarian." The Congress greeted his words with warm applause.

Next the concepts underlying the platform of the new party were outlined by Andor Jaross. "It is an evolutionary, progressive program," he said. "It is modern when so required by the tempo of the new life; it is conservative where we have to dip into the well of ancient law and historical tradition, because we want to provide new values, as well as rescue values from the past to serve the present and, indirectly, the future as well. There is room in this program for every Hungarian and Czechoslovakia.

"We respect the religious faith and convictions of every citizen and when we place Christian morality and national goals on our flag, we do not wish to exclude from our camp Hungarians of the Jewish faith, who have been fighting on our side with unwavering energy for our common national goals. We honor them for their past efforts and we count on them in the future, as well," Jaross said.

Next, legislators of the two parties, as well as members of the Slovakian and Subcarpathian Ruthenian legislature were introduced. Then, the Congress having approved the proposed platform of the united parties, Dr. Geza Szullo declared that the platform has been adopted.

Janos Esterhazy was next, with a bilingual speech in Hungarian and Slovak. First, as required by the merger of the two parties, he announced his resignation as national chairman of his party. Then, amidst warm applause, he said: "We draw the two parties which had accomplished so much into a joint front, placing them on a common platform, so that the expanded efforts of the Hungarians may be greater and even more successful than before."

Following Esterhazy's address, Dr. Geza Szullo, chairman of the Congress, announced to great jubilation that the Congress has declared the establishment of the United National Christian Socialist and Hungarian National Party. The Congress was adjurned following closing remarks by Dr. Bela Szilassy who urged all participants to join in the common effort.

The newly chosen party leadership met in the afternoon to elect members of the presidium and executive committee for the united party. Following a motion by Dr. Geza Szullo, the following were elected:

Andor Jaross, national chairman; Janos Esterhazy, national executive chairman. Dr. Geza Szullo, as head of the party's parliamentary caucus and Deputy Jozsef Szent-Ivany were elected to the presidium. Peter Balazsy, Lipot Gregorovits, Dr. Endre Korlath, Bela Pinter, Dr. Bela Szilassy and Barna Tost were elected vice chairmen.

Following the election of the executive committee, the leadership decided to establish two legal aid offices, one in Pozsony (Bratislava), headed by Dr. Marcell Szilard and one in Rimaszombat, headed by Dr. Jozsef Torkoly.

Andor Jaross, the new national chairman emphasized in his inaugural address that "in order to create complete spiritual harmony, we want to bring about a united spirit among the Hungarian minority. That means that every member of the Hungarian minority should take a united stand on the issues of today and tomorrow."

Jaross' inaugural address was received with great enthusiasm. Janos Esterhazy the party's new national executive chairman was the next speaker. He was greeted with warm applause as he asked for the party's confidence and promised that "Just as in the past, I will continue to perform my assigned tasks in the interest of the Hungarian people with all my strength and enthusiasm."[215]

Among the other national minority parties in Czechoslovakia, the German Christian Socialist Party is worth noting. It was one of the so-called activist groups which submitted its demands in a petition to Prime Minister Hodza. The demands included participation in the country's economy, cessations of efforts to strangle the national character of minorities, elimination of illegalities in the educational system, participation in governmental administration and reform of the census system.[216]

In Hungary itself, Regent Miklos Horthy's late August, 1936, meeting with Hitler in Berchtesgaden was an important news event. According to notes presented to Hitler, the negotiations probably dealt with Yugoslavia, Czechoslovakia, the Rumanian-Soviet pact and the question of Hungary's rearmament.[217]

The serious political situation where the Czechs had found themselves was illuminated by the talks between Frantisek Chvalkovsky, the Czechoslovak Minister to Rome and his Hungarian counterpart, Frigyes Villani. According to Villani's report, Chvalkovsky had told him, "if the Prague government is unable to settle its relationship with Italy and Germany in a satisfactory manner, it will be compelled to depend entirely on Russia because it cannot count on help from the French." Villani added that in view of the Czechs' pro-Russian sentiments, such a policy would be popular and it would be well received by Slovaks and the Subcarpathian Ruthenians also because -- as the Czech diplomat admitted -- they are dissatisfied with the present conditions.[218]

Benes Extends Another Invitation to Janos Esterhazy

A most significant event in the life of the Hungarian people in Czechoslovakia was President Benes's invitation to Janos Esterhazy for a meeting on September 11, 1936. He received Esterhazy in Kistapolcsany, asking him to treat the meeting confidentially and not to issue any public statement.

Benes began by stating that conditions have improved since his last visit to Slovakia. He emphasized that he will always respect the rights of the minorities. He gave an overview of the international situation and said that certain European states may be threatened by revolution. He hinted that Hungary might be one of them.

Benes further stated that revision, as demanded in Hungary, is out of question. But he would be willing to enter the most far-reaching negotiations with Hungary, provided the Hungarians do not raise excessive demands. Benes said he had never been offended by Count Apponyi's demands for a complete nullification of the peace treaties because he was aware that an old man could not be expected suddenly to give up something which he held sacred through a long life. By the same token, the Hungarians should not be surprised either that he, Benes, is not willing to compromise his life's work.

Next, Benes invited the Hungarians to join his government. He said he knows and feels that the Hungarians have grievances against the Czechoslovak government but these grievances could be corrected. Benes hinted that the Hlinka Party may soon enter the government and suggested that the Hungarians, too, might get a cabinet seat without portfolio, along with a certain budget allocation. Benes added that he would very much like to see Esterhazy in that post because he could not see anyone from the older generation taking it.

Finally, Benes brought up the questions the Hungarian political leaders had submitted before the presidential election. He said he is persuaded that none of the requests have been met but he has issued instructions to take care of this matter. And then Benes asked for Esterhazy's reaction to his proposals.

Esterhazy thanked Benes for the briefing. Regarding Benes' statement on the improvement of conditions in Slovakia, he said that in his opinion, just the opposite is true. Slovakia is sinking ever deeper into poverty and the impact of the Czechoslovak societies to strangle the national character of the minorities is being increasingly felt. This, he said, does not make the Hungarians any calmer. They can endure just about everything except the efforts to deprive them of their national identity.

"The Hungarians who live here," said Esterhazy, "know all too well that the Lord did not create the Hungarian race and did not help it to develop and survive through vicissitudes of a thousand years only to allow that after 1,022 years, as the consequence of an unfortunate war, a good part of that race be transmuted into another.

"Throughout their long history, the Hungarians have been stricken by much adversity but their loyalty to their mother tongue and their insistence to use it have always helped them to overcome every calamity. If the Hungarians survived the disaster of Mohacs[219] and managed to live through the long Turkish rule, I am quite certain that the day will come when in this land, too, the Hungarians will determine their own fate and nobody will raise obstacles to the use of their language and culture.

"I deemed it necessary to preface my words with the foregoing," Esterhazy continued, "to make it clear to you, Mr. President, that even though I may not belong to the older generation which, as you said, is not inclined to cooperate, all Hungarians living in this land, no matter what their age, are Hungarians, will remain Hungarians and want to serve the Hungarian cause."

In response to the offer of a cabinet post without portfolio, Esterhazy said that in view of the fact that nothing has happened since December 18 to make the life of the Hungarians easier, it would be very difficult for him to explain to his party why he should bestow his endorsement on the regime. It is up to the Czechoslovak authorities to earn that trust, Esterhazy added.[220]

On September 29, 1936, the United Hungarian Party held a rally in Leva, which turned into a celebration of Hungarian unity. Janos Esterhazy emphasized in his speech that "the nation can achieve its goals only if it works through the party for the common cause."[221]

Previously, on September 2, the United Hungarian Party submitted a memorandum to the government. This memorandum came to be regarded as one of the most basic documents of Hungarian minority politics. Right at the outset, it declares that at the signing of the peace treaties, the government of the Czechoslovak Republic made a solemn promise to the Allied Powers to maintain the right to their language of the national minorities transferred to the new state and would grant members of the racial, religious and linguistic minorities the same rights that are enjoyed by all citizens of the republic.

Another treaty undertaking of the Czechoslovak government is not to alter these obligations without the approval of the Allied Powers. On March 6, 1920, the constitutional assembly of the Czechoslovak republic enacted a law about the use of minority languages. This law entered force as soon as it was enacted. The Hungarians were not represented in the constitutional assembly, even though the government could have provided for such representation because delegates to the assembly were not elected. They were appointed by the government.

Contrary to both the letter and the spirit of the Treaty of St. Germain en Laye, as well as the Czechoslovak constitution itself, the language act links the exercise of minority language rights to a 20 percent ratio. The decree to implement the law, issued at the urging of the national minorities, granted only the most minimal rights and even these were not enforced by the authorities.

Te memorandum stated that before they would turn to the Council of the League of Nations, as provided by the peace treaty, "in keeping with our previous practice, we request the government first to remedy our grievances." With that, the memorandum outlined in general terms the grievances, stating that if the government so desired, complete, detailed documentation would be furnished.

The list of grievances included the following areas: language usage in the courts; establishent of judicial districts; the use of the Hungarian language in public administration (in Slovakia and Subcarpathian Ruthenia, there were more than a thousand villages and towns which were entitled by the law to use Hungarian in their official correspondence); a Hungarian version of the laws (often, laws were translated into Hungarian only after they had been repealed already); right to use the Hungarian language in parliament; extension of the language act to the Post Office and the railroads; Hungarian administrators in counties populated by Hungarians; educational grievances and demands, and other demands relating to the use of language.

The memorandum stated that rule of the law is a major precondition for the peaceful development of the state and it rests on the public's respect for the law. "We, Hungarians, are law abiding people, therefore it is our just demand that the responsible government respect and enforce all the laws. And that includes rectifying grievances," the memorandum declared.[222]

In October, 1936, Prime Minister Gyula Gombos of Hungary died and was replaced by Kalman Daranyi. One of his first foreign policy moves was to try to establish a relationship with England and the other Western powers. Following the establishment of the Berlin-Rome Axis, Italy took on a diminished role -- a fact of major significance for other nations, as well. Italy's firm stand against the *Anschluss* between Germany and Austria had weakened. Also, Hungary's rejectionist stance against the *Little Entente* underwent a change because of Daranyi's intention to negotiate with the *Little Entente*. He made the question of national minorities the focal point of these negotiations. As a result of these efforts, the Germans came to distrust Daranyi's policies.

Janos Esterhazy's Speeches in the Budget Debate

Meanwhile, the Prague parliament enacted a law to devalue the currency. Janos Esterhazy sharply criticized this move. He said, "Before attempting to devalue the crown we should have assured that it is not followed by a general price increase."[223] On October 16, he lodged a protest against forcing the Hungarian students of Bajanhaza to attend a Slovak school.[224]

In a committee hearing on the budget, on November 4, 1936, Esterhazy declared, "Slovakia and Subcarpathian Ruthenia, along with the Hungarian question, are the most burning problems of the state, in need of the most urgent solution."[225] Addressing the same committee, on November 11, he sharply criticized the Prime Minister's plans for minority reforms. On November 14, he criticized the educational budget, noting that since its establishment, the Czechoslovak state had spent 24,000 million on education but only a tiny fraction of that sum went to the Hungarians.[226]

On December 2, 1936, Esterhazy delivered a major, comprehensive speach in the house budget debate. "It is said," he began, "that we are not satisfied. Well, let us look and see objectively, who is satisfied in this republic. The Czechs are not satisfied because they are afraid of bankruptcy. The Slovaks are not satisfied because they have not been granted autonomy, the same as the Ruthenians, even though it has been guaranteed by international treaty. Neither are the Germans satisfied, nor can the Hungarians be satisfied because their minority rights, guaranteed by the peace treaty and the constitution have not been granted.

"We have thousands of grievances. In villages with all-Hungarian population we do not have elementary schools. In the two-room school of the pure Hungarian Macsola, a Czech school was set up to accomodate the children of a handful law enforcement officers. As a result, there is one Czech teacher with 35 students in one room, while in the other room, two Hungarian teachers are taking turns teaching 124 Hungarian students. The Hungarian school of Ipolyker was closed in 1935. The village of Machaza has repeatedly petitioned for a school for its 42 children, to no avail. In the village of Sirak, 58 parents requested the introduction of Hungarian teaching, to no avail.

"In Aknaszlatina, a two-room auxiliary building serves as the schoolhouse. One room is occupied by a handful of Czech children, while 470 Hungarian children take turns with Ruthenian children in the other. In Palyi, some 100 Hungarian families have requested the non-compulsory teaching of the Hungarian language. The school principal did not even bother to forward the request to higher authorities."

And so continued Esterhazy's litany of grievances. He pointed to a similar situation with the secondary schools also. "These, gentlemen, are crimes crying to high heavens," he said. "And legislators from the governing party calmly ignore our grievances, saying that the Hungarians have all the rights they are entitled to; that there is nothing amiss here; that the republic is threatened by the murderous Hungarian revisionism and the murderous German Hitlerism, therefore they are rushing into an alliance with Stalin.

"Eighteen years ago, the responsible leaders of the republic promised autonomy to Slovakia and Subcarpathian Ruthenia. Let the government, at last, grant those two provinces autonomy so that we and our Slovak brethren may determine the destiny of Slovakia."

Esterhazy's speech was repeatedly interrupted by hecklers but he just brushed them aside.[227]

On December 14, 1936, the first flag of the United Hungarian Party was dedicated by the Hungarian farmers of Abauj county. The large, festive celebration was marked by a rousing speech by Esterhazy.[228] On December 19, in Zsolna, he addressed the United Hungarian Party's executive committee.[229]

Those "crimes crying to high heavens," that is to say, the various measures depriving the Hungarians of their treaty rights, which Esterhazy had frequently complained about in the Prague parliament, did not cease. They were becoming increasingly grievous as time went by. Eventually, as we shall see, the Hungarian government joined the leaders of the Hungarian minority in addressing these problems. The tactical moves of Hodza, such as his November 10, 1936 statement about the solution of the problems of the minorities, as described in Part One, or his February 18, 1936 meeting with the Sudeten German activists, which has been so much ballyhooed by the Czechs, did not bring any change in the lot of the minorities.

Diplomatic Negotiations
between Hungary and the *Little Entente*

The increased participation of the Hungarian government in the attempts to solve the problem of the national minorities was actually promoted by the *Little Entente* powers through their approach to Hungary in early February, 1937. On January 19, Kobr, the Czechoslovak Minister to Budapest, spoke to Foreign Minister Kanya about the moderation of the sharp war of words between the Hungarian and Czechoslovak news media. He also brought an offer of a non-aggression treaty between Hungary and Czechoslovakia in return for recognition of Hungary's right to military parity.

Kanya referred to the April, 1935, talks in Venice where, he recalled, he had set conditions regarding full military parity and the condition of the Hungarian national minorities. On the same occasion many others, including British Foreign Secretary Eden, acknowledged that Hungary was pursuing peaceful policies.

"It is a well-known fact," said Kanya, "that all the international problems experienced by Czechoslovakia can be traced back primarily to the Prague government's treatment of its national minorities... Several European powers, including Italy and Austria, share our position regarding military parity, therefore any concession on our part is out of question.

"In my opinion, a rapprochement between Czechoslovakia and Hungary will be possible only if the Czechoslovak government recognizes our right to military parity and, with a noble gesture, remedies at least the most basic grievances of the Hungarian minority in Czechoslovakia," Foreign Minister Kanya concluded.[230]

On June 10, 1937, the Hungarian Minister in Prague reiterated to Foreign Minister Krofta that a declaration on mutual non-aggression would be conditioned on a concurrent, far-reaching gesture by the *Little Entente* powers toward their Hungarian minorities. Krofta's response was that under no circumstances would the Czechoslovak government allow it policies toward the minorities become the subject of an international agreement.[231]

Meanwhile, Hodza, too, discussed resumption of relations with Hungary in a conference of the three *Little Entente* prime ministers.[232] That resulted in August 30, 1937, meeting in Sinaia where Hungary was represented by Laszlo Bardossy, the Hungarian Minister in Bucharest.

Bardossy presented a four-point proposal which included: 1. recognition of the right to military parity; 2. declaration that a state may order certain administrative measures on its own accord. Following a previous agreement, these are listed in an attached confidential annex; 3. Hungary's declaration of non-aggression, reciprocated by her neighboring states; 4. the responsible authorities of the *Little Entente* states establish contact with leaders of their Hungarian minorities to negotiate a far-reaching settlement of the conditions of those minorities.[233]

In his talks with Krofta, Minister Bardossy remarked that the annex about the administrative measures would contain the memorandum submitted in December, 1935, by Esterhazy to Benes, following his election to the presidency. Benes had promised to comply with the requests in the memorandum in return for Hungarian support in his election campaign, but subsequently he failed to do so. Krofta replied that this question can be settled only on the basis of mutuality, securing the rights of Hungary's Slovak minority as well. Bardossy rejected this condition, saying that the situation of the Slovaks in Hungary is not comparable to the situation of the Hungarians in Czechoslovakia. Krofta, however, insisted on his condition.[234] With Kanya's agreement, the negotiations continued and it was decided that they would be resume in Geneva.[235] On September 13, the *Little Entente* states met in Geneva, but nothing was accomplished.

The Hungarian view at the time was that even though the *Little Entente* states had agreed to bring up their national minority policies in international negotiations, "in their narrow-mindedness they failed to do the very thing they should have done, they failed to meet numerous just demands of their Hungarian minorities."[236]

While this was going on, Janos Esterhazy was unceasingly lobbying the Prague government, demanding that the endless grievances of the Hungarian minority be remedied. On January 30, 1937, he submitted a question to Minister Derer compelling him to act on a question submitted earlier, in 1936, regarding the use of the Hungarian language in the court at Ersekujvar. On February 18, Esterhazy demanded government assistance to Hungarian college students. On February 18th, in the house agriculture committee, he demanded revision of the agricultural reform. On June 4, in a speech in parliament, he demanded establishment of a Hungarian university.

On June 15, Esterhazy was the first speaker in the debate of the government's bill about the authority of the governor of Subcarpathian Ruthenia. On June 19, he and Holota requested that the grievances of the small paprika growers be remedied. On June 21, at a demonstration by 8,000 United Hungarian Party supporters in Nyitra, he demanded autonomy for Slovakia. On October 6, Esterhazy declared, "the fulfillment of our rights can be achieved only through autonomy." On October 10, he submitted a question in parliament regarding the naming of a chief judge in the Rimaszombat district and demanded to know why are there no Hungarians appointed to leading positions in the judiciary. On November 10, Esterhazy questioned the Minister of Interior about the violation of Hungarian language rights in the Feled, Galanta and Ersekujvar districts.[237]

It became clear by November, 1937, that in order to steer the German expansionist efforts towards the East, the Western powers became willing to accept Hitler's plans for the reorganization of Central Europe. This fact left its imprint on the whole continent. It affected every foreign policy move.

The Hungarian political leadership, too, was guided by this recognition in its negotiations. It was aware of the fact that the moderate policies it had pursued for a long time, especially with regard to territorial demands, particularly the efforts to have these demands satisfied in a peaceful and mutually acceptable fashion, would no longer satisfy the aggressive German policies, sanctioned by the Western powers. And that is what came to pass.

The Czechoslovak-Hungarian diplomatic negotiations from October through December, 1937, also demonstrated the same narrow-minded attitude of the *Little Entente* states, which we have noted before, in sharp contrast with the great patience that Foreign Minister Kanya had displayed in the matter of the Hungarian national minorities. That was conceded by not less a person than Czechoslovak Foreign Minister Krofta on October 17, 1937, to the Hungarian Minister in Prague. The Minister reported that Krofta "spoke with admiration about the great patience" displayed by Foreign Minister Kanya in this matter.[238] But this did not prevent two days later Kobr, the Czechoslovak Minister to Budapest, from telling Kanya that Czechoslovakia cannot accede to the demand of the Bardossy memorandum that the

138

Prague government keep the promises it had made to Szullo and Esterhazy. Kobr used the occasion to attack Szullo and Esterhazy.[239]

Two months later, on December 21, in a conversation with Gabor Apor, permanent deputy to the Hungarian Foreign Minister, Kobr asked Apor about his talks with French Foreign Minister Delbos who had stopped in Budapest on his tour of Central Europe. Delbos's moderating influence of the *Little Entente* states and his efforts at compromise were reflected in his own attitude. He stated his own view that "the question of the minorities must be solved, it is a matter of life or death for Czechoslovakia."

Delbos was certain about a Czech-German compromise and said that this would be automatically beneficial for the Hungarians, too. "If the Rumanians are not willing to go along," he said, "a bilateral solution may be possible, without their participation or, perhaps, together with the Yugoslavs." He always stressed, however, that these were his personal opinions.[240]

This possibility was underscored by a report from the Hungarian *charge d'affaires ad interim* in Prague. He reported that President Benes had briefed Austrian Minister Marek about his talks with Delbos and stated, among others, that "The national minorities may not be a subject of international negotiations, however Czechoslovakia may be willing to discuss the question with its friends (sic!)."[241]

Leading Hungarian Politicians Visit Germany

It was against this background that leading Hungarian politicians traveled to Germany. Lord Halifax, the British Foreign Secretary, had just visited Hitler and Hitler, satisfied that England would not interfere with the annexation of Austria and Czechoslovakia, invited Prime Minister Kalman Daranyi and Foreign Minister Kalman Kanya to see how Hungary would react to such a move. It soon became apparent that Hitler had in mind a very active role for Hungary.

Daranyi and Kanya met with Goring first, on November 21. Goring criticized Hungary, for not taking a sufficiently decisive stand against a proposed Vienna-Prague-Budapest bloc, or the rumored Hungarian offer of armed help to Austria in the event of a conflict between Austria and Germany.

Goring tried to intimidate the Hungarian statesmen to line them up behind the German plans. He said: "It is Hitler's opinion that the present generation of Hungarians must be content with taking an aggressive attitude in one direction (Czechoslovakia) and thus regain its lost territories." Rapport with Yugoslavia should be restored, even at cost of recognizing the present boundaries. There should be some *modus vivendi* found between Hungary and Rumania because, even though Hitler is not opposed to the Hungarian revisionist efforts, he thinks such moves should be postponed. Goring was a past master of playing off neighboring states against each other and manipulating them in the furtherance of German political goals.

Daranyi and Kanya met Hitler on November 25. Like Goring before him, Hitler, too, was pressing for action against Czechoslovakia.[242] Even though the Hungarian delegation was emphasizing the identity of the German and Hungarian goals, the possibility of an *Anschluss* gave rise to deep concern among the Hungarians.

Meanwhile, the debate on the budget was continuing in the Prague parliament. The general debate was concluded on November

140

16, followed the next day by the debate of specific items. The Sudeten German politicians were to first to attack Hodza's address. Dr. Rosche, a Sudeten German Deputy, pointed out that "even though the Germans of Czechoslovakia were given the concept of the state they do not see the concept of the Fatherland. Relations with states which have national minorities living in Czechoslovakia, such as the Germans, Hungarians and Poles, can be improved only after the Czechoslovak government improves its relations with those nationalities," Rosche added.

Esterhazy's Response in Parliament to Hodza's Speech

Janos Esterhazy also delivered a speech in response to the address by Hodza. "I have never heard such an empty, meaningless statement by a Prime Minister," he said. Regarding the condition of the national minorities, Esterhazy quoted from a speech the late President Masaryk had delivered on July 6, 1892, in Vienna: "Those of us in Bohemia will not rest as long as we must feel that we are only tolerated. The more educated our people becomes, the more it will be aware of the foreign rule and I must say that a government which fails to understand the spirit of a people represents a foreign rule."

Esterhazy then added, "We, Hungarians, who live here today, find ourselves in the same situation where the Czechs were at the time President Masaryk delivered that speech. Two full years have gone by since Prime Minister Hodza became head of the government. We have heard him say repeatedly that the condition of the minorities will be improved but, the truth be told, unfortunately there has been no tangible measure taken toward that end.

"There will be no domestic tranquility in this republic until a complete and radical solution is found for the problem of the minorities. It is in the interest of the state to find that solution as soon as possible. The solution to the problem of the minorities, in my opinion, depends primarily on the chauvinism of the present regime," said Esterhazy. Then he quoted a December 9, 1908, statement by Masaryk:

"Chauvinism is basically devoid of character. The chauvinist is willing to use any scoundrel who is willing to betray his people. The chauvinist keeps insisting on the purity of the race, the righteousness of thinking, but embraces even the most unprincipled individuals if they betray their race."

Esterhazy called on the government and the majority party to pay heed to Masaryk's words. And with reference to the so-called Hodza Plan, he called its promotion an exaggeration when the author of the plan cannot restore order even among the national minorities of the country entrusted to his care, while, at the same time, proposing a solution to the problems of the Danubian Basin.

Next, Esterhazy raised questions relating to Hungarian teacher training, the University of Pozsony, the issue of citizenship and the settling of disputes about language rights. "If the Czechoslovak government truly wanted to create a peaceful atmosphere with Hungary, the Prime Minister should have paid more attention to our condition and many of the oft-stated promised should have been fulfilled. We have had more than enough statements and promises," said Janos Esterhazy.[243]

In Part One, we mentioned Benes's broadcast at Christmas, 1937, when he promised once again a remedy for the grievances. We also noted that Derer, a Slovak cabinet minister with Czech sentiments, called Father Hlinka and his colleagues, rascals. We reviewed Beran's sensational proposal in the New Year's issue of the newspaper *Venkov*, suggesting that both the Sudeten German Party and the Slovak Peoples Party should be given a seat in the Prague government. And we quoted Henlein who had surveyed the previous 20 years and found that there are many dissatisfied Germans, Slovaks, Hungarians and Poles living in Czechoslovakia, and yet the government lacks any understanding.

The Prague government's response, as we know, was an even more vehement attack against the national minorities. At this stage, the Sudeten German Party sent emissaries to Father Hlinka in Rozsahegy (Ruzemborok) to discuss cooperation between the two parties. From there, the delegation went to Budapest. Before discussing that visit to Budapest, first a look at the overall situation in Central Europe and the conditions in Hungary.

The possibility of an impending *Anschluss* raised understandable concern in Hungarian government circles. The appearance of Hitler's might in the vicinity of the Hungarian border placed a severe restriction on the government's freedom of action. Therefore, in search for the best solution in a difficult situation, Kanya began looking once again at the concept of the "horizontal axis." Because even though the revision of the peace treaties it has deemed unjust remained one of the most important goals of the Hungarian government, it wanted to accomplish that by peaceful means, through mutual agreement, and never under conditions dictated by Germany. Nevertheless, it was already known that Hitler had assigned Hungary an active role in the summary solution of the Czechoslovak question.

It was under these circumstances that in February, 1938, Regent Horthy paid a state visit to Warsaw. At a February 10 press conference in Warsaw, Foreign Minister Kanya declared: "The discussions were characterized on both sides by the bond of ancient friendship between the two nations. I consider that friendship of special value because of its significant contribution to the improvement of the atmosphere in the Danubian Basin, which is equally in the interest of both Hungary and Poland."

During the discussions of the "horizontal axis," Polish Prime Minister Beck made repeated references to the German threat, but Kanya emphasized that "in the event plans for a Polish-Hungarian and Yugoslav-Italian combination were to come into being in order to establish a balance, it would pursue friendly policies toward Germany."[244] In connection with this plan, there began an active diplomatic effort to transfer Subcarpathian Ruthenia to Hungary and thus establish a common border between Hungary and Poland. This plan had the support of Italy, too.

In the course of discussions between the Hungarian Minister to Warsaw and French Minister Leon Noel, the French diplomat spoke in the most complimentary manner about "the moderate and intelligent conduct of Hungarian foreign policy." According to Kobylanski, chief of the political division in the Polish Foreign Ministry, "the Czechs, too, are recognizing the errors of their previous policies. Sooner or later, Prague will be compelled to make very far-reaching concessions to the Sudeten Germans and this will be accompanied by a solution of the Hungarian and Slovak questions, too. Whether Prague wants to or not, it will have to enter this path."[245]

According to confidential information reaching Petrovich, the Hungarian consul in Pozsony, Sudeten German Deputy Frank had promised Father Hlinka that if the Slovak Peoples Party is willing occasionally, in certain matters, to cooperate with the Henlein Party and the United Hungarian Party against the government and thus form a joint opposion front of the national minorities against Prague, the Sudeten German Party would support the Hlinka group's demands for autonomy. The February 27 edition of the *Slovak* newspaper published statements by Henlein, Esterhazy and Pjescak, a Ruthenian deputy from Slovakia, about the questions of autonomy and communism, a statement which could be regarded as a manifestation of a united opposition front of the national minorities.[246]

Hitler Occupies Austria

On March 13, 1938, as it had been expected for quite some time, Hitler occupied Austria and annexed it to Germany. This move created a totally new situation for Hungary. Not only did the mighty German empire become a next-door neighbor across the country's western border, it also became a determining factor in the entire Danubian Basin. It became a factor which the peoples of the region had to deal with, whether they liked it or not.[247]

Foreign Minister Kanya told the foreign affairs committe of the Hungarian parliament that "blood and territory" were the only things Hitler was interested in. The threat that Germany might draw much of Europe under its rule became increasingly apparent.[248]

The Hungarian political leadership was trying to maintain a free hand as much as possible under those difficult circumstances. It tried to postpone any major decision to the time when it would be clear what commitments would serve its best interests. Hungary had hoped that London would play a greater role in European politics. That is why Hungary wanted to have diplomatic relations both with the Western powers and with Moscow, while maintaining its membership in the League of Nations.[249]

Around May 20, Czechoslovakia ordered a partial mobilization along its borders with Germany and Hungary. Certain German troop movements were given as the reason. The mobilization created a tension between Hungary and Czechoslovakia. On May 30, Hitler approved the plans, code-named *Fall Grun* for a possible attack on Czechoslovakia.[250]

It should be noted here that Hitler plans anticipated a very active role for Hungary and during their meeting in November, 1937, Hitler had promised Daranyi and Kanya that Slovakia would be turned over to Hungary. Kanya, however, had already stated that Hungary does not want to use force in support of its revisionist claims and does not want to trigger a war. At the same time, Kanya raised the possibility of a settlement with Yugoslavia.[251]

In pursuit of the political goals outlined earlier, the Hungarian government launched an intense diplomatic activity, partly to promote a rapprochement with the *Little Entente*, and toward Poland, Italy and Germany. Kanya and Polish Foreign Minister Beck had agreed that they would demand the same rights for their national minorities in Czechoslovakia as Germany was demanding for the Sudeten Germans.

While these diplomatic efforts were going on, Daranyi, who had been moving to the extreme right, was defeated as Prime Minister. He was succeeded by Bela Imredy. The negotiations with the *Little Entente* took place during his administration.

Getting back now to the situation in Slovakia, on a tour of Eastern Slovakia, Janos Esterhazy addressed the Hungarians of Saros and Zemplen counties, who gave him an enthusiastic reception. In a speech on February 22, he stressed that "autonomy is the joint demand of all the original inhabitants of Slovakia." In Szepsi, he pointed to "several recent statements on the part of the governing majority, expressing the desire for reconciliation with the national minorities." He noted that "the government has not yet carried out the February 18 agreement with the Germans, even less so with the Hungarians. There has been no trace yet of the promised reforms 'with the stroke of a pen.'" Esterhazy added that "the nationalities living in this land must join forces to secure their rights."[252]

In an interview with the editor of the newspaper *Slovak*, Esterhazy was asked if he saw any parallels between the Hungarian and Slovak nationality policies. He replied: "Those who have been paying attention to the policies of the local Hungarian parties since the new state came into being, may see that their main goal has been to maintain the Hungarian nation in Slovakia, to nurture its national consciousness and to work for the full recognition and securing of their rights as guaranteed by international agreements. That is the basis of the parallel between the Slovak Peoples Party and our political movement," he added.[253]

The Sudeten German Party Sends a Delegation to Hlinka, then to Budapest

We have noted in Part One that a delegation from the Sudeten German Party called on Father Hlinka in Rozsahegy (Ruzomberek) to discuss cooperation and to name liaison persons. From there, the delegation went to Budapest to explore the possibility of cooperation with the United Hungarian Party. Sudeten German deputies Kunzel and Frank held unofficial discussions with Tibor Pataky, Secretary of State in the Hungarian Prime Minister's office. They briefed Pataky of their negotiations with the Slovaks and told him of plans for a joint Slovak-Hungarian-German demonstration in Pozsony to mark the 20th anniversary of the Pittsburgh Agreement. The Sudeten German emissaries were also received by Daranyi and Kanya. At the request of Esterhazy, they also met former Prime Minister Istvan Bethlen.[254]

As we have noted earlier, Janos Esterhazy also met with the leaders of the Slovak Peoples Party. On May 10, Szullo, Jaross and Esterhazy had an hour-long meeting with Prime Minister Hodza. On May 11, in a speech in parliament, Esterhazy demanded that the government honor the *status quo* of the national minorities.[255]

The March 22 edition of the proceedings of the house of deputies included a question submitted by Esterhazy back in February, complaining of the lawless behavior of local government officials and gendarmerie in Kiralyhelmec. According to the question, similar acts of lawlessness had occurred, among others, in Czernochova, Boly, Ladmoc and Kaponya.[256]

On March 29, Hodza announced in a broadcast speech that he will submit a proposal for a comprehensive law embracing all the rights of all the national minorities.[257]

The United Hungarian Party's Appeal
to the Hungarians of Slovakia

On March 30, the United Hungarian Party issued an Appeal to the Hungarians of Slovakia, calling on "all Hungarians, regardless of social class or religion... We consider all Hungarians our brethren... The national minorities of the republic are uniting before our very eyes. The minority Germans have formed one camp, so have the minority Slovaks and Poles. Let us, minority Hungarians, join in our united camp!" The Appeal was signed by Dr. Geza Szullo, Dr. Janos Holota, Jozsef Szent-Ivany, Dr. Miklos Pajor, Andor Jaross, Dr. Endre Korlath, Kalman Fussy, Dr. Bela Szilassy, Janos Esterhazy, Geza Porubszky, Karoly Hokky and Lajos Turcsanyi.[258]

On April 1, 1938, in a dictatorial manner, the Minister of Interior banned all public assembly, with the obvious intent of preventing the opposition parties from informing the public of their program for the upcoming municipal elections.[259]

On April 6, 1938, in an address to the house of deputies, Janos Esterhazy called parliamentary, provincial and municipal elections.[260]

On April 8, the Hungarian *charge d'affaires ad interim* in London reported to Foreign Minister Kanya that statements made by Chamberlain in his March 24 speech are still regarded an expression of government policy. That means that England would not necessarily join France in an armed conflict in Czechoslovakia.[261]

On April 11, 1938, the permanent deputy to the Hungarian Foreign Minister instructed the Hungarian Minister in Berlin to inform the German Foreign Minister of "the firm intent of the Hungarian government to grant the widest autonomy to the Slovak and Ruthenian residents of the Highland in the event it were to be returned to Hungary."[262]

In an effort to promote more moderate and conciliatory policies, on April 18, 1938, Kanya informed the Hungarian Minister to Bucharest that the situation has substantially changed since the

September, 1937, meeting in Geneva with representatives of the *Little Entente*. The Czechs have drawn the appropriate conclusions from the altered situation and are preparing new legislature on the national minorities. The minorities are looking forward with great anticipation to the concessions to be granted by the Prague government. "We have to wait and see what the new legislature contains," Kanya said.[263]

The Sudeten Germans' Eight Points in Karlsbad

On April 24, 1938, at a Sudeten German Party rally in Karlsbad, Henlein pointed out that in 1918, the Sudeten Germans had believed in President Wilson's principles of self-determination. That is why they have turned so many times to the League of Nations to complain over the violation of those principles, but to no avail. They have repeatedly tried to negotiate with the Prague government, also. Henlein summed up the Sudeten German demands in eight points:

1. The same legal rights and equal status for members of the German minority and the Czechs.

2. In securing of such equal status, recognition of the Sudeten German minority as a legal entity.

3. Designation and recognition of the territories inhabited by Germans.

4. Introduction of autonomous German administration in all spheres of life whenever the interests of the German minority are involved.

5. Introduction of legally valid measures to protect citizens who live outside their designated national minority territories.

6. Putting an end to the wrongs inflicted on the Sudeten Germans since 1918 and redress for the damages they have suffered.

7. Recognition and application of the principle that territories inhabited by Germans should be served by German officials.

8. Full freedom to declare adherence to the German nationality and German political philosophy.[264]

The Sudeten German demands were rejected by the Czech news media.[265]

The *Pragai Magyar Hirlap* Sums up
the Hungarian Demands

We have noted in Part One that the *Pragai Magyar Hirlap*, the official newspaper of the opposition, summed up the Hungarian demands. Following a sloppy and often erroneous publication in *Narodny Listy*, on May 11, the Hungarian newspaper reprinted the memorandum which had been submitted one month earlier to the Prime Minister's office by Andor Jaross and Janos Esterhazy.

It was emphasized in the memorandum that "these demands are not complete. They pertain to legal, cultural and economic matters and do not include the party's political program which embraces full equality and self-government for every nation in the republic, as well as territorial autonomy for Slovakia and Subcarpathian Ruthenia.

"Revision of the constitution, or drafting of a new constitution, is required to carry out this program, and that must be done with the participation of representatives of every nationality in the republic. We are convinced that only a complete and organic refurbishment of the state can secure a harmonious coexistence for the nations which make up Czechoslovakia; protecting the ethnic identity of each nationality, based on political, economic, cultural and social equality, free development and equal opportunity that will form the fundations for peaceful relations among Czechoslovakia's nationalities.

"This great, comprehensive, truly historic effort must be preceded by an internal national reconciliation to restore the fully Hungarian character of the Hungarian minority."

The demands contained in this memorandum outline this preliminary task in full detail in 81 points. The parliamentary forum had summed these up in general terms in 12 points.

The article emphasized that the present program and political goals of the United Hungarian Party are identical with the program established by the party's predecessors nearly 20 years earlier. If the government were to agree to the 81 points, it would restore the na-

151

tional *status quo* without which any solution to the Hungarian question would be nothing but a worthless document written in a vacuum.[266]

British-French Diplomatic Moves
Regarding the Sudeten German Question

The rigid attitute of the Czechoslovak government in the Sudeten German question generated ever greater anxiety, especially in British political circles. In the course of the April 18 and 29 English-French discussions in London, Chamberlain and Halifax finally persuaded Daladier, the new French Prime Minister and Bonnet, the new Foreign Minister, that under the given circumstances it would be impossible to defend Czechoslovakia against a German military attack. They decided, therefore, to increase the pressure on the Czechoslovak government for an urgent solution to the Sudeten German question.[267]

This alteration of political course had most far-reaching consequences on the politics of the entire European continent. This was manifested, among others, by a sudden burst of diplomatic activity. We will take a look at the most important moves, in chronological order, as much as possible.

On April 25, Henderson, the British Ambassador to Berlin, visited Budapest where he met Regent Horthy, Daranyi, Imredy and Prince Primate Seredy. Next, Henderson went to Prague and met with Benes and Hodza. He also saw, twice, Dr. Geza Szullo.[268]

Osusky, the Czechoslovak Minister in Paris reported that in return for full support, Paris expected full readiness to compromise on the part of Prague.[269] On May 7, the British and French minister to Prague delivered seperate *demarches* to the Czechoslovak government. Henderson told Secratary of State Woerman that the *demarches* were intended to promote a general settlement of the question.

Meanwhile, between May 7 and 10, Hitler and Ribbentrop were in Rome where they met Mussolini and Ciano. Their meeting put the brakes on the efforts of the Italian and Hungarian politicians to establish a "horizontal axis" because from here on, the Italians exercised the greatest caution in this matter.[270] This fact only served to confirm the long-standing Hungarian policy to seek the settlement of territorial questions by peaceful means and to stay away from European conflicts of any description.

The Prague government, however, apparently did not attach much urgency to the solution of the problem. That is clear from the May 10 report by the Hungarian *charge d'affaires ad interim* in Prague. The report concluded with a prophetic prediction for the future.

According to the Hungarian diplomat, the Czechs wanted the country and the world to believe that they are feverishly working on a new national minorities law. His understanding was that the Prague government was unable to reach agreement even about general principles. Foreign Minister Krofta himself had said that it is a very slow process but hopefully it would be ready for presentation to parliament during the current session. The Hungarian envoy was of the opinion that "the Czechs want to solve the question or postpone the solution, with long-range promises which the Sudeten Germans will never accept and suddenly we may face a situation which is dangerously reminiscent of the final days of independent Austria."[271]

The British government demonstrated the great importance it attached to the solution of the Sudeten German question by inviting Henlein to visit London in May.[272] According to those present at the meeting, "Henlein made a generally good impression and behaved in a diplomatic manner." Churchill himself spoke with satisfaction about Henlein in an interview. Henlein was demanding autonomy but did not ask that Prague break up its alliance with Russia.[273]

As noted earlier, Hungarian Prime Minister Daranyi, who had shifted too far to the right, was replaced on May 13 by Bela Imredy. Three days later, the Hungarian Minister in Rome called on Ciano and proposed, among others, a new, secret agreement to replace the Pact of Rome.[274] Both Mussolini and Ciano received the proposal with skepticism. This attitude, as we have noted, can be attributed to the talks between Hitler and Mussolini around May 10. Later, Ciano told the Hungarian Minister that the issue would be discussed with Imredy and Kanya during their visit to Rome. Ciano had repeatedly raised the question of Hungary leaving the League of Nations. Imredy kept postponing this move because he wanted to avoid a confrontation with the very powers with which he was anxious to improve relations.

On May 16, the *Le Temps* newspaper called Henlein's demands just. Earlier, on May 2, the *Times* of London published a report to the effect that Prague would be advised to accept the majority of Henlein's demands. Meanwhile, Dr. Szullo and Jaross received an invitation from the Hungarian committee of the English parliament.[275]

According to a coded telegram from the Hungarian Minister to Berlin, dated May 19, "a German cabinet minister has voiced German concern over the fact that the Czechs are negotiating with each national minority separately and play them off againt one another. He thinks it would be necessary for the Hungarians to raise the same demands the Sudeten Germans do."[276]

On May 20, Hodza declared in a statement to the press that the Pittsburg Agreement is morally binding.[277]

Probably in order to counter German troop movements, on the night of May 20, Prague ordered a partial mobilization. This move stretched almost to the breaking point the already existing tensions. On May 20, Ribbentrop reported to Hitler that he was told by Henderson that England would not remain idle in the event of a German attack on Czechoslovakia.[278] On May 21, the Czech and British ministers to Budapest lodged a protest against the alleged mobilization of five Hungarian age groups.[279] Kanya reassured the British diplomat. Benes, in a speech to the military, declared: "We are not afraid of anything."[280]

We have mentioned in Part One Father Tiso's negotiations in Budapest, at the end of May, when he attended the Eucharistic Congress.

Meanwhile, the advocates of autonomy won a great victory in the municipal elections. The Hungarians won with unprecedented margins in Nyitra, Vagsellye, Losonc and Galanta. In the meantime, Hodza received Henlein.[281]

Following the deep crisis of May, German Admiral Canaris sent General Staff Major Pruck to Budapest. Pruck emphasized that Germany wants to maintain peace under all circumstances.[282] This more cautious was also reflected in statements by Goring and Weizsacker before Sztojay, the Hungarian Minister to Berlin. They had called for caution in dealing with the Czechoslovak question because Hitler did not want to be swept into a European war.[283]

On May 27, the British government sent William Strang as an observer to Prague. From Prague, he went to Berlin.[284]

Osusky, the Czechoslovak Minister to Paris, briefed French Foreign Minister Bonnet about the new legislation dealing with national minorities.[285]

In Part One, we have mentioned a visit by a Slovak American delegation to Rozsahegy. We might mention as a sidelight that there was a crowd at the station, as early as four in the morning, waiting for the train which was due at seven. Dr. Hletko was the first to step off the train as it arrived from Warsaw, with a case holding the Pittsburgh Agreement in his hand. Karl Sidor greeted the delegation on behalf of the Slovak Peoples Party. Father Hlinka received the delegation Saturday noon. For the first time, Dr. Hletko took the Agreement out of its case. There, for all to see, was the signature of Masaryk. It was a great moment in Slovak history.[286]

The Russian central committee of Subcarpathian Ruthenia met on May 30 to honor the delegation of American Ruthenians. Pop, a member of the delegation, pointed out that because his group had voted in America for attaching Subcarpathian Ruthenia to the Czechoslovak republic, they are morally bound to help the Ruthenian brethren to secure their autonomy.[287]

The Secret Talks between Hungary
and the *Little Entente* Continue

Even though the policies of Benes never showed any serious intent beyond words to remedy the grievances of the Hungarians, Benes remained hopeful that the Imredy government would seek closer relations with Czechoslovakia. These hopes had been fanned by the Western powers, based largely in Imredy's British orientation. However, the Hungarian political leadership had always held the same views about the grievances of the Hungarians, regardless of who was at the head of the government.

This was clearly demonstrated in Kanya's address to parliament on June 1. He said, among others: "After the end of the world war, when with the assistance of its friends among the great powers, Czechoslovakia established a state where the so-called national minorities constitute a majority, it also acquired large Hungarian territories. Many had hoped that this circumstance would prompt the Czechoslovak government to do everything it can for a reconciliation with Hungary and establish at least the basis of a normal economic relationship with us. However, the official Czech policies had run on a totally different track and were probably based on the belief that it would be possible to maintain for a long time the Czechoslovak Republic's extremely advantageous postwar position which was resting exclusively on the power of bayonets."[288]

Much earlier, on April 6, Bakach-Bessenyey, head of the political department in the Hungarian Foreign Ministry, told Czechoslovak Minister Kobr quite frankly and without mincing any words that he regards the *Little Entente* responsible for its failure to reach out to Hungary before it was too late: "All opportunities have been buried by now and the Danubian nations face a unrelenting fate very soon. In one form of another, they will become satellites of Germany. It will happen to Czechoslovakia because of the Sudeten German problem. Hungary will become a satellite of Germany on account of their comradeship in arms. Rumania and Yugoslavia will find themselves in the same situation because of economic pressure."[289]

Nevertheless the secret negotiations with the *Little Entente* had continued and, as we will see, concluded with the Bled conference in August, unfortunately without any substantive result. Again, the main reason was the refusal of the *Little Entente* to recognize the realities and to work for a rational settlement. Even among the *Little Entente* member states themselves there was a lack of unanimity on many issues, often they fought each other, each pursuing its own interests. No wonder then that the alliance established in 1919 for the maintenance of the *status quo* was bound to collapse under such circumstances.

Hodza, in the meantime, kept promising a solution for the problem of national minorities. In a statement to the *Pesti Hirlap* newspaper, on June 2, he held out the promise of local autonomy as the solution.[290]

At the Pozsony meeting of the United Hungarian Party, it was announced that the national minorities act was still under preparation. The party leaders reiterated that their position remains the same. They continue to demand Hungarian national self-government within the territorial autonomy to be granted for Slovakia and Subcarpathian Ruthenia.[291]

In early June, both the Ruthenian National Council and the Sudeten German Party submitted their demands to Hodza.[292]

A very large crowd attended the municipal elections rally of the United Hungarian Party. Esterhazy reiterated once again that "We Hungarians are law abiding citizens and for twenty years we have fulfilled our civic responsibilities to a degree beyond our strength. We did not preach revolution but we did not hesitate openly and bravely to step before domestic and foreign forums and with frank words and truthful propaganda inform the world of our situation.[293]

The United Hungarian Party won a great victory and Hodza announced that within the next few days the government would introduce legislature on the status of the national minorities.[294]

The Hodza government held two meetings with the Sudeten German representatives. Hodza and Krofta informed the cabinet about the negotiations with the Germans.[295]

Jaross and Esterhazy sent a long telegram to Hodza, protesting a petition campaign and fund raising for national defense throughout Slovakia.[296]

One June 27, the Hungarians of Subcarpathian Ruthenia demanded immediate autonomy. On this occasion, the United Hungarian Party held a congress in Subcarpathian Ruthenia.[297]

In the course of his meeting with representatives of the various national minorities, on June 29, Hodza received a Polish delegation. On the same day, he also received the Hungarian delegation. According to a press release about the hour-long meeting, Hodza was briefed about the contents of a memorandum which the party had submitted at an earlier date. The Hungarian delegates had an opportunity to inform Hodza in some detail about the conditions of the Hungarians in Slovakia.[298]

Hodza, reportedly, did not mention the proposed legislation about the statutes of the national minorities, nor was anything said about revising the constitution, which would be unavoidable if equality before the law for the national minorities was to be secured. Consequently, the national minorities were anticipating the new legislature with some apprehension.

The first detail of the legislation, as disclosed to the Sudeten German Party, dealt with amending the law on language rights.[299]

On July 4, Hodza informed representatives of the Slovak Peoples Party about the proposed legislation.[300]

According to American press reports, Ruthenians in the United States had requested President Roosevelt to press for autonomy for Subcarphatian Ruthenia.[301]

On July 13, Slovak and Hungarian speakers at the national legislative assembly demanded autonomy for Slovakia.[302] Foreign Minister Krofta, in a statement to the *Petit Journal* newspaper, declared that the national minorities would be given major concessions.[303]

On July 20, Hodza met for an hour with the Hungarian leaders. He promised that the final draft of the legislature would be published to following week.[304]

Kanya, in an interview with a Brussels newspaper, declared that the most important issue, as far as Hungary is concerned, is the condition of the Hungarian population in the *Little Entente* countries.[305]

Kanya's statement was closely linked to the increased Hungarian diplomatic activity following Imredy's appointment to the office of Prime Minister. One of the main goals of Hungarian diplomacy was rapprochement and coming to terms with Yugoslavia. The importance of this goal was underscored by the appointment of Kanya's close personal friend, Bakach-Bessenyey, as Hungarian Minister to Belgrade. Earlier, the Hungarian Minister to Rome reported to Kanya about his conversation with Kristic, the Yugoslav Minister to Rome. Kristic, who had accompanied Yugoslav Prime Minister Stojadinovic on his tour of Italy, told the Hungarian diplomat that Stojadinovic wants to reach an agreement with Budapest.

"Kristic has the poorest possible opinion of Benes and regards him the despoiler of Czechoslovakia," reported the Hungarian Minister. "His (Benes') worst mistake was the decisive influence he had exerted on the drafting of the peace treaties. He compounded this mistake with his subsequent policies which were based on the assumption that the postwar weakness of the German empire could be maintained indefinitely.

"Benes has managed to earn the hatred of all his neighbors. He had alienated his allies in the *Little Entente* by assuming a posture of supremacy and trying to act as *primus inter pares*. A proud nation like the Serb, which resembles in many respects the Hungarian, could not welcome and permit such a behavior. Consequently, Belgrade has gradually developed a strong antipathy to Benes and his country which lacks all the natural requisites needed for its continued existence," said Yugoslav Minister Kristic, as quoted by his Hungarian counterpart in Rome. The Hungarian diplomat added that Kristic is a most thoughtful, serious man with great political savvy, who used to be chief of staff to Yugoslav Prime Minister Pasic.[306]

On July 12, Bakach-Bessenyey reported to Kanya that he had met Stojadinovic in his villa at Bled and briefed him about the Bucharest discussions regarding the *Little Entente*. The Rumanian treatment of the Hungarian minority raises great obstacles to any rapprochement, even though the Rumanians ought to know that the Hungarian government and public opinion attach the greatest importance to this question. With regard to Czechoslovakia, it is the position of the Hungarian government that no agreement is possible until the Prague government reaches a settlement with the leaders of the Hungarians in the Highlands. Following a discussion of the condition of the Hungarian minority of Yugoslavia, Stojadinovic spoke. "He considered our conception correct," Bakach-Bessenyey reported, adding that for the time being, the Yugoslav Prime Minister did not want to make a political committment regarding the nations of the *Little Entente*.[307]

On July 15, Istvan Csaky, chief of staff of the Hungarian Foreign Ministry, received Kean, foreign affairs editor of the *Sunday*

Times. He told Csaky that it is his understanding that Hitler and the German general staff do not want war under the present circumstances, while Goring and lower-ranking leaders of the National Socialist Party would not mind going to war. This state of mind is all the more dangerous because, according to Kean, Csaky was absolutely right that "certain Czech circles have assumed a provocative posture because they regard the current circumstances favorable to take care of an armed conflict which seems to be inevitable." Kean also said that he had heard of a memorandum by Colonel General Brauchitsch, requested by Hitler, laying out order of battle plans for an attack on Czechoslovakia. He had also heard that these plans made no mention of Hungary, either as an ally or as an opponent.[308]

On July 18, Imredy and Kanya met Mussolini and Ciano in Rome. According to notes prepared for the meeting -- presumably by Kanya -- the Czechoslovak situation was to be the first item on the agenda. The notes make it clear that "Hungary has never considered an offensive move against Czechoslovakia on its own. However, in the event of an armed conflict between Germany and Czechoslovakia, Hungary could not remain a bystander. But Hungary would participate in the military solution of the Czechoslovak question only if it could remain 100 percent certain that Yugoslavia would remain neutral and would not attack Hungary in the rear."

The notes express doubt that about such neutrality at the moment, regardless of what Stojadinovic may have told Ciano. This remark was a hint at Stojadinovic's two-faced politics. The Bucharest negotiations between Hungary and the *Little Entente* and between Hungary and Rumania are making very little progress, largely because of the attitude of the Rumanian government. They would consider any settlement only on the basis of our (Hungary') legal equality and reconfirmation of the Kellog Pact, while a general statement about the national minorities would have to be negotiatied separately with each member of the *Little Entente.*

On the question of Hungary quitting the League of Nations -- something about which the Italians are very insistent -- the notes point out that the League of Nations is the only forum where "we have been able to bring before the public opinion of the entire world the pathetic fate of the Hungarian minorities, torn from us by the peace treaty. On the other hand, Geneva is the place where we can have, at least once a year, direct contact with the great Western powers. By that, I have mostly England in mind because it has always shown some interest in the Hungarian problems."

With reference to the "horizontal axis," the notes observe that "from our point of view, there are two further preconditions (in addition to keeping an eye on Germany) to its establishment. One is the absolute necessity of a common border between Hungary and Poland; the other, a satisfactory settlement of the relations between Hungary and Yugoslavia, without which we could not join the axis."

The notes also mention the German invitation to Regent Horthy, which he was pleased to accept, having already visited two other friendly powers, namely Italy and Poland.[309]

Large Scale Hungarian Diplomatic Activity:
Esterhazy in Warsaw

Janos Esterhazy took an active role in the diplomatic efforts when he visited Warsaw for talks with Foreign Minister Beck. Beck emphasized the true friendship between Poland and Hungary. He predicted that in the event of Czechoslovakia's disintegration, Slovakia in its entirety would be returned to Hungary.

The Polish Foreign Minister recalled his conversation with Sidor, a leader of the Slovak Peoples Party, whom he had received some time earlier. Beck told Sidor that Poland has no territorial claims against Slovakia, therefore it should go in its entirety to Hungary. He reassured Sidor that he was familiar with the intentions of the Hungarian government about the Slovak question. Hungary, he said, was planning to grant Slovakia far-reaching autonomy.

Beck's statement reassured Sidor who said that the Slovaks are not afraid of the Hungarians of the Highlands because they understand each other, but are somewhat apprehensive about the attitude of the Hungarians in Hungary itself.[310]

A report from the Hungarian Minister in Warsaw to Foreign Minister Kanya reviewed the Polish views about the general international political situation: "The farther away we get from the critical days in May, the more the bellicosity of the great Western powers decreases. As far as France is concerned, the dominant factor is to save the appearance of loyalty to the allies. They do not want to have this loyalty tested, therefore the French no longer rule out the establishment of a federated state in Czechoslovakia, which would lead ultimately to the separation of the various alien nationality groups.[311]

Early July, the Hungarian Minister in Bucharest reported to Kanya that "the Rumanian government is delaying the settlement of the nationalities' question for fear that following publication of the new Czech law on the minorities, the minorities in Rumania would raise new demands, invalidating all previous measures.

In facing Rumanian public opinion, Foreign Minister Comnen became a prisoner of the carelessly posited thesis that the question of the minorities is strictly a domestic affair and none of the Hungarian government's business. At the same time, he wants to create the impression abroad, especially among the great powers which have shown interest in the nationalities' question, that Rumania is solving the problem of its national minorities with the tacit agreement, or consent, of the Hungarian government. Creating that impression would greatly strengthen the position of the Rumanian governmment against demands that the securing the rights of the minorities should go beyond the minimal program envisioned by the Rumanian government.[312] This delaying tactic had greatly impeded negotiations with the *Little Entente.*

A highlight of the intense diplomatic activity among the great powers was the proposal by the German Minister to London to call an international conference for the solution of the Czechoslovak problem. The conference would be attended by England, France, Germany and Italy, and it would mediate between the Prague government and the Sudeten Germans. France supported this move at first, but then turned against it.[313] The plan found warm reception in the British press.[314] The great interest shown by the British government was reflected in the fact that Basil Newton, the British Minister to Prague, had two meetings with Hodza on July 23.[315]

On July 26, in an interview with *The Daily Telegraph*, Henlein declared that defense and foreign affairs should be the responsibility of the central government, while all the other matters belong to an autonomous popular assembly.[316]

Prague Publishes the Nationalities Act
in a Piecemeal Fashion

The nationalities act was completed by the end of July but it
was published in a piecemeal fashion. Essentially, it provided a skele-
ton which was to be fleshed out through further negotiations. Much of
it was drawn from measures which were said to have been based on
providing equal rights.[317] Apparently, the intent had been to complete
and publish the hastily prepared legislation before the arrival of
the Runciman Mission. It was reported in *The Daily Telegraph*
newspaper on July 26, and subsequently announced by Chamberlain in
the House of Commons that the Prague government and Sudeten
German Party have agreed to the appointment of Lord Runciman to
mediate the disputed questions.[318]

The roots of this British diplomatic initiave go back to a
period prior to the news report in *The Daily Telegraph*. They can
be traced back to the infinite stubbornness of Benes' politics.
Prague's attitude toward the Sudeten Germans, as well as toward all
the other national minorities, had been more provocative than conciliatory and showed little inclination for a rational settlement. The
British government was deeply disturbed by this attitude because it
knew that Prague's stubbornness would push the national minorities,
like it or not, into Hitler's arms.

The Sudeten German issue was the most explosive of them all
because it involved the mighty German Empire. The earliest solution
of this problem had top priority. Dealing with the grievances of the
other minority groups was relegated to the background. A question
directed at the Prime Minister in the House of Commons by Captain
Plugge, made the point. The question was whether the Prime Minister
was willing to convene a conference to review the grievances Hungary
had suffered for a long time at the hands of its neighbors and as a
result of the Treaty of Trianon, and to seek a remedy for those grievances. The question was prompted by the fact the Britain had been

165

one of the signatories of the Treaty of Trianon. Even though there were no plans for such a conference, the question reflected the view that neither the Hungarian minority groups, nor the Hungarian government were interested in a solution by armed force. What they wanted was a negotiated solution.

Notwithstanding the fact that the *Anschluss* had given Germany a disproportionate impact on Hungary's economy, Hungary's sympathies were with England. Hungary had made every effort for a sincere rapprochement with the West, only to be abandoned by the West and, contrary to its interests, forced into the German sphere of political influence. The Hungarian national minorities have been forced to endure historically unprecedented injustices and the time has come to find a legal and peaceful remedy for those injustices.[319]

Negotiations by Lord Runciman

As noted earlier in Part One, on August 3, 1938, Lord Runciman arrived with his wife and entourage in Prague. The United Hungarian Party's welcoming message, in English and Hungarian, appeared on the front page of the party's newspaper.

The message reminded him that twenty years earlier, "the peace treaties took into account only the two polarities of battles lost and battles won, and forgot the fact that only states can be defeated for a while, but nations can not. The Czechoslovak Republic came into being through recognition of victory by the Czech, Slovak and Ruthenian, while the German, Hungarian and Polish nations living in the same territory were made to bear the entire moral and material burden of a lost war. Twenty years' efforts at nation building had but one goal: to employ the strength of the majority in the establishment and broadening the *Lebensraum* of the Czechoslovak nation at the expense of the Germans, Hungarians and Poles.

"Such a development was unhealthy and contrary to nature and was bound to result in conflicts. All that has been needed was a shift of balance among the great powers which are shaping the history of Europe.

"There is more than a German-Czechoslovak, Polish-Czechoslovak, Slovak-Czechoslovak or Ruthenian-Czechoslovak problem. There is also Hungarian-Czechoslovak problem. We feel that 20 years ago we were deprived of the right proclaimed with prophetic inspiration by President Wilson, the right of self-determination. Only securing that right can restore an equitable state which guarantees equal development under equal conditions for all nationalities."[320]

In Part One, we have touched upon Lord Runciman's negotiations. Here is now a somewhat more detailed look at their Hungarian aspects. As noted earlier, Lord Runciman's main mission was to mediate in the Sudeten German problem. Nevertheless, leaders of the other national minorities, including the Hungarians, also tried to bring their grievances to his attention.

Leaders of the United Hungarian Party spared no effort to secure an appointment with Lord Runciman. They saw him on August 12, and Lord Runciman's office issued a brief official communique about the meeting. It stated that Lord Runciman received the delegation of the United Hungarian Party at 12 noon. The delegation was composed of Dr. Geza Szullo, Andor Jaross and Janos Esterhazy, who briefed him about certain points in a memorandum which was submitted earlier.

Because of the confidential nature of the talks, the Hungarian side also refrained from giving a more detailed account. It was understood, however, that the one-and-a-half hour meeting took place in the Hotel Acron in Prague and the Hungarian leaders had an opportunity to brief Lord Runciman and his experts on all questions involving the Hungarians in Czechoslovakia. It was thought likely that further negotiations might follow.[321] According to other sources, Lord Runciman had said that whatever rights the Sudeten Germans may be granted, such rights would be automatically extended to the Hungarian population of Czechoslovakia.[322]

The grievances presented by the Hungarian delegation included the following: excessive number of Czechoslovak civil servants in Hungarian districts; a shortage of Hungarian civil servants; excessive taxation; restrictions imposed on the use of the Hungarian language in the courts and before administrative agencies; often insurmountable obstacles put in the path of those who want to obtain proof of citizenship; severe damage to industry and agriculture; serious shortcomings in education, and reparation for the damages inflicted since the end of the war.

Even though coexistence for the Hungarians in Czechoslovakia is not at all assured under the present conditions, the United Hungarian Party would be willing to accept a *modus vivendi*, Lord Runciman was told.[323]

It should be noted that several members of the party had urged to emulate the Sudeten German Party as the only way to succeed with Lord Runciman. Democratic methods, they said, bring no results. Esterhazy's response was, "Never! The violent methods employed by the Sudeten Germans are contrary to our democratic convictions," he said.

The delegation of the United Hungarian Party had a second meeting with Lord Runciman on August 25. This encounter took place after the Bled conference between Hungary and the *Little Entente* and the Kiel meeting of Hitler and Horthy. The agenda of the second meeting with Lord Runciman included once again the small number of Hungarian civil servants in the Hungarian districts; the way Prague was taking advantage of the so-called activists, or collaborators; educational matters, including the appointment of teachers by the Czechoslovak authorities; the absence of a Hungarian university, and the appointment of non-Hungarians to Hungarian chairs.[324]

Hungary and the *Little Entente* Meet in Bled, Hungarian Statesmen Visit Kiel

The scheduled visit by Hungarian leaders to Germany had a major impact on preparations for the Bled conference. Hitler's invitation to Regent Horthy, delivered in May by General Raeder, soon became common knowlegde and raised deep concern among the *Little Entente* governments. They began speeding up the diplomatic negotiations with Hungary so that an agreement might be reached before Horthy and Hitler meet. The Czechoslovak government became more conciliatory and was ready to accept the first part of the formula proposed by Kanya but continued to reject the second part, insisting that it would be another interference in Prague's domestic affairs.

The Hungarian government, too, eased its position and was willing to come to terms with all three *Little Entente* states regarding parity in armaments and the question of a non-aggression treaty. The change in the Hungarian attitude was due to diplomatic intervention by the British government on August 16 and 19.[325]

A joint communique was issued on August 23 simultaneously in Budapest and Bled. According to the communique, the *Little Entente* accepted parity in armaments for Hungary and all four states had come to an agreement about non-aggression in accord with the Kellog-Briand Pact.

Hungary had also reached secret agreements with Yugoslavia and Rumania regarding their Hungarian minorities. Czechoslovakia, however, refused to accept a similar draft statement. Some light had been shed on this during a meeting between Kanya and the British *charge d'affaires ad interim*. Kanya told the British diplomat that "Bossy, the Rumanian Minister to Budapest, had shown great understanding regarding our demand to Prague for a more far-reaching statement on national minorities than the one issued by the other two *Little Entente* states -- demand which even Prague had recognized

170

as justified. We could not accept the statement proposed by Prague, first because of Czechoslovakia's internationally known record in the treatment of its minorities, and, second, because Benes is held in an extraordinary distrust here by eveyone without exception, because of all his unkept promises."[326]

Thus, Kanya himself regarded the Bled agreement a temporary measure which "will be considered final with the signing of a Hungarian-Czechoslovak minorities agreement." The *Little Entente* powers were unable to bring themselves, even at the twelfth hour, to find a realistic compromise which would solve the problem once and for all. The Bled agreement never came into force. The *Little Entente*, doomed to failure from the beginning, demonstrated that the prophecy of so many observers has been fulfilled. It could not pass the test of history. As a result, each of its members ended up on Hitler leash, as predicted by the Millerand government as far back as 1929.

The Bled agreements,limited as they may have been, stirred quite a dust in the European diplomatic arena. It goes without saying that each state judged their significance according to its own interests. The Western powers wanted to see an anti-German victory in the agreements, coming at the time when it appeared that Hungary might be swept by Germany into a coming war against Czechoslovakia. This is demonstratred by the tone of the British press. Such as an August 24 editorial in the *Daily Herald*, paying tribute to the extraordinary flexibility of Hungarian diplomacy.[327] The British *charge d'affaires ad interim* in Budapest told Kanya of Foreign Secretary Halifax's satisfaction on August 30.[328] The *Little Entente* was raving about the unity among the three member states and hailed the agreement as their great success, even though Prague knew all too well what the facts were.

Berlin, on the other hand,was dismayed by the news from Bled. It showed that the Hungarian diplomacy was trying to secure itself a back door, a kind of emergency exit, toward the Western powers and, at the same time, attempting to increase Hungary's influence. Thus, Hungarian diplomacy held two cards simultaneously, hoping to play them as the occasion arose. Toward Germany, it could raise the prospect, or at least the appearance of an agreement with the *Little Entente*. That card could have been played, for example, if Germany were unwilling to guarantee Yugoslavia's neutrality.[329] The same card could have been played if Germany had assumed a threatening posture against Hungary, as it had done with Austria.[330] The

Hungarian diplomacy had to brace itself against potentially strong pressure to join immediately a military campaign against Czechoslovakia, which could easily drag the entire continent into war.

The Bled agreements obviously ran counter to Hitler's plans and the German leaders made no bones about that during the Kiel talks with the Hungarian leaders, which had just begun. On August 23, Ribbentrop and Kanya met aboard the *Patria* where a self-assured Kanya kept fending off Ribbentrop's queries about the Bled agreements. But the German foreign minister kept remonstrating. The agreements, he said, made it appear as if Hungarian wanted to keep itself apart from the German-Czechoslovak conflict and had given up its territorial demands.

While in Kiel, the Hungarian leaders were told by the Hungarian Chief of General Staff that the Germans had scheduled their attack on Czechoslovakia for late September or early October. They were also told that Hitler had refused to listen to the advice of his own generals who were opposed to the early date because they needed more time to make preparations.[331]

Ribbentrop easily dismissed Kanya's concern over the neutrality of Yugoslavia by saying that "he who wants revision (of the borders) must be an opportunist." In the course of the meeting, Kanya made several sarcastic remarks which Ribbentrop could never forget.[332] Hitler who met Imredy the same afternoon had an angry outburst, saying that he "wanted nothing from Hungary." That put Imredy, reportedly, at ease but soon thereafter Hitler told him that "he who wants to participate in the feast cannot stay away from the kitchen."[333]

In the evening of August 23, there was probably another meeting where the Hungarians proposed a compromise solution, namely that Hungary would join 14 days after the German intervention.[334] Kanya must have thought that after 14 days, it would become obvious what the attitude of Britain and France were and Hungary could act accordingly.

The impact of the Bled agreements on the Western powers became fully clear only on August 24. By then, the Western capitals, as well as those of the *Little Entente*, were hailing the agreements as an anti-German victory. To a certain degree, even Budapest contributed to this. Kanya had not anticipated such a tremendous press reaction and it made the continued negotiations awkward. It took the greatest effort on the part of the Hungarian statesmen to refloat the negotiations which had run aground. On August 25, Imredy and

Kanya held a press conference where they declared that the Bled agreement will not enter into force before an agreement is reached with Czechoslovakia about the national minorities.[335]

For some time by now, Kanya had lost the Germans' sympathy. There have been stories leaked to the effect that the Germans were eavesdropping on his telephone conversations with Kiel and Budapest.[336] Ribbentrop made no bones about this during the August 25 session. Kanya had no choice but to tell frankly all about the background of the Bled agreements, their motives and their temporary and preliminary nature. Ribbentrop, however, retained his rigid posture and Kanya had to alter his position regarding the timing of the intervention. He was in a difficult situation and, probably as a tactical move to gain time, gave October 1 as the earliest date. Ribbentrop did not even answer him.[337]

On August 25, in a discussion between Horthy and General Brauchitsch, the general remarked that he had shared Horthy's apprehensions about the outbreak of war. This had come to Hitler's attention and he reproached Horthy during their afternoon session, provoking an irritated response.[338]

Next, Hitler tried to pressure the Hungarian leaders through General Ratz, the Hungarian Minister of Defense. He also brought up the Polish threat, saying that should Poland intervene, Slovakia would fall into its lap and Hungary would be left with nothing. But the Hungarian Defense Minister did not yield to these arguments and noted that the Hungarian army was undergoing a reorganization. He also referred to the uncertainty of Yugoslavia's neutrality. So, this meeting, too, remained fruitless, except perhaps for Hitler agreement to continued discussions between the Hungarian and German general staffs.[339] The Potsdam talks of August 26 between Ribbentrop and Imredy remained similarly unsuccessful.[340] The same day in the afternoon, Horthy met Goring in the latter's hunting lodge at Karinhall, again without any substantive agreement. The entire visit to Kiel was best characterized by Kanya's outburst a few days later to a Hungarian diplomat: "That madman wants to trigger a war at all costs.[341]

Among the events with a direct bearing in that period on the fate of the Hungarians in Slovakia, we must mention that in its response to the Prague governments draft reform of the administrative machinery, the United Hungarian Party demanded legislative authority for the provincial assemblies.[342]

In a speech at the Stockholm Congress of European National Minorities, Dr. Geza Szullo painted a shocking picture of the lot of the minorities. Even though they are protected by international treaties and the individual states have assumed obligations toward their minorities, their grievances would fill volumes, said Dr. Szullo. He spoke of the various methods of robbing the minorities of their national identity, such as language tests, the critical shortages and abuses in the educational system, discriminatory practices in the hiring of teachers, dilution of legislative bodies with political appointees alongside the elected members and the overall state of corruption in public life. Dr. Szullo concluded his address by saying: "It is a fact that the problem of European national minorities demands an urgent solution."[343]

We have noted in Part One that in the talks with Lord Runciman, Prague was employing delaying tactics, presenting a second and then a third plan to divide the German-inhabited areas into four administrative districts.[344] Hodza discussed this plan with Jaross and Esterhazy also.[345]

The Daily Telegraph reported that Imredy was asking that the Hungarian minority be given equal treatment with the Sudeten Germans.[346]

The Sudeten German Party Rejects
Hodza's Plans for the National Minorities

The Sudeten German Party did not accept the third plan, based on a cantonal system, because it failed to recognize the national minorities as legal entities and did not grant them the right of self-determination.[347] In the meantime, Henlein met Hitler and Ribbentrop and delivered a message from Lord Runciman.[348]

On his return to Prague, Henlein handed to Lord Runciman the so-called Hitler Plan.[349] The plan stirred intense diplomatic activity because, reportedly, Hitler had demanded further concessions which would have been tantamount to granting the Sudeten Germans autonomy.[350] Meanwhile, very important negotiations were being conducted in Prague between Aston-Gwatkin of Lord Runciman's staff and Henlein and Hodza, and between Lord Runciman and President Benes. Hodza also saw the leaders of the Slovak Peoples Party.[351]

Up to the middle of September, the Hungarian press exercised great moderation in presenting the events, compared, for example, with the *Volkischer Beobachter*. It had still maintained its British orientation and employed a calm but determined tone in bringing attention to the pitiful lot of more than one-million Hungarians in Czechoslovakia. Imredy's speech in Kaposvar, on September 6, was an exception, with a sharp attack on the nationalities policies of the Prague government.[352]

We have noted in Part One that the political parties of the four national minorities held a joint meeting in Prague to form a Hungarian-German-Slovak-Polish Unity Front.

On September 7, in Ostrava, there was a clash between Sudeten Germans and the Czechoslovak police. As a result of the incident, the nationalities talks were interrupted. On September 8, Lord Runciman asked Janos Esterhazy to warn Frank, the deputy leader of the Sudeten German Party, not to use the incident as a pretext to undermine the negotiations because that could lead to war. Frank promised Esterhazy that the negotiations would be continued. Then he went to see Lord Runciman and the two men kept talking until almost two in the morning.[353]

Janos Esterhazy's Negotiations with the Authorities about Questions Relating to the Hungarian Schools

Even in this politically charged atmosphere, Janos Esterhazy found time to bring the grievances of the Hungarian schools to the attention of the Prague government authorities. He called on the Minister of Finance, urging prompt payment of the funds needed for the furnishings of Hungarian State Gymnasium (senior high school) in Pozsony.

Esterhazy visited the Minister of Education to discuss the construction of numerous Hungarian schools. The talks included enlarging the elementary school of Pozsonyret and the establishment of Hungarian elementary schools in Nyitra, Nemetgurab, Makranc and Csecs. The last two villages have been struggling for a Hungarian school for 15 years, even though the Hungarian population constituted an absolute majority in both villages and the Czechoslovak minority had its own schools.

Esterhazy also brought up the demand of the Hungarian population of Ligetfalu for the establishment of parallel Hungarian classrooms. Ninety Hungarian children had already applied for enrollment. Esterhazy put in a strong word also for the establishment of a Hungarian Gymnasium in Ungvar -- something the people had been demanding for nearly 20 years already.

Social support for Hungarian college students was another thing Esterhazy had been lobbying for. One of his requests was that applications of Hungarians for scholarships and other grants be screened by the organization of Hungarian college students, rather than the Czechoslovak student organization.[354]

The Hungarians of Leva (Levice) turned directly to Lord Runciman regarding the reopening of the Hungarian gymnasium which was confiscated in 1918.[355]

We have noted in Part One that in a September 10 radio address, President Benes called once again for moderation.

We have also noted the appeal of the Slovak Peoples Party, printed in the newspaper *Slovak*, entitled "Our Patience Has Also Reached Its End." The appeal's conclusion was that "Twenty years of patience have stretched human patience to its absolute limit."

In the meantime, Hodza briefed the Sudeten German leaders about his "fourth plan." As we have reported, the plan was rejected both by Sudeten Germans and the Slovak autonomists.

Lord Runciman's Final Report Highlights the Prague Government's Faulty Policies

At a party rally in Nuremberg on September 12, Hitler delivered a sharp speech, demanding the right of self-determination for the Sudeten Germans. We have noted earlier that the Czechoslovak government had declared a national emergency, dissolved the Sudeten German Party (because of Henlein's demands to attach the Sudeten German territories to Germany). Lord Runciman's negotiations had broken off and he returned to London to prepare a final report for the British government. It is worth to describe a few sections of the report because they show us in what light the British statesman viewed the crisis in Czechoslovakia.

No matter how he condemned Henlein and Frank for breaking off the talks, Lord Runciman understood in many respects the feelings of the Sudeten Germans, their bitterness and their hopelessness.

"I sympathize with the cause of the Sudeten Germans," he wrote. "It is very difficult to live under alien rule. I am leaving with the impression that the rule over the Sudeten German territories in the last 20 years, even though it cannot be called actual tyranny and certainly not terror, could be characterized as insensitive, lacking any understanding, impatient and discriminating to the point where the anger of the German population was beginning to border on rebellion.

"The Sudeten Germans also felt that there have been too many promises in the past, followed by very little or no deeds, at all. This experience created an open lack of confidence in the leading Czech politicians. Local abuses only fueled the more serious grievances. Many Czech civil servants and gendarmes who spoke little or no German were sent to pure German districts. In the course of the land reform, Czech settlers were encouraged to settle in German areas; many schools were built for the children of the Czech intruders; Czech businesses were given preference over German ones...

"Even at the end of my mission, I saw no intention to remedy for these grievances. For any number of reasons, including the foregoing, three or four years ago the Sudeten Germans regarded their situation hopeless. The Nazi power has given them new hope. I consider it a natural development that they would turn to their ethnic kin and want to be transferred to the German empire.

"It goes without saying, in my opinion, that the region along the German-Czechoslovak border with its overwhelming Sudeten German majority should be entitled to full self-determination. Should certain transfer of land be unavoidable, and I think it is, it should be carried out at once. In territories where the German majority is not so overwhelming, I would propose local autonomy in accord with the 'fourth plan,'" wrote Lord Runciman.[356]

ut it is noteworthy how an impartial British diplomat regarded the Sudeten German griavances and the attitude of the Czechoslovak government regarding their remedy. The other national minorities had the same grievances and, again, the attitude of the Prague government was the same. Nevertheless, Prague expected loyalty from the minorities and when, naturally, such loyalty was not forthcoming to the degree it had been expected, the national minorities were accused of disintegrating the republic.

Hitler's sharp speech in Nuremberg, announcing that Germany would secure the right of self-determination for the German population of Czechoslovakia, generated considerable diplomatic activity throughout Europe. Hungarian diplomacy, too, swung into action.

The Hungarian government's goal was to see to it that every concession given the Sudeten Germans should be automatically extended to the Hungarians. It was working for the achievement of this goal in accord with the Western powers' conciliatory policies, through compromise rather than by force. Therefore, the first priority in Hungarian political circles was to secure the goodwill of the British and French governments. The main obstacle to that had been the fact that the Western powers were interested in little else beside a solution to the Sudeten German problem so that war with Hitler may be avoided. They were not concerned over the grievances of the other national minorities even if they had a stronger cause in demanding a remedy for those grievances. That is why Chamberlain extracted a promise from Hitler not to bring up the matter of the other nationalities -- a promise that Hitler failed to keep.

The Czechoslovak propaganda had also raised the argument that if the matter of the Hungarian and Polish minorities were to become subject of an international settlement parallel with the Sudeten Germans, it would lead to disturbances in Czechoslovakia and clashes with the neighboring countries would become inevitable.[357] This had greatly contributed to putting the Hungarian and Polish questions on the back burner and leaving the solution to bilateral negotiations.

The Hungarian government was negotiating with the Polish government, too. On September 13, immediately following Hitler's speech, the Hungarian Minister to Berlin met the Polish Ambassador who raised the possibility of a common border between the two countries. Regarding Slovakia, he said a plebiscite should be prepared as soon as possible.[358]

The Hungarian *charge d'affaires ad interim* in London reported on September 13 that the British government was determined to push for a plebiscite in Czechoslovakia. But he did not think this would extend to the Hungarian question. Subsequently, the chief of staff of the Hungarian Foreign Ministry instructed the envoy to convey the message that "up to now, the Hungarian government has exercised the greatest patience and moderation over the events in Czechoslovakia. To a large degree, this can be attributed to the heretofore calm behavior of the Hungarians in Slovakia. However, should there be any discrimination regarding the legal status of the various national minorities in Slovakia, it could have unforeseeable consequences."[359]

In a coded message to the Hungarian Minister in Warsaw, the Hungarian Foreign Minister expressed the opinion that either there will be war or, with British support, plebiscite will be held in the Sudeten German territories. "We must do everything in our power therefore to have the plebiscite extended to the territories with Hungarian inhabitants," he said.[360]

On September 14, the Hungarian Minister in Warsaw reported to Foreign Minister Kanya that according to the Secretary of State of the Polish Foreign Ministry, "the present conditions may be just right to have at least some of the Hungarian demands fulfilled."[361]

On the same day the Hungarian *charge d'affaires ad interim* in London reported to Kanya that he had told most emphatically to Ingram, the head of the South European Division, of the most serious consequences if any concessions to the Sudeten Germans, including a plebiscite, would not be extended to the Hungarian minority. "Ingram replied that for the time being, all attention is being concentrated on the Sudeten Germans, therefore he cannot say any more at the moment, except that he will take note of my communication and make it part of the official record."[362]

Foreign Minister Kanya met the Polish Minister to Budapest on September 15. In his notes of the conversation, Kanya stated that the Gentlemen's Agreement between Hungary and Poland has come into force. The Polish Minister remarked that the Hungarians are too soft and in the event of a plebiscite in Czechoslovakia, will not be able to represent the interests of the territories with Hungarian inhabitants with sufficient force. Kanya denied this allegation.[363]

On September 15, the Hungarian Minister in Warsaw reported to Kanya that he was told by the Polish Foreign Minister the following, among others: "I am entitled by our friendship to ask the Hungarian government in these fateful days to demand the most forcefully a plebiscite in the Hungarian Highlands. We can now really speak only in terms of moments because, as soon as England has come to terms with Germany, it will no longer pay attention to the others. If Hungary does not change its restrained attitude, it will miss a historic opportunity," said the Polish Foreign Minister.[364]

Hitler and Chamberlain Meet
in Berchtesgaden and Godesberg

The news of Chamberlain's announcement on September 15 that for the sake of preserving the peace he would be willing to meet Hitler anywhere in Germany, spread like wildfire. As it came to light later, the news was a shocking surprise even to the German generals because, as Chief of General Staff Halder was to testify, Chamberlain's visit to Germany thwarted an imminent *coup d'etat* by the generals against Hitler.[365]

This unexpected move was tantamount to the capitulation of England and France and the sacrificing of the interests of Czechoslovakia. It also presented a new situation the Hungarian government had to face.

Chamberlain met Hitler on September 15 in Berchtesgaden. Hitler, in a threatening tone of voice, demanded the unification of the Sudeten Germans with the motherland. In response to a question by Chamberlain, Hitler did concede that the Poles, Hungarians and Ukranians also had demands, but declined to act as their spokesman. Only the Sudeten German issue was discussed in Berchtesgaden and Chamberlain agreed to the transfer of territories with Sudeten German majorities to Germany.[366]

The German government blamed Hungary for the failure to act on the Hungarian claims. Hitler was not fully satisfied with the Berchtesgaden agreement because the new *status quo* had greatly restricted his freedom of movement in the fulfillment of his further plans. In order to change the *status quo* without taking the blame for increasing the risk of war, Hitler resorted to fanning the Hungarian and Polish demands. He felt certain it would aggravate the situation without anybody blaming him for it.

On September 17, Foreign Minister Kanya briefed the Hungarian Minister in Warsaw about the latest Hungarian diplomatic moves. He said, "Through our Minister in London we informed the

British Foreign Secretary that the Hungarian government would draw the farthest-reaching conclusions if the Hungarian minority were to receive a different treatment than the Sudeten Germans and we will assume no responsibility for the consequences of any resulting discrimination which the Hungarian government, too, would find intolerable.[367] In the presence of the Prime Minister, I gave the same message, in the strongest terms, to the British Minister in Budapest."[368] In Geneva, the Hungarian Minister held a similar conversation with the British envoy.

The Hungarian government requested Mussolini and Ciano to support Hungary's position. Regent Horthy sent a handwritten letter to Hitler.[369] The Hungarian Minister in Berlin addressed a similar appeal to Goring.[370] Not long afterward, Regent Horthy went hunting with Goring and they, too, discussed the question.

On September 17, the United Hungarian Party met in Pozsony and issued a proclamation, demanding the right of self-determination and plebiscite for the Hungarian minority.[371] The proclamation noted that as a consequence of the Paris peace treaties the members of the Hungarian minority had to live in Czechoslovak territory but never had any doubt that they, too, like every nation and nationality, were entitled to all the rights enshrined in the laws of God, man and morality. For 20 years, this Hungarian national minority has always fulfilled its obligations as one of the most disciplined nationalities of the republic, but during those 20 years, the possessors of power have never taken into consideration the interests of the other nationalities, including the Hungarians. Every one of their legislative acts served only the concept of the Czech national state. It has been a faulty policy, running counter to the interests of Europe as a whole and endangering the peace of the world. The Hungarian national minority in Czechoslovakia wants to take charge of its destiny and wants to exercise the right of self-determination which was granted only to a few nations in 1918.[372]

On September 18, Kanya summoned Maugras, the French Minister to Budapest, to discuss the just-concluded British-French talks in London and the agreements reportedly made there. It was said that instead of ordering a plebiscite in the Sudeten German territories, those territories would be transferred to Germany.

Kanya made it clear that the Hungarian government would consider most dangerous any solution which would entail discrimination against the Hungarian minority. "Order cannot be restored in the Danubian basin without meeting the just demands of all the national minorities in Czechoslovakia and it goes without saying that any solution which is discriminatory against the Hungarian minority would bring about an extremely tense situation between Czechoslovakia and Hungary. We decline in advance any responsibility for the consequences," reported Kanya in notes about his meeting with the French diplomat. He added: "The policies of the Hungarian government, I stated, have not been belligerent until now. Rather, we have been seeking compromises, as demonstrated by the Bled agreement, but we could not ignore the great outrage which, fed by rumors, is already palpable throughout the country..."[373]

Barcza, the Hungarian Minister in London, was negotiating with Sir Alexander Cadogan. Cadogan had been representing Lord Halifax. In his report to Kanya on September 18, Barcza said: "I made absolutely clear the position of the Hungarian government that it demands without fail that the nearly one million Hungarians in Czechoslovakia receive the same treatment as the Sudeten Germans. The most basic justice and logic demand that there be no discrimination between the various nationalities. I noted that given the outstanding sense of justice and fair play which has been developed and honored by the British people and government over the centuries, I would not even dare to presume that a national minority which has tolerated for twenty years with exemplary patience the sufferings of living under foreign rule and which has demonstrated an amazing calm even in the turmoil of recent weeks, would be punished because it constitutes the second largest minority of Czechoslovakia and because instead of the bayonets of a nation of 75 million, it can depend only on the support of a government which is in search of a peaceful solution, and on justice itself.

"If England," Minister Barcza continued, "would not show the same concern over the just demands of the Hungarians in Czechoslovakia as it does over the Germans, it would no longer appear in the eyes of the world as the voice of justice, law and freedom, rather it would be seen as one who had bowed to the threats of the bully. I am convinced that England does not want to and will not accept the moral disgrace of such an action in the eyes of the entire civilized world."

Following the remarks of the Hungarian envoy, the British official remarked that "it is his purely personal opinion that from a moral point of view, there can be no doubt that rights which are the accorded one minority are the due of another also. But," he added, "it would be much more difficult to meet this demand than one would think because it would bring up the problems of national minorities in every country of the world." Cadogan also raised the question, what would be left for the Czechs if all the national minorities were to secede from Czechoslovakia?

Minister Barcza continued: "My response to Mr. Cadogan's first objection was that, in my opinion, with the mission by Lord Runciman and through Mr. Chamberlain's magnificent peace-keeping efforts, England has assumed the voluntary role of the world's foremost *arbiter pacis* in the problems of the minorities in Czechoslovakia. For the sake of peace and justice, it must maintain this role to the very end, playing it both firmly and impartially. And by no means would this mean that England would have to assume a similar responsibility regarding any or all of the world's other national minorities."

In response to Cadogan's second objection, Barcza declared: **"Following the secession of the territories inhabited by its national minorities, Czechoslovakia would survive in the shape and size it should have been originally established. That is to say, the state created in 1919 should have conformed to the right of self-determination of various nationalities, as invented, proclaimed but, unfortunately, not applied by the victorious powers. Had they acted differently, had they not run counter to political foresight, historic, economic and moral consideration in putting together this artifical and -- as we are unfortunately witnessing today -- nonviable state, world peace would not be threatened today."**

Cadogan did not reply to these remarks but promised to relay the Hungarian Minister's message to Lord Halifax the same day. And he expressed his appreciation for the peaceful policies of the Hungarian government.[374]

In his September 19 message to Kanya, Minister Barcza reported that Prime Minister Chamberlain has received the memorandum of the Hungarian government. He replied: "I fully sympathize with Hungary, she has no need to worry. I will carefully remember Hungary's situation. **I fully approve the peaceful and calm behavior Hungary has manifested heretofore and urge her to continue to do so."**

In the same message, Minister Barcza made reference to another of his reports about information he had received from Grandi, the Italian Minister to London, to the effect that the British and French governments would consent to the transfer of the Sudeten German territories.[375]

The Hungarian government had learned from another Italian source, as well, about the question of the Sudeten German transfer. According to Ciano, the French government has not yet agreed to the British plan and, in any event, the plan was intended to satisfy the Germans only and it would not extend to the Hungarians and the Poles. Accordingly, the Hungarian Minister in Rome reported, "Mussolini has recommended that we should use every available means to give voice to our demands loudly, forcefully and most emphatically."[376] The French government did have initial reservations about the British plan, but eventually agreed to it.[377]

On September 20, Lord Halifax received Hungarian Minister Barcza and told him that the question of the Hungarian minority in Czechoslovakia has been discussed repeatedly, both in the cabinet and with members of the French government. The British government has taken note of the Hungarian diplomatic moves. At the moment, he said, the question of peace or war depends on finding a solution to the German-Czechoslovak problem, therefore the British government is totally preoccupied with this issue.

Lord Halifax said that even though the British government fully understands the Hungarian government's interest in the future of the Hungarian minority, it hopes that the Hungarian government has confidence in the British government. He urged the Hungarian public and the Hungarians in the detached territories to remain calm in this delicate situation. Lord Halifax "expressed his great appreciation for the Hungarian minority's discipline and calm and expressed the hope that this will remain unchanged. At the same time, he acknowledged the Hungarian government's proper and peaceful attitude."[378]

On September 22, Kanya instructed the Hungarian Minister in Prague to request an immediate appointment with Foreign Minister Krofta and inform him that the Hungarian government demands for the Hungarian minority the same rights that will be granted the Sudeten Germans. Krofta took note of the message but reproached the Hungarian government for taking advantage of Czechoslovakia's difficult circumstances.[379]

The Polish government called up several age groups and deployed them near the Czechoslovak border. Several clashes had occurred and Polish minority leaders demanded self-government for the Polish minority.

The Polish government was beginning to exert a growing influence on Hungary to change its reserved posture toward a more assertive stance. Polish Foreign Minister Beck had several discussions to this end with the Hungarian Minister in Warsaw. As early as September 16, he told him in greatest confidence that in the event of a German attack against Czechoslovakia, Poland, too would join the attack for fear that otherwise the Germans might not take into account the Polish interests. He also told the Hungarian Minister that in the event Hungary decides to make a military move against Czechoslovakia, Poland would be ready to conclude a political agreement, followed by a military alliance with Hungary, and the two nations would coordinate their joint military action.[380]

On September 21, the Prague government complied with a strong British *demarche* from the day before and accepted a British-French note which had been delivered two days earlier. The note contained a demand to cede the Sudeten German territories to Germany.[381] Hodza was one of the few in Prague who supported this Western move.

On September 22, Kanya instructed the Hungarian Minister in Rome to relay the Hungarian government's thanks for the effective support from the Italian government. "Now that the Czechoslovak government has accepted the British-French proposal for the solution of the Sudeten German problem, we request the return of the territories inhabited by Hungarians without any further negotiations. Moreover, we request full rights of self-determination for the Ruthenians and the Slovaks," said Kanya.[382]

Also on September 22, the Hungarian Minister in Warsaw reported to Kanya that the Polish Foreign Minister had sent the following message to the Polish Minister in Prague and the Polish Consul in Pozsony: "As he has the national fate of the Slovaks on his heart, he wishes to bring to their attention that the Hungarian parts of Slovakia will secede and if they want to prevent a territorial division they urgently should come to terms with Hungary. It is time to make a decision regarding a transfer to Hungary."[383]

As the next meeting between Chamberlain and Hitler had been scheduled for September 23 in Godesberg, the Hungarian government thought it necessary to discuss Hungary's position with the German leaders. On September 18, Goring invited Horthy for a hunt. On September 20, Imredy and Kanya met Hitler in Obersalzberg. **Hitler reproached the Hungarian leaders once again "for their indecisive behavior during the current crisis. This is the last moment for Hungary to join, otherwise he would not be able to take a stand for the Hungarian interest..."**

Hitler called on Imredy and Kanya to 1. immediately demand a plebiscite in the territories they wanted; 2. to give no guarantees whatsoever for the possible new boundaries of Czechoslovakia and 3. to have Hungary quit the League of Nations at a later date.

The notes taken during the Obersalzberg meeting reportedly show that Hitler had proposed to Imredy that Hungary should launch military action against Czechoslovakia at the time of the Godesberg meeting because there is a risk that the Czechs may occupy everything and if that happens, the complete liquidation of Czechoslovakia would have to be postponed.[384]

In the discussion of the Berchtesgaden negotiations we have noted that the agreement reached there was not really satisfactory for Hitler because the newly created respite greatly restricted his freedom of action as far as his further plans were concerned. He thought the fanning of the Hungarian and Polish claims would be the most suitable means to change this situation freeing him of blame for any new tensions.

Hitler's idea was that a Hungarian military move would provide him with an excuse to break off the Godesberg negotiations. That would make it possible to solve the Czechoslovak question on a territorial, rather than ethnic basis, in line with Hitler's original intentions.

The Hungarian leaders rejected any military move because they did not want to risk a political defeat. That would have created a confrontation between Hungary and the other two *Little Entente* states or even with the Western powers, too. Moreover, a military clash with those states also seemed inevitable.

Thus, the Obersalzberg talks generated a new conflict between Hungary and Germany, which made itself clearly felt when the Hungarian claims were introduced. The Hungarian leaders gave Hitler a memorandum listing the Hungarian demands and Hitler promised that he would present those demands in Godesberg -- all in vain. Only the German demands were brought up in Godesberg. The same thing happened with regard to the Polish demands, despite Hitler's earlier promise to the Polish Ambassador in Berlin.[385]

At about the same time, as we have noted in Part One, Father Tiso went to Prague to see Benes. Concurrently, he was also negotiating with the Hungarian government. As a result, he summed up in three points his conditions for having Slovakia attached to Hungary. As we have noted, the Hungarian government informed Father Tiso of the acceptance of those conditons.

When the Godesberg negotiations broke off and the situation in Czechoslovakia became critical, a branch of the Slovak Peoples Party, led by Sidor, obtained significant concessions from Benes who was forced to do so by the circumstances. That, in turn, had a decisive impact on the talks between Father Tiso and the Hungarian government because, from then on, the Slovak Peoples Party was no longer interested in any offers made by the Hungarian government.[386]

According to a coded message No.229 from the Hungarian Minister in Warsaw to Kanya, Sidor's declaration of loyalty, as broadcast by the Czechoslovak radio, caused quite a consternation in the Polish Foreign Ministry. Up until then, Father Tiso and his colleagues have shown an interest in coming to terms with Hungary. According to the Minister, "the Slovaks are apparently continuing their two-faced games."[387]

The Sidor solution was basically more favorable for Hitler who wanted to extend his influence not only the Sudeten German territories but, sooner or later, over the entire Czechoslovakia.[388] This was behind the obviously two-faced German ploy, as we have noted in Part One, with Goring constantly inciting Hungary and reproaching it for the moderate nature of its demands on Czechoslovakia, while at the same time, assuring the Rumanian Minister in Berlin that Germany does not want Hungary to become too strong.

In the meantime, Hungarian public opinion became aroused and there was a massive demonstration in Budapest, demanding the return of the Highlands. Several age groups were called up, provoking a protest note from the British government.[389]

The Hungarian Minister in London once again explained to the Foreign Secretary, Lord Halifax, that "even though the lot of the Hungarian minority, as the whole world knows, has been the most difficult, the Hungarian government has never ceased to urge a peaceful solution, both in Geneva and in direct negotiations. However, all of these peaceful and well-intentioned efforts were thwarted by the stubborn opposition of the *Little Entente*.

"The time has come, however, for us to enforce our claims to the same degree as the Germans do. And I believe we are justified in expecting that Britain, in its impartiality, will give the same weight to the just demands of the Hungarian minority as it does to the Germans. It is true that the Hungarians cannot depend on the military bayonets of a nation of 75 million but I assume that instead of yielding to German force, Britain pay heed to justice which is as much behind our cause as of the Germans."

In response to a question by Lord Halifax, the Hungarian diplomat outlined the geographic distribution of the Hungarians in Czechoslovakia, noting that **"a homogeneous group of some 800,000 Hungarians live in a territory immediately adjacent to the mother country, consequently their return to Hungary could be accomplished very simply and easily."**

When Halifax wanted to know why these territories were incorporated into Czechoslovakia in 1919, the Hungarian Minister explained that **the Czechs themselves had been forced to admit at the time that there was no ethnographic or political reason, they had claimed strategic and economic necessity for demanding the territories with a pure Hungarian population."** Halifax said the British government would keep the Hungarian question in mind and consider it "at the appropriate moment."[390]

The Hungarian government's assessment of the situation at the time was that "there appears to be willingness on the part of the French and the British to find a satisfactory answer to our claims regarding the territories with Hungarian inhabitants, but our demand for the establishment of a Polish-Hungarian corridor has met strong resistance."[391]

Once again, as could be expected, Goring reproached the Hungarian Minister in Berlin over the alleged assurances given by the Hungarian Minister in London to Lord Halifax that Hungary does not intend to take up arms against Czechoslovakia. He warned the Hungarian government that if Hungary were to stay away from the military action in which Poland is certain to participate, Hungary would be left out of the solution. "While the Poles are engaged in heavy combat, nobody hears of the Hungarians," Goring said.[392]

The situation in Czechoslovakia became increasingly tense. On September 22, when the Hodza government accepted the British-French note, there were large demonstrations against the government's willingness to compromise. The Czechoslovak Communist Party was the loudest in demanding that the government resign. The combined opposition forces managed to overthrow Hodza and General Sirovy was named the new Prime Minister.

The new government did not accept the demands contained in the British-French note. Hitler was threatening with military action.[393] The Western powers demanded most emphatically that Prague meet the demands because they were afraid that otherwise war may break out. Further consultations were held in London around September 25 among Chamberlain, Halifax, Daladier and Bonnet. Daladier was the only one to oppose concessions to Germany but finally he was forced to yield.[394]

It was in this highly tense situation that the Western powers turned to Mussolini to exert his influence for rescuing peace. Mussolini's response on September 28 was a proposal for a summit meeting among the four great powers. The proposal was accepted, the date was set for September 29 and Munich was agreed upon as the site of the conference.

The Road to the Munich Agreement
and the Vienna Decision

Hitler, who blamed Imredy and Kanya for the overly cautious nature of the Hungarian foreign policy, was reluctant to bring up in Munich the question of non-German minorities. Thus, at the suggestion of the Hungarian Minister in Berlin, Csaky was sent as an observer in Munich, with a letter of introduction from Horthy to Mussolini and another letter from Imredy, and was armed with ample statistical material.[395] Thus, it was to Mussolini's credit that the Hungarian question was brought up in Munich, and it was Csaky who gave him a thorough briefing. The Hungarian demands included immediate transfer to Hungary of territories which were determined to have been inhabited by Hungarians by the 1910 census. Hungary also demanded a plebiscite within one month in Western Slovakia, Eastern Slovakia and Subcarpathian Ruthenia.[396]

Csaky had instructed the Hungarian Minister in London also to request the Prime Minister's support at the conference.[397] While in Munich, Csaky met Hitler also.

In his opening address at the conference, Hitler did emphasize that the German, Hungarian, Slovak, Polish and Ruthenian minorities had been forced against their will into a state against which they were now revolting. But he added that he could speak only on behalf of the German minority.[398] It was obvious that fanning the Hungarian and Polish demands was only meant to serve Hitler's tactical goal which was to increase tensions.

Following Mussolini's proposal for the solution of the Hungarian and Polish questions, a counter-proposal was tabled by Sir William Malkin, the legal expert of the British Foreign Office, and that served as the basis of the solution incorporated in the Munich Agreement.[399]

We have reviewed in Part One the decisions of the Munich conference. The immediate transfer of the Sudeten German territories to Germany; a three month moratorium with regard to the Hungarian and Polish questions, and direct negotiations between the interested governments -- these were the main decisions. The decisions in the Hungarian and Polish questions accomplished Hitler's purpose. He knew very well that the bilateral negotiations would lead nowhere. And Hitler also knew the Western powers would not interfere with those negotiations, therefore the decision would remain in his hands.

We have also seen that Poland did not accept the Munich decision. It sent an ultimatum to Prague and then it occupied Teschen. We have pointed out that **Hungary did not emulate either the German or the Polish example and did not use force because it had hoped to be able to have its just demands met by peaceful means, with the support of the Western powers.** We have emphasized at the same time that having failed to use force, Hungary had been pushed more and more into the embrace of the totalitarian powers.

We have also reviewed the Hungarian diplomatic moves following the Munich conference. At this time, we would like to present material pertaining primarily to the Hungarian demands, as well as information in support of **Hungary's peaceful and patient policies in contrast with the coercive moves of Germany and Poland. This information should serve as bountiful source material to reach conclusions especially about the two-faced policies of the Germans and the Western powers -- policies which were swinging between exaggerated promises and harsh denials.**

On October 3, Kanya instructed the Hungarian Minister in Prague to tell Foreign Minister Krofta that "the Hungarian government considers it most important to conduct its negotiations with Czechoslovakia in a friendly spirit and peaceful atmosphere. Therefore, it deems it necessary to raise certain preconditions to create a peaceful atmosphere." He listed in five points the preconditions which could be met without any difficulty, such as release of political prisoners, discharge of soldiers of Hungarian nationality, protection of life and property, and as a symbol of territorial transfers to come, transfer to Hungary of two or three towns near the border, and commencement of direct negotiations on October 6.[400]

On October 4, Kanya instructed the Hungarian Minister in Prague the tell Krofta immediately of the Hungarian government's surprise that "we have not yet received a reply to yesterday's note, even though Krofta had promised his reponse for today. We request immediate response," Kanya said.[401]

Also on October 4, the Hungarian Minister in London reported that he had told Cadogan, the British Deputy Foreign Secretary: "We have been admonished to be patient with our demands because of the threat of a world war. Now, with that threat having disappeared and even the question of Polish minorities having been solved, I believe we have reached the 'opportune moment,' mentioned by Lord Halifax in his letter of September 24, to support and solve the question of the Hungarian minorities.

"I stressed the great patience we have demonstrated under difficult conditions, as well as our constant willingness to find a peaceful solution. However, it is now high time for the Czechoslovak government to take practical steps to grant the right of self-determination to the Hungarian minority, as provided by the Munich Agreement.

"Now is the time to settle this question amicably in such a manner that it would not have a harmful effect on future relations between Czechoslovakia and Hungary. Therefore I consider it most important for the Czechs not to wait until the end of three months, as provided by the Munich Agreement, but settle the question at once," said the Hungarian Minister in London. Cadogan assured him of the support of the British government.[402]

Germany and, undoubtedly, Britain played the leading roles in the global crisis that had just ended. A report from Barcza, the Hungarian Minister in London to Foreign Minister Kanya on October 4 provided perhaps the best summary of Britain's role.

"Prime Minister Chamberlain's policy of "peace at any price" to the very end was mainly prompted by the recognition, as I was confidentially told by sources in his entourage, that a world war would have unforeseeable consequences for Europe, including England. I have heard that Mr. Chamberlain was concerned that an undoubtedly long war, with a massive toll in lives and material losses on both sides, would have increased Moscow's influence, bringing Europe ultimately under Bolshevik rule. In order to avoid this ultimate danger at all costs, he sacrificed the interests of the French and the Czechs. That was the price he paid for peace. Thus, the solution to the global crisis is nothing but 'defeat in a gift wrapping.'

"The Foreign Office, I understand, is very critical of Mr. Chamberlain's policies which it considers as deeply humiliating for England and dangerous for the future. Czechoslovakia is being referred to in these circles as "poor little Czechoslovakia" and its amputation is being labeled the greatest injustice of the century, forgetting the fact that this state came into being in 1918 through the much more unjust vivisection of three nations. Czechoslovakia is the 'victim' deserving full sympathy and it was immediately extended a loan of 10 million pounds.

"With the threat of a world war gone, I believe I am not mistaken in saying that with the signing of the annex to the Munich Agreement, the British government considers its commitment to us for the time being fulfilled. In the British view, the settlement of the question of the Hungarian minorities has been shifted to the track of direct Hungarian-Czech negotiations.[403]

The Czechoslovak government, in view of its domestic political crisis, requested a delay in commencing the negotations. This crisis culminated in the abdication of President Benes. **It ended an era of more than two decades which had a decisive influence on the destiny of Hungary and its neighbors, as well. Benes' abdication demonstrated that the political conception so closely tied to his name, which was built on force and the formation of military blocs rather than mutual reconciliation, could not be maintained for more than two decades. With changes in the European balance of power, his system collapsed like a house of cards. A regime which can be swept away so easily by any change in the balance of power of the European great powers carries the seeds of its own destruction.**

In Part One, we have told about the Slovak interparty conference of October 6. **The three Slovak parties, meeting in Zsolna (Zilina, Sillen) declared Slovakia's autonomy.**

On October 5, Csaky, chief of staff of the Hungarian Foreign Ministry, flew to Warsaw to discuss questions relating to the establishment of a common border between Hungary and Poland. In a message to Kanya, Csaky reported that Polish Foreign Minister "Beck shares our views about the need for a common border."[404]

The Hungarian Minister in Prague had personally discussed with Prime Minister Imredy a draft resolution he was proposing for the corthcoming major meeting of the The United Hungarian Party in Pozsony. In his daily report, the Minister said that since he could not see Janos Esterhazy until the next day, he would have the Hungarian Consul in Pozsony deliver the draft resolution to the United Hungarian Party. The Minister emphasized that "as far as Kassa (Kosice) was concerned, the Slovaks must understand those deep, emotional ties which link the Hungarians to this sacred shrine of their history. I am convinced that it will be possible to come to an agreement, based on brotherly understanding, on this as on every other issue.[405]

On October 7, Janos Esterhazy and Andor Jaross broadcast a major speech on Pozsony radio, outlining the resolutions of the United Hungarian Party. They included the following demands: 1. Withdrawal of the Czechoslovak army from territories inhabited by Hungarians. 2. Immediate discharge of all Hungarian soldiers in the Czechoslovak army. 3. Immediate release of all Hungarian political prisoners and hostages. 4. Immediate return, or appropriate indemnification for all property, horses, carriages and motor vehicles that the Hungarian population was compelled to turn over to the military. 5. Immediate indemnification of the Hungarian population for all losses suffered at the time of the mobilization. 6. Handing over of governmental authority in the Hungarian territories to the United Hungarian Party and, in the interim, securing freedom of press and assembly. It was also announced that the Parliamentary Club of the United Hungarian Party has formed a Hungarian National Council to represent the interests of the Hungarians in Czechoslovakia until the question of the borders is settled.[406]

On October 9, the Hungarian-Czechoslovak negotiations began in Komarom (Komarno). We gave a detailed account of the negotiations in Part One. The Czechoslovak delegation was led by Dr. Jozef Tiso, the new Prime Minister of Slovakia, and the participants included the future Foreign Minister, Dr. Ferdinand Durcansky, who was Minister of Justice at the time. During the negotiations, the Slovak statesmen, as we have reported, had repeatedly flown to see Hitler. **By this time, the Slovak political leadership was bidding for Hitler's favors and made all sorts of promises to secure his support.**[407]

To counter these moves, the Hungarian government decided to send Daranyi to Germany. His trip was set for October 14. In the meantime, the Hungarian government declared the Komarom negotiations terminated because, to quote the official statement: "We are persuaded that we cannot hope to be able to bridge at this conference the wide gap between the views represented by the two delegations about the basic principles of the settlement."[408]

For a background to this statement, we would refer to Part One where it has been stated that the Slovak statesmen clearly must have known about Hitler's latest designs for Slovakia and that would account for their rigid and uncompromising attitude. **They refused**

to agree to as little as 10 percent of the Hungarian territorial demands. The Hungarian government had to turn to the four signatories of the Munich protocols to request prompt settlement of the territorial demands. As we have noted earlier, Janos Esterhazy and several other deputies of the United Hungarian Party stayed in Komarom during the negotiations, available for any assistance to the Hungarian delegation. **In Part One, we provided a detailed account of the feverish diplomatic activity following the Komarom negotiations, with both parties bidding for the favor of the great powers, especially Germany.**

With regard to the Daranyi visit we might add that once again, Hitler did not fail to bring up the cautious and hesitant policies of Imredy and Kanya, which had resulted in the loss of a favorable opportunity. Hitler did not accept the Hungarian request for the convening of the four-power conference, nor the demands for plebiscite in Slovakia and Subcarpathian Ruthenia. At that point, Daranyi had to make different promises, such as Hungary joining the Anti-Komintern Pact, quitting the League of Nations and establishment of closer economic ties with Germany. Obviously, this was exactly what Hitler wanted. He instructed Ribbentrop to take care of the details.[409]

Despite lengthy diplomatic negotiations, as we have seen in Part One, the four-power conference could not be reconvened. Finally, German-Italian arbitration was agreed upon.

We wish to emphasize again that the Western powers were reluctant to interfere in Central European affairs. They provided ample evidence of that. Thus, according to a report by the Hungarian Minister in Paris, **"when it became known that we and the Czechoslovak government had requested arbitration by Germany and Italy, no objection at all was raised in the press to the exclusion of the Western powers from the settlement of this question of such a vital importance for Central Europe."**[410]

On October 28, the Hungarian Minister in Rome reported that "the British Ambassador stated last night that his government would have no objection against a four-power conference but would much prefer arbitration by the Axis powers."[411] The French Minister in Warsaw told his Hungarian colleague that it may be better for Hungary not to bring its case to a four-power conference because this time France may not abandon Czechoslovakia.[412]

We have discussed the Rome talks between Ciano and Ribbentrop where Ciano had persuaded the German Foreign Minister to give up the idea of the so-called Ribbentrop Line and agree to the transfer of the contested towns to Hungary. But he had to give up on the common border between Hungary and Poland.

We have also spoken about a journey to Rome by Janos Esterhazy and a delegation from the United Hungarian Party to brief Ciano. Ciano had told the Hungarian Minister in Rome that Hungarian claims on Pozsony are hopeless because of resistance on the part of the Germans and the concessions indicated by Esterhazy have no chance of success, except perhaps in cultural and religious matters. The Minister further stated that he and Esterhazy would arrive in Vienna Tuesday night.[413]

The arbitration session was formally opened in November 2 in the Belvedere Palace. We have given a detailed account of the proceedings and the decisions. We have quoted from an address by Slovak Prime Minister Tiso as broadcast by the Pozsony and Besztercebanya radio stations. Here is some more: "The responsibility rests on the shoulders of the Czechoslovak politicians who have been deciding our fate for twenty years without asking us about it. That is why the Vienna decision is unjust because strangers have judged us as if we were vanquished, without giving us any chance to influence the outcome." At the same time, much attention was paid to **an editorial in the Agrarian Party daily *Vecer*, with close ties to the Foreign Ministry, openly stating that the policies of Benes were responsible for the dismemberment of Czechoslovakia.** The *Vecer* editorial was the first to say what had been hinted at for some time between the lines, but prevented by the censorship from being expressed openly in the newspapers.[414]

It is worth stressing over and over again that **the Western powers bear a tremendous moral responsibility for admitting only the victors to the peace talks at Trianon and excluding the vanquished. It is an irony of fate that it was the dictatorial powers, into whose arms the vanquished nations had been pushed, which granted them this right in 1938.**

The Vienna Decision and the International Law

We have already discussed the impact of the Vienna Decision on the Hungarian people. Now, a look at various views, first of all by Hungarian scholars, on the question whether or not the Vienna Decision should be considered valid according to international law.

The Vienna Decision of 1938 was the only available peaceful solution for the ever growing problems that had existed for nearly 20 years. None of the other attempts for solution, short of using force, brought the slightest result. On the other hand, both interested parties had freely agreed to submit and abide by the arbitration.

It is a generally accepted fact that the roots of the Vienna Decision can be traced to the Paris peace treaties of 1919.

As a result of those treaties, Hungary suffered huge losses in population and territories. More than three million Hungarians were transferred without being asked to the newly established states, along with the country's most important mineral resources. For nearly two decades, Hungary had been seeking remedy at the League of Nations. **But neither the countless grievances submitted to the League of Nations, nor direct negotiations with the successor states had any result.** As it became increasingly obvious, the League of Nations had only served to preserve the *status quo*, while the direct negotiations with the successor states led nowhere because of the stubbornness of Benes' self-serving policies.

Hungary, thus, had no choice but to turn to the states which were against the *status quo* and, with their support, work peacefully for the fulfillment of its just demands. As we have pointed out earlier, it became clear as far back as 1920 to the makers of French foreign policy that the vanquished states would sooner or later fall into Germany's orbit, and they came up with a new conception to prevent it. But, again, the shortsighted policies of Benes prevailed and the *Little Entente* system of alliances came into being. Unfortunately, it enjoyed the support of the Western powers until

1938 when, as a result of shifts in the European balance of power, the entire system collapsed under its own weight. **That is how Hungary came under the influence of Italy, at first, then Germany.**

Hitler's Germany demanded a very high price for supporting Hungary's just demands: armed participation in his designs on Czechoslovakia. We have seen how Hungary had tried to refuse to do so, despite great difficulties and under tremendous pressure, with the German leaders, such as Hitler and Goring promising to meet the Hungarian territorial demands to the fullest extent. **Hungary, by consistently rejecting Hitler's demands, lost the sympathy of the German leadership and that became very obvious in every encounter with them.**

Following the failure of the Komarom negotiations, both parties, in accord with the Munich decisions, turned to the four great powers. Of the Western powers, Britain showed willingness to participate in the four-power arbitration process and the British government informed Ciano that it was in principle in favor of transferring to Hungary territories with an overwhelmingly Hungarian population.[415]

On the other hand, as the Hungarian Minister in Rome reported on October 28, "the British Ambassador stated last night that **his government would have no objection against a four-powerconference but would much prefer arbitration by the Axis powers.**"[416]

As we have seen, the French government had no intention, either, to participate in the arbitration process.[417] The French have apparently accepted Hitler's explanation to French Ambassador Francois-Poncet to the effect that by declining to act on Hungary's request to the four great powers, Germany has prevented a potential conflict among the great powers and forestalled a peril which would have arisen.[418]

It is a historical fact that the solution to the two decades' old problem between Hungary and Czechoslovakia had been discussed by the four great powers in Munich and they called on the two countries to find a solution through direct negotiations within three months. If they fail to do so, the four great powers would decide it for them.

As we have seen, the direct negotations brought no result and on October 24, the two interested states requested the four powers to make a decision.[419] The Italian *charge d'affaires ad interim* informed of this the French government the same day. Mussolini suggested that the foreign ministers of the four great powers meet early the following week either in Venice or in Brioni. Later, probably under German pressure, he withdrew this suggestion.[420] Ciano sent word that the Italian initiative to convene the conference has been cancelled and on behalf of Mussolini he recommended that if the direct negotiations fail to bring prompt results, German-Italian arbitration should be requested. And he repeated his regret over the cancellation of the conference.[421]

According to the October 23 report of the Hungarian Minister in Rome, Ribbentrop had said he was not in favor of arbitration and asked Ciano why could not this matter be entrusted to the four great powers? Ciano replied that that is what he had proposed on October 14.[422]

Kanya telegraphed the Hungarian Minister in Berlin that according to the Czechoslovak Foreign Minister, since the Hungarian government has not found the latest Czechoslovak offer satisfactory, the Czechoslovak government has agreed to submit the question of the Hungarian minority to arbitration by Germany and Italy. Kanya also said that if Ribbentrop continues to refuse arbitration, Hungary would request the immediate convening of the four great powers.[423]

On October 28, the Hungarian Minister in Rome reported in a telegram that he had spoken with Ciano. He reported that the Italian Foreign Minister, "citing the agreement of the British government, was demanding the most emphatically that Ribbentrop agree to arbitration."[424]

On October 29, the Hungarian Minister in Rome reported that Ribbentrop who was in Rome at the time, has agreed to arbitration. The meeting will be held on November 2 in Vienna.[425]

Prague did not agree to the Hungarian government's demand for a plebiscite, based on the 1910 census, in the contested territories. Therefore, Prague "wishes arbitration by the Axis powers but would like to know the British government's position in this matter." The British reply stated: "**His Majesty's government saw no objection to the settlement of the Czech-Hungarian question by means of arbitration by Germany and Italy, if the Czechoslovak and Hungarian governments agreed to settle their differences this way**... If the two parties to the dispute preferred to refer the matter to the four Munich powers, His Majesty's government would be ready to join in any discussion."[426]

Speaking of the Hungarian-Czechoslovak negotiations, Lord Halifax declared in the House of Commons on October 24: "I hope indeed that the rectification of the frontiers according to the racial distribution of the population which is now taking place in Central and

South-Eastern Europe may contribute to the stability of peace. **What we are now witnessing is the revision of the Treaty of Versailles, for which provision was made in the Covenant of the League (of Nations), but which has never till now been made effective.**"[427]

According to the Hungarian view, the procedure in the League of Nations just cited by Lord Halifax, which has been ignored for many years, along with the growing severity of the situation with the expansionist efforts of the German empire which had repeatedly brought the directly involved states to the brink of war and might have resulted in a conflagration throughout Europe, provided the legal basis for negotiations as prescribed by the four power agreement in Munich and, following the failure of the negotiation, for arbitration. This procedure made it possible to find a quick solution for the problem and did not run counter to any provision of international law.[428]

The absence of Britain and France from the arbitration did not render the procedure illegal, according to the Hungarian view.

The charge that Czechoslovakia was under "irresistible duress" to accept arbitration by the Axis powers, does not stand up, partly because it had been urged by the Slovak leaders and also because the two Western powers would have been willing to participate if requested by the interested states, but no such request had been forthcoming.

Speaking in the House of Commons on October 14, Chamberlain declared: "The Czechoslovak and Hungarian governments have agreed to accept arbitration by the German and Italian governments and to abide by their final decision. Accordingly, there has been no need for any further action by His Majesty's government.[429]

It has also been argued by authorities on international law and by political writers that the Vienna Decision of 1938 ran counter to the procedures of international law. One argument has been that the decision was based on and was a direct consequence of the Munich Agreement. According to this argument, the Munich Agreement ran counter to international law and, consequently, so did the Vienna Decision. However, the *de facto* legality of the Munich Agreement did not cease until Hitler's Germany turned Bohemia and Moravia into a protectorate and, at the same time, established the independent Slovakia under German sponsorship.

According to the Hungarian view, the Munich Agreement and the Vienna Decision were two distinct transactions. Procedures for the Munich Agreement were chosen and agreed to by the four great powers as a mechanism sanctioned by international law to resolve the

German-Czechoslovak question. On the other hand, the Vienna Arbitration was a procedure chosen by the two interested states, Hungary and Czechoslovakia, because it offered the best chance to reach a mutually agreeable solution to the questions which had been unresolved between them for nearly twenty years.

The roots of the Hungarian-Czechoslovak question, as we have seen, go back to the Paris peace treaties of 1919, long preceding the Sudeten German-Czechoslovak questions. Thus, the Vienna Arbitration was not a direct consequence of the Munich Agreement. Munich had only served as a trigger to launch bilateral talks. The Vienna Arbitration came about as a result of an agreement between the Czechoslovak and Hungarian governments. After the failure of the bilateral talks, they agreed to choose this procedure and committed themselves to abide by its decision, whatever that may be.[430]

The decision of the Vienna Arbitration was based on the application of ethnic principles. This has been in sharp contrast with the economic, strategic and other considerations applied in the drafting of the Paris peace treaties of 1919. The application of ethnic principles, as noted by several authors, was by no means perfect or entirely free of bias. Nevertheless, its main strength was that it had been resting on the mutual consent of the interested parties.

In 1942, the British and French government declared the Vienna Decision null and void. It was invalidated *de facto* by the arrival of the Soviet army in late 1944 and the transfer to Czechoslovakia of the territories in question. It was set aside *de jure* by the 1947 Paris Peace Treaty. That restored the pre-Munich borders between Hungary and Slovakia. Subcarpathian Ruthenia was ceded by Czechoslovakia to the Soviet Union.

The Period Following the Vienna Decision

Returning to the situation following the Vienna Decision, we must take note of the festive session, on December 3, of the Upper House of the Hungarian parliament where the return of the Highlands Hungarians to the motherland and the recovery of the lost territories were celebrated. On the same occasion, a decision was made to invite the Hungarian deputies from the Highlands. Geza Szullo and Andor Jaross were present and received an enthusiastic welcome.

Aladar Huszar made the following statement amidst the warm applause of the members of the Upper House: "I believe I would be amiss if I did not extend greetings from this place to **Janos Esterhazy and his colleagues. They remained beyond the borders to become leaders, protectors and guardians of the Hungarians who were left behind the new borders. Our affection and prayers accompany their work and struggles. We implore the Allmighty to bless and protect their every step.**"[431]

On December 3, Janos Esterhazy had a long talk with Dr. Tiso, the Prime Minister of Slovakia about the affairs of the Hungarian minority in Slovakia and the issue of equal rights for Hungarians living in Pozsony.[432]

Also on December 3, Czechoslovak Prime Minister Beran said in Prague, that "following the settlement of the border issue, we wish to establish wide-ranging cooperation with Poland also, especially in the realm of economics, culture and transportation. The same is true of Hungary."[433]

In his Christmas, 1938, statement Janos Esterhazy declared that "the strength of the Hungarians remains unbroken under the new circumstances."[434]

Following the Vienna Decision, the diplomatic efforts of the Hungarian government were aimed at the securing of Subcarpathian Ruthenia and the establishment of a common border with Poland. The international situation appeared to be favorable, with the rationale being that both the Western powers and the Soviet Union would rather have this territory under Hungarian rule, instead of strengthening Germany's military might which was already too great. Germany was opposed to any independent action by the smaller powers. It consented to such an action only if it could serve, directly or indirectly, German interests. Berlin wanted to take advantage of any unilateral action, either as a *quid pro quo* or as a tactical move against its neighbors. Accordingly, a Hungarian military move that had been planned for November 20, had to be cancelled in the face of German and Italian protests.

On November 23, Hungarian Prime Minister Imredy submitted his resignation but Regent Horthy asked him to try to form a new government. At the same, Count Istvan Csaky became the new Foreign Minister, replacing Kalman Kanya who had lost the confidence of the Germans.

A December 5 message from Ribbentrop hinted at certain changes. As a result, Ribbentrop was told that Csaky would accept his invitation for a visit next January.

Meanwhile, at the suggestion of Ciano, the Hungarian diplomats were trying to determine the likely impact among the Western powers of Hungary's anticipated joining the Anti-Bolshevik Pact. The news from the Western capitals was favorable. Only Soviet Foreign Commissar Litvinov was making threatening statements.

On November 13, 1939, Hungary did join the Anti-Bolshevik Pact and the Soviet government broke diplomatic relations with Hungary.

Even though on the advice of the Axis powers Prague had shown a degree of rapprochement toward Hungary, the Tiso government which was unable to accept the Vienna Decision and kept demanding that it be changed, was inciting border incidents and staging demonstrations. In Subcarpathian Ruthenia, Volosin displayed a similar attitude.

The most serious incident took place on January 6 at Munkacs where the Czechoslovak army opened artillery fire on the city, resulting in several dead and wounded. The day before there were reports of troop concentrations near Munkacs. Apparently, the incidents had been aimed at the retaking of Munkacs. The Germans did not interfere because the growing tension fit well into their political designs. Volosin was supported by Ukrainian guerillas.[435] The incidents had Karmasin's support also.

Csaky's negotiations with Hitler and other German leaders began on January 16. Hitler, as was his wont, recited his accusations against Hungary. He found it particularly objectionable that even during the Czechoslovak crisis, Hungary's policies remained indecisive and hesitant; that Hungary had signed the Bled agreement and helped revive the *Little Entente* against Germany. Poland had acted at once, while Hungary did not do anything, Hitler claimed, adding that "**Germany will not sacrifice itself for its friends who refuse to help at the decisive moment.**"

Csaky tried to put up a defense against Hitler's accusations, but without success for quite a while. Hitler calmed down only when Csaky promised that all German demands would be met.[436] Hitler hinted that he was planning military action against Czechoslovakia in March. And in return for the many promises he made, Csaky received almost nothing, except a half-promise of sorts regarding Subcarpathian Ruthenia.

Following Csaky's visit, Ribbentrop invited Czechoslovak Foreign Minister Chvalkovsky to Berlin. To his great disappointment, Ribbentrop treated him in a very patronizing manner, produced a long list of accusations and raised new demands. This was natural beause the fate of Czechoslovakia had already been decided by then and Chvalkovsky was made aware of this.[437]

Soon thereafter, **on January 28, Durcansky** and another Slovak minister visited Germany. **Goring told them that they can count on the requested financial help only if they agree to Czechoslovakia's dismemberment.**[438] **To give the point greater emphasis, the German leaders loved to bring up the Hungarian territorial demands, saying that Germany was prepared to honor them provided that Berlin finds them suitable; that is, if the Hungarians do not secede from Czechoslovakia.**

The decisive force behind these events was Hitler's newly reached decision to let Hungary have Subcarpathian Ruthenia. This was due to Csaky's total German orientation, the easing of Polish-Hungarian relations and **realization by Germany that it would gain much more by establishing an idependent Slovakia and recognizing its "independence."**

Meanwhile there were changes in government both in Hungary and Yugoslavia. To the great regret of the Axis powers, Stojadinovic had been set aside and Cvetkovic was appointed Prime Minister. And in Hungary, Imredy who had drifted too far to the right, was replaced by Count Pal Teleki, a move which was not designed to please the Germans, either.

Teleki became Prime Minister on February 16 and began at once an intense diplomatic campaign to regain Subcarpathian Ruthenia. But instead of invoking the ethnic principles, he laid the emphasis on the economic facts of life which appeared to be much more convincing. Memoranda containing his views were sent London, Paris, Berlin and Rome. The French government received the moves of the Hungarian government with particular understanding.[439]

Beyond trying to secure the support of the Western great powers for the return of Subcarpathian Ukraine, he made a similar attempt in Prague. He sent the permanent deputy to the Foreign Minister to Prague to talk with Chvalkovsky. The Hungarian envoy spoke of good neighborly relations with Chvalkovsky and mentioned the possibility of other rewards. Chvalkovsky displayed some interest in the offer but left its acceptance up to President Hacha.[440]

When the German learned that there was no complete agreement among Slovak leaders regarding the secession of Slovakia -- notably Sidor was opposed to it -- they informed Tiso and Sidor that with the dismemberment of Czechoslovakia being a foregone conclusion, it should coincide with the declaration of Slovak independence.

Prague, however, decided to rely on its army. On March 10, Beran replaced Tiso as Prime Minister. Tuka, Mach and others were jailed, Durcansky fled to Austria. With that the Germans exerted heavy pressure on the Slovaks and, once again, raised the specter of a Hungarian threat. All these moves favored the Hungarian political efforts.

Teleki spared no effort to regain Subcarpathian Ruthenia without any German assistance, if at all possible. On March 10, he obtained the Cabinet's agreement to have the Hungarian army occupy Subcarpathian Ruthenia when Slovakia declares its independence, even if the Germans do not agree to that. **However, in view of the events in Slovakia, the Germans decided to give Hungary a free hand.** On March 11, the German Minister in Budapest delivered a note, informing the Hungarian government of this decision.

The Germans set a few conditions, most of them of an economic nature, although some of them were political, pertaining to the rights of the ethnic Germans in Hungary, and the like.[441] Hungary accepted the conditions.[442] Hitler personally informed the Hungarian Minister in Berlin of these developments, saying that "Hungary has 24 hours to resolve the Ruthenian question.[443]

C.

From the Declaration of Slovakia's Independence to the Restoration of the Republic of Czechoslovakia in 1945

The Declaration of Slovakia's Independence

From here on, events began to move much faster. Following the rejection by Sidor, the Germans invited Tiso to Berlin. There is a detailed account of that meeting in Part One. What happened, in effect, was that **Slovakia seceded from Czechoslovakia and declared its independence. On March 14, 1939, the Slovak parliament gave its unanimous approval.** Hungary and Poland recognized Slovakia's independence the very next day. Later, under rather dramatic circumstances, the German leaders persuaded Tiso to conclude a defense treaty with Germany. **Tiso signed the treaty on March 18** and the Slovak parliament took due note of it.

Slovakia accomplished at last what its "brother" Czechs had promised and failed to deliver, that is to say, autonomy within the Czechoslovak Republic, and much more than that, independence for Slovakia, although it was granted not by the Czechs but came about with the support and under the "guardianship" of the German Empire. This had suited the German interests no less than the Hungarian military occupation of Subcarpathian Ruthenia, which was also about to take place. With the declaration of Slovakia's independence, the Slovak struggle for autonomy and independence entered a new chapter.

Before we examine this period which was very important for the struggles of the Hungarians also, it is time to take a look at the conditions of the Hungarians who had remained in Slovakia, and the activities of Janos Esterhazy.

The first item on Esterhazy's agenda in 1939 was to act on the old wish of the Hungarians in Slovakia, the establishment of Hungarian Houses. He knew all too well how important this was in order to gather together and better utilize the Hungarian forces, and also to promote their economic wellbeing.

On January 1, 1939, Esterhazy issued an appeal to the Hungarians in Slovakia. It said, among others: "Let us build a Hungarian House in Pozsony, first of all. Let us build then Hungarian Houses in Nyitra, Nagyszombat, Eperjes, Iglo -- in every town or near towns where Hungarians live in sizeable numbers. The Hungarian House of Pozsony should be built before the end of 1939.[444]

On January 8, 1939, Janos Esterhazy registered a forceful protest against the treacherous attack on Munkacs, mentioned earlier.[445]

The Executive Committee of the United Hungarian Party met for the first time since the Vienna Decision on January 19, 1939. Janos Esterhazy expressed his warmest thanks to the Hungarians from Czechoslovakia who have been returned to Hungary. He turned first of all, to "the brethren who have gone back to the motherland, thanking them for their faithful perseverance through 20 years of adversity...

"We shall never forget that, whether they were intellectuals or blue-collar workers struggling through two decades of oppression, in towns and villages, through all the hardships of minority life they have loyalty to the Hungarian language and the Hungarian land, nurtured their Hungarian consciousness, and tolerated no blemish on the Hungaian honor. It gives us satisfaction if they are now able to enjoy the fruits of their long suffering...

"The classification into second or third class citizenship must cease," Esterhazy said. And he emphasized that just as in the past, the Slovaks will continue to be able to count on him in the future, as well.[446]

On January 27, 1939, Esterhazy met with Tiso to discuss the question of discharged workers and trade union matters. On the same day, he sent a telegram to the President of the republic regarding the dissolution of the Subcarpathian Ruthenia branch of the United Hungarian Party. On the 28th, he visited Saros and Zemplen.[447] On February 8, he spoke over the Budapest radio about the Hungarian Houses in Slovakia, emphasizing that "today, ten times fewer Hungarians must maintain the concept of the Hungarian nation in Slovakia and Subcarpathian Ruthenia."[448]

An extraordinary episode worth noting was the encounter in Pozsony between Janos Esterhazy and Czechoslovak General Viest.

Esterhazy had known the general from the Komarom negotiations. On March 15, 1939, he spotted the general in the Cafe of the Hotel Carlton. The general wore civilian clothes and appeared to be very dejected. With a friendly gesture, Esterhazy invited him to his table. They were talking for a good while about Hitler's aggression and the general confided in Esterhazy that he was organizing the resistance and soon he would be going to London to see Benes who, the general was certain, would take charge of the resistance movement.

Esterhazy knew that the Germans would not permit the general to leave. He assured therefore the general that he would help him go through Hungary. Esterhazy did so because was convinced that the small nations must join forces against Hitler's imperialism.

In addition to General Viest, Esterhazy saved many Czech patriots from the *Gestapo* by arranging for them to cross the border and travel through Hungary and Yugoslavia on their way to London.

Esterhazy gave an interview the *Uj Hirek* newspaper about the sitation in Subcarpathian Ruthenia. He said, "Since Volosin came to power, he has been systematically suppressing the Hungarians of Subcarpathian Ruthenia and has demonstrated such a lack of understanding regarding the most basic rights of the national minorities that as long as he stays in power, or at least until the Hungarian grievances are rectified, Volosin can look forward to nothing but a total lack of confidence on the part of the Hungarians in Subcarpathian Ruthenia.

"I will find a way," Esterhazy continued, "to prove before an international forum how the Hungarian population of Subcarpathian Ruthenia is being treated by a Prime Minister who has managed to garner only 7,000 votes at the peak of his career."[449]

The *Magyar Nemzet* Newspaper Hails Esterhazy

On February 28, 1939, the Budapest newspaper *Magyar Nemzet* paid a glowing tribute to Esterhazy. The paper wrote, among others: "Those who are the most familiar with the events and movements of the Highlands in the last 20 years know very well the deeds of Count Janos Esterhazy in the defense of Hungarian justice during the mad binge of Czech tyranny. The entire national Christian public opinion knew that Janos Esterhazy would have been completely within his rights to accept the honorable offer which had been extended to him from the highest official places. **By remaining and continuing to fight in the 'lion's den,' he has demonstrated and continues to do so with the greatest eloquence that he is imbued to the marrow of his bones with the motto of the ancient poet, 'The Fatherland above all else!'** His entire psyche is totally apart from the self-serving patriotism of the loudmouths with their eternal toasts and noisy celebrations. **Instead of the comfort of a velvet seat in the cabinet room he chose the tribulations of the thorny path until he reaches the final triumph of his nation's cause.**"[450]

In response to an article, entitled "False Auslehnungen," by Sudeten German Deputy Karmasin in the February 26 edition of the newspaper *Grenzbote*, Esterhazy reminded the author of the following: "The first permanent, organized state in this land was established first of all by St.Stephen and the other kings of the Arpad Dynasty, amidst, and in spite of invasions from East and West. And through the centuries, iron and blood have forged the community of nations in the lap of the Carpathians."[451]

With regard to the declaration of Slovakia's independence, Esterhazy told the *Uj Hirek* newspaper, "I deem it necessary to state that **the Hungarians living in Slovakia have been greatly pleased over the Slovak declaration of independence... I am sure that now, as it guides its country's destiny truly on its own, the Slovak government will show understanding toward Slovakia's Hungar-**

ian population and its just demands. I believe the results of that understanding will benefit both sides... Let everybody, to the best of their abilities, support the newly independent Slovak nation."[452]

Radio Pozsony, in its Hungarian program on March 20, broadcast Janos Esterhazy's festive proclamation to the Hungarians on the occassion of the establishment of the independent Slovak state. He greeted the Slovak sister nation and outlined the tasks of the Hungarians within the framework of the new state. "We live in historic times," he said, "with events moving around us at speeds almost beyond the comprehension of the human brain.

"In these historic times I find it necessary to make direct contact with Hungarians wherever they may live in Slovakia, with the Hungarians of Pozsony and its environment, with my Hungarian brethren living in the linguistic islands of Nyitra and its vicinity, with my kins who have preserved their Hungarian identity in the diaspora of Central, North and East Slovakia.

"I must speak to you, Hungarian Brethren because those of us who have remained behind constitute an inseparable family... What we were unable to accomplish over 20 years with a centralist Czechoslovak regime, we will obtain without any pressure from the responsible leaders of the independent Slovak state who are imbued with the greatest goodwill toward the Hungarians. They have told me so repeatedly, I have their assurances.

"The Czechoslovak Republic was created by the dictate of the Paris peace treaties. These peace treaties were inspired by individuals whose hearts have not been permeated by Christian brotherly love. **The Czechoslovak Republic, created by the Paris peace treaties, have thrown us Hungarians under the greatest oppression and, along with us, they have also driven our Slovak brother nation under the yoke of Czechoslovak rule. Part of the shackles placed on us Hungarians were broken on November 2, 1938. The Slovaks got rid of their shackles on the Ides of March, 1939, when they declared their independence.**

I am convinced that the Slovak government is fully determined to maintain the most friendly relationship with its neighboring states. **Therefore, it will avoid the error which became the downfall of the foreign policies of Benes. He was friendly with the Soviets, he was friendly with the French, he was friendly with faraway nations, but he failed to come to terms with his immediate neighbors, the Hungarians, the Germans and the Poles. The**

German occupation of Prague served as the closing curtain for this faulty foreign policy.

Hungary and the Hungarians living in Slovakia have been always pleased over the efforts to gain freedom for the Slovak people and have been happy to welcome Slovakia's independence. I wanted to bring this to the attention of my Hungarian brethren on the eve of the day when every community in Slovakia is about to celebrate its independence."[453]

In his Easter message of 1939, Esterhazy told the Slovaks once again that "I have often volunteered for constructive work with the greatest sincerity on behalf of the Hungarians living here. In this respect, I would like to recall the statements I have made on behalf of the Hungarians before the first Slovak parliamentary elections of 1938, and most recently, on March 18, 1939 when, again on behalf of the Hungarians, I spoke out in support of the declaration of Slovakia's independence and called on my Hungarian brethren to work to the best of their abilities for the independent Slovakia. Thus, with the greatest sincerity, we have publicly declared our determination to work with and assist our Slovak brethren."[454]

The Return of Subcarpathian Ruthenia

Meanwhile, the long-festering problem of Subcarpathian Ruthenia has been also resolved. As we have noted, the events in Slovakia had brought about a change in Germany's previous position on Subcarpathian Ruthenia and the German government gave Hungary a free hand to achieve its political goals. There was some sympathy among the Western powers also toward Hungary's goals in Subcarpathian Ruthenia because both Slovakia and Subcarpathian Ruthenia have become tools of the German interests. By transferring the latter to Hungary, it could be prevented from having the same fate as Slovakia. At the same time, the common Hungarian-Polish border could be also realized -- something that seemed desirable for the Western powers concerned about the German expansionism.[455]

As we have mentioned before, on March 12, Hitler personally told the Hungarian Minister in Berlin that Hungary had 24 hours to resolve the Ruthenian question. On March 14, there were border incidents at Munkacs and Ungvar, and on March 15, units of the Hungarian army started marching into Subcarpathian Ruthenia. There was sporadic resistance by the so-called Szics Guard but, the Germans having refuse to defend the Volosin government as it had requested, the Hungarian army reached the Polish border in a short time.[456]

The national leadership of the United Hungarian Party met on May 12 in Pozsony. Janos Esterhazy gave a major speech. He said, among others: "First of all, I must register the good news that last March Hungary regained Subcarpathian Ruthenia, fulfilling a long-standing desire for a common Hungarian-Polish border. In the extraordinarily eventful month of March, Slovakia became independent amidst revolutionary circumstances. On behalf of the Hungarian minority, with full candor and sincerity, I offered our constructive contribution. Unfortunately, our sincere goodwill was either not understood or has been misunderstood in certain circles. I can find no other explanation for the substantial deterioration of our condition in every respect since last March.

"Let it suffice for me to point out that since it became independent, Slovakia has banned the newspaper *Uj Hirek*, prohibited the activities of the Hungarian Cultural Association of Slovakia, and the ban on assemblies still continues. On top of that a number of very important petitions we have submitted have not been acted on for several months, even though they pertain only to purely social and cultural matters. Most recently, the government's failure to pay pensions had the greatest impact on large numbers of Hungarian families for whom the small pension is the only source of income.

"**I want to emphasize again that we and the Slovaks have our roots in the same soil. It was not power play but rather the forces of nature, economics, geopolitics and the like which have forged common bonds between Slovaks and Hungarians. The souls of the Hungarian and Slovak peoples can and must be brought into harmony because we share so much of a common spirit. If Hungarian and Slovak turn against one another, both will suffer for it. Any attempt to break up the spiritual and economic bonds of interdependence among the peoples in the Carpathian Basin would run counter to nature and is doomed to failure. It goes without saying that this is true of the relationship between the Hungarians and Slovaks also.**

We should have learned from our history that nobody can escape Divine justice, even if he has managed to avoid human justice. We should have learned also that causes which have martyrs will triumph.[457]

Several major events had taken place in the international arena also. Prompted by the ever greater German pressure on Poland, a mutual assistance agreement was concluded on April 6, 1939, between Great Britain and Poland. France ratified a French-Polish treaty. On April 13, Great Britain and France concluded economic agreements with Greece and Rumania.

In view of the growing German pressure on Poland, Hungary was trying to conduct its foreign affairs with the goal of staying out of the war. It wanted to maintain its armed neutrality in the event of a war between Germany and Poland, which was expected to come at the end of August, 1939. **Accordingly, Prime Minister Teleki declared in letters to Hitler and Mussolini that** unless there is a major change in circumstances, **"Hungary is not in the moral position to enter hostilities against Poland."** Berlin, naturally, was out-

raged over Teleki's letters. On August 8, Hitler and Ribbentrop received Hungarian Foreign Minister Csaky in Berchtesgaden. Hitler reproached Csaky over the letters. Csaky had to promise that the letters would be withdrawn. The letters were withdrawn, as promised.

The signing of a German-Soviet Non-Aggression pact on August 23, 1939, was another highly significant event. The new situation it had created raised the specter of a confrontation between Germany and the Western powers as the result of a German-Polish war. Teleki sent a secret message to Halifax, assuring him that Hungary will not support Germany against Poland and wishes to remain neutral.

On September 1, 1939, Germany invaded Poland and on September 3, Great Britain and and France declared war on Germany.

Slovak Incitements against the Hungarians

Returning to the situation in Slovakia, Janos Esterhazy who has always had the destiny of the Hungarian youth on his heart, announced the results of the Hungarian fund raising in Pozsony. The sum of 122,000 Crowns that was raised exceeded all expectations. Esterhazy expressed his gratitude in the *Uj Hirek* newspaper.[458]

Esterhazy told the *Felvideki Magyar Hirlap* newspaper about the indefinite postponement of the Slovak-Hungarian economic negotiations scheduled for July 26. He said he had urged the Hungarian government repeatedly to get these much needed talks underway as soon as possible. However, he has just been informed by Foreign Minister Csaky in Budapest that the negotiations had to be postponed because "increasingly strong anti-Hungarian sentiments that have been voiced in recent weeks at various rallies and celebrations which were broadcast by the Slovak radio, most recently in Kistapolcsany... It is the position of the Hungarian government that the success of the economy talks should not be endangered by holding them in an atmosphere heavy with political tension."

Esterhazy added: "We hope the Slovak government will take the most forceful steps to curb developments which tend to raise obstacles to the conclusion of an economic agreement.[459]

On July 26, Janos Esterhazy declared in Parliament: "We expect a new spirit in the new administrative law."[460]

Sandor Petho, Editor in Chief of the Budapest newspaper *Magyar Nemzet*, spent his vacation in the High Tatra Mountains and that gave him a chance to study the conditions in Slovakia at some length. Commenting on the wonderful unity of the Hungarians, Petho concluded that the unity rests on the unprecedented and unlimited trust felt by young and old, intellectual and farmer, artisan and urban dweller, toward the leader they have chosen. "The persona of Janos Esterhazy is truly providential," Petho wrote.

"I watched a meal of 300 children from Hungarian poor families, who were vacationing in the Tatra. I exchanged only a few words with the dedicated teachers from Pozsony who were supervising this happy crowd of youngsters. I must confess that I have never felt the unbearable pain and happy pride of my Hungarian identity as I did in the midst of little people in whose souls the sacred flame of Hungarian consciousness is being nurtured by these tender and noble-hearted women, many of whom have already paid a heavy price for being Hungarian. To these people, **the name Esterhazy represents the Hungarian nation itself, the parental home, the protective power, the ultimate shelter.**"[461]

On September 7, *Uj Hirek* printed a request by Janos Esterhazy, calling on Hungarian women and girls to help those who through no fault of their own have fallen into poverty. He asked that the women, in cooperation with the United Hungarian Party, seek out every opportunity, official or unofficial, to participate in programs, such as nursing the sick or helping alleviate hardships caused by the hostilities.[462] His appeal was well received by the Hungarian women.

In early September, the *Magyar Nemzet* of Budapest reported that Janos Esterhazy has been placed under police surveillance, along with Artur Polnisch, leader of the Hungarians in the Szepes district. Andor Nietzsch, a former German Deputy of the Hungarian Party was jailed. The paper wrote of Esterhazy: "We do not need to explain to anyone what the person of Janos Esterhazy has meant to the Hungarians of Slovakia: his matchless energy, his uncommon courage, his sincerity, his tactful skill to bring into harmony the universal Hungarian goals with the unique interests of the peoples of the Highlands, his views rooted in the noblest ancient Hungarian political traditions, as well as his day-to-day activities -- all these characteristics have predestined him to be the chosen leader of Hungarians of the Highlands."[463]

The relations between Hungary and Germany became increasingly tense because of the growing German diplomatic pressure for permission by the Hungarian government to open up a front along the common Hungarian-Polish border for the German war on Poland. On September 9, Ribbentrop called Csaky on the phone, asking for the use of the railroad line to Kassa to transport German troops. Next day, Prime Minister Teleki moved in the Council of Ministers that the German request be denied. On Ribbentrop's repeated request, permission was granted to ship war materiel only, under strictly defined conditions. This did not assuage the resentment of Hitler and the other German leaders toward the Hungarians. **As Ciano noted in his Diary, "Some day, the Hungarians will have to pay for this."**

Meanwhile, through its envoys in London and Paris, the Hungarian government was engaged in intense diplomatic activity to counter the plans of Benes and Hodza for Czechoslovakia's postwar future. The country's independence and the restoration of its borders were in the focus of these plans. The two Western governments have shown a degree of understanding.

On September 24, 1939, diplomatic relations were restored between the Soviet Union and Hungary.

The economic and trade negotiations which began on October 11 in Budapest, helped raise hopes of improvement in Hungarian-Slovak relations. Janos Esterhazy said, "I am facing the near-future with confidence because, as I see it, the ice has broken, the ice which has prevented the leaders and the public opinion of the two countries from becoming better acquainted with each other. Our attitude toward the Slovak state has been positive from the first moment. Even though I cannot say that our condition has improved in the past year, in some respects it has become worse, it has not discouraged me for one minute. I would like to believe that the pending questions will be soon resolved and the Hungarians of Slovakia will be able to nourish their language and culture and take care of their social problems without any hindrance. With that and with their sincere goodwill, they will contribute to the constructive labors for which they have volunteered from the moment the independence of Slovakia has been established."[464]

Dr. Josef Tiso the new president of Slovakia took his oath of office on October 26. He rode to the presidential palace in a four-horse carriage, followed by automobiles carrying Dr. Tuka, the Deputy Prime Minister and Minister of the Interior, Foreign Minister Durcansky, War Minister Catlos, army commander and propaganda chief Alexander Mach and other leading personalities. The end of the motorcade was brought up by Dr. Kirschbaum, General Secretary of the Hlinka Party. Next to him sat Dr. Murin, the secretary to the president.

President Tiso received greetings in the presidential palace. Janos Esterhazy was also present, accompanied by several others. He said, among others: "The Hungarians of Slovakia fully share the joy and happiness which fills the heart of every Slovak this day when, for the first time, they may behold a son of their independent and free nation as their chief of state. We, Hungarians in Slovakia, come this day with respect and trust to your presence, Mr. President, to express the emotions accumulated in our hearts with manly candor and openness. May I be permitted to hope that in your person, Mr. President, the Hungarians of Slovakia will find that well-intentioned and just supreme forum which will assure full equality to all Slovak citizens of Hungarian nationality within the boundaries of this country."

Hitler sent Dr. Tiso the highest German decoration, the Grand Cross of the Order of the Eagle.[465]

On October 28, Janos Esterhazy discussed presidential elections in a broadcast on Pozsony radio. He recalled his 1935 talks with Benes in Prague before the presidential election, when Benes made many substantive promises to the Hungarian leaders. Even though the Hungarians had cast their votes for Benes, subsequently he refused even to hear about his promises. This time there were no such talks before the election, said Esterhazy.

"It is not necessary to enumerate facts and figures to show that **especially in recent times, the fate of the small states, small peoples and small nations has been threatened more than once by assorted difficulties and dangers. On their own, no matter what virtues thay may possess, they are too weak to wrestle with the burden of adversity. This is the time, if ever, when we must strengthen the solidarity, derived from the interdependence of small nations, without which more than one precious element of our national identity may be lost forever.**

"I have had this always in mind, I have always worked toward this end and if I have been misunderstood, if I had obstacles thrown in my way, if I have been attacked, it does not matter because I am convinced that I have been right. **It is in our mutual interest with the Slovaks to develop harmonious cooperation within the boundaries of the state, as well as among all the nations of the Danubian Basin, which would provide peaceful living and the pursuit of happiness for all, including the smallest.**"[466]

On November 28, 1939, Janos Esterhazy delivered a speech, more than an hour long, in the parliamentary debate of the Tuka government's program. He gave a detailed, comprehensive overview of the current condition of the Hungarians in Slovakia. The speech was a panoramic view of the various grievances, complaints, demands and hopes.

The theme of Esterhazy's address was constructive cooperation and that is why he discussed in detail all the phenomena which hinder the development of a sense of trust and satisfaction. He noted the need for realism in politics, as well as in everyday life. And he discussed the relationship between the various nationalities and the Slovak national state.

"I am concerned," Esterhazy said, "over the great attention that is being paid to the concept of the 'national state.' Experience has taught us about the practical consequences of pursuing that concept. We must see to it that we do not repeat the experience of the last 20 years, which gave rise to so much bitterness, dissatisfaction and complaints, that the sons of the Slovak nation would become the first class citizens, with members of the other nationalities relegated to second or third class citizenship. I would hope, Mr. Prime Minister, that you will dispel this concern of mine in the course of this debate."

Esterhazy also touched upon the anticipated new laws. He noted the absence of proposed legislation to secure individual freedom, equality, equal treatment by the law, freedom of press, as well as failure to define and secure the rights of the nationalities. He mentioned that the use of the Hungarian language has been severely restricted. Equal language rights are non-existent. There is still in force a decree requiring government employees not to speak in Hungarian even in their private lives and social contacts. It is virtually impossible for a Hungarian to obtain public office and he risks dismissal if he continues to maintain his Hungarian identity. There are confidential decrees and instructions providing for "gentle" pressure toward this end.

Hungarian workers, Esterhazy continued, no matter where they may be employed, face the greatest uncertainty. Firings are the order of the day and if their official residence is in the territories which have been returned to Hungary, they also face the threat of expulsion.

"I hope this is not the first step toward a population transfer or an attempt to do so," said Esterhazy, adding: "I must state, *sine ira et studio* that the economic condition of the Hungarian minority is worse off today than it was under Czechoslovak rule. Where are the Hungarian factories? Where are the Hungarian factory owners? Is there any Hungarian manufacturer left?" he asked. The Hungarians of Slovakia, Esterhazy continued, "are being squeezed out systematically from all areas of the economy, things have deteriorated so badly."

There are many strange things going, Esterhazy concluded and raised the question: "What good is being derived from all of this?

222

After all, with a little goodwill, the lot of the Hungarians could be improved easily, even in the spirit of reciprocity," he added.[467]

On December 23, Janos Esterhazy delivered a major address in the budget debate in parliament. The speech was widely reported not only in the Hungarian press but in Slovak, German and Austrian papers also. The German-language *Grenzbote* of Pozsony featured the passage dealing with reciprocity. The *Neues Wiener Tagblatt* of Vienna cited the efforts aimed at Hungarian-Slovak rapprochement. The Slovak press and the Budapest papers also reported about the speech in great detail. We would like to quote here just a few passages from the long speech.

On the question of reciprocity, he said: "Every time I raise a concrete Hungarian grievance and request its remedy, everybody from the Prime Minister down, at every level of government, invokes the idea of reciprocity, instead of doing something about our grievance. With the fullest objectivity, I would like to bring to the attention of the honorable government that such a frequent and usually groundless invocation of reciprocity is a dangerous game in my opinion. I am entitled to say so because ever since I entered politics, I have been most sincerely trying to smoothen the path of Slovak-Hungarian coexistence.

"In my opinion, the small nations in the Danubian Basin most find each other, especially in this warlike atmosphere, in order to safeguard their independence and thus secure peaceful life in the Danubian Basin or, if you prefer, the Carpathian Basin. It naturally follows then that I believe the Slovaks in Hungary must be granted all the rights that God has given every nationality. At the same time, I cannot renounce any of the rights of the Hungarians in this country, especially not rights which we had to fight hard to secure in the Czechoslovak Republic that was formed following the Peace Treaty of Trianon -- rights which we have brought with us after the collapse on Czechoslovakia to the independent Slovak state.

"I hope the Slovak government and my fellow deputies here know that I have never raised any demand which could not be met or would have in any way touched or weakened the sovereignty of the Slovak state. I have tried to secure only the most basic rights for the Hungarians living in this country. Unfortunately, more than once I was unsuccessful.

"I do not deny that there have been instances in the territories returned to Hungary, a few low-ranking officials carried out measures contrary to the interests of the Slovaks in Hungary. But such measures ran counter to the Hungarian government's official position in the question of national minorities, and I immediately intervened at the most appropriate authorities. I can assure you, Gentlemen, of one thing: Whenever I presented a realistic complaint which could be proven, remedy was forthcoming immediately," said Esterhazy.

Esterhazy was angered more than once when told of mistreatment of Slovaks in Hungary. He told the Hungarian authorities that such grievances will shake the trust of the Slovaks, destroying what he had done for many years to earn the sympathy of the Slovak people.

Most of the abuses were triggered by display of the Slovak colors. Another frequent incident was the singing of the Slovak national anthem which some overzelous officials were trying to prevent. Janos Esterhazy reported such grievances immediately to the Hungarian government and every time he was given a firm promise to rectify them.

One such incident occurred in Komjati. Esterhazy learned of it from his sister, Louise who drove to the scene at once. When the local priest confirmed the incident which had to do with the flying of the Slovak flag, she drove to Dictric Governor Jozsef Majtenyi who was shocked to learn of the incident. He went immediately to Pozsony to give a full report to Janos Esterhazy. Esterhazy, in turn called the Hungarian Minister of Interior who promised immediate action. The minister kept his word. Two days later, an investigating committee arrived in Komjatice. As a result of the investigation, the mayor was immediately transferred to another part of the country.

Esterhazy's remarks about the so-called "St.Stephen's Concept" were received with great interest. **It is the sovereign right of the Hungarian government and people,"** he said in a speech in the Slovak parliament on December 22, 1939, **"to determine the foundations of their policies and the sources of their political morality, and nobody else is entitled to interfere with that. Hungary has existed as an independent state for more than a thousand years and will remain so, God willing, remaining faithful to the traditions of St.Stephen, which remind the Hungarians forever of their first king who not only established the Hungarian state but who is also credited with turning Hungary into a Christian cultural nation.**

"St.Stephen's policies, in my view, can be explained only one way: resting on a Christian national foundation, he honors the national consciousness of people speaking a different tongue. St.Stephen's Concept has never tolerated any suppres-

sive efforts or any attempt to deprive others of their national identity. St.Stephen's Concept never allowed the forcible extension of power to dominate the land of others. With regard to Slovakia, the only meaning of St.Stephen's Concept is to secure the happy and peaceful coexistence of the two nations in the sign of his apostolic cross, equally revered by Hungarians and Slovaks."

In the rest of his speech Esterhazy criticized the government's budget, particularly the Hungarians' share in it. He noted the planned census and the propaganda budget, saying that they do not apply an equal measure. Finally, he brought up the question of bank mergers which regards as somewhat anti-social.[468]

On January 1, 1940, the *Uj Hirek* newspaper carried a signed New Years Day editorial by Janos Esterhazy, which was most interesting from the perspective of this work. Here are some of its highlights:

"Last March we witnessed the disintegration of one state and the establishment of another. **Many lessons can be learned from the disintegration and I wish they were taken to heart throughout Europe by those who regard it their calling to decide the fate of states, nations and peoples. Using modern terminology it is said that there are certain geopolitical realities which cannot be overthrown and can be resisted only for a short time.**

"I would express the same idea by saying that there have been, there are and there will be Divine and natural forces which determine the destiny of peoples and nations. These forces do not allow that those whom fate had combined into one community in a given region be torn asunder, separated and, segment by segment, attached to other spheres of influence. I am thinking of the millions of people, living side-by-side on the slopes of the Carpathians, who will develop and find happiness only if they seek together, in peaceful coexistence, the path to a better future. There is and there can be no other solution."[469]

The Rapidly Changing International Scene

The most important international development in 1940 occurred on **May 10 when Hitler launched his Western offensive.** Soon, Italy too, joined the war. Following Denmark, Norway, Belgium and The Netherlands, France too, capitulated. Although the German maneuver at Dunkirk did not quite turn out as it had been expected because 340,000 men of the Western armies managed to escape, the Germans occupied Paris.

Hitler had begun preparations to attack to Soviet Union and that required settlement of the long-standing Hungarian-Rumanian territorial issues. Following the 1938 recipe, he tried to settle the question by bilateral talks, knowing all too well that the talks would not produce any results so that, once again, he would be able to make the final decision.

That is how it happened. As a result of the German-Italian arbitration decision, signed on August 30, 1940, 43,000 square kilometers of land were returned from Rumania to Hungary, with 2.5 million inhabitants, including more than one million Hungarians. Some 400,000 Hungarians remained in Rumania.

In return, Hungary was compelled to render many different kinds of services to the Germans. The most important of these was permission to move so-called "training divisions" from Germany through Hungarian territory to Rumania, which made possible the marshalling of the German forces for the invasion of the Soviet Union. Also, Hungary had to adhere to the tripartite pact of Germany, Italy and Japan, which took place on November 20, 1940, in Vienna. Soon thereafter Slovakia and Rumania also joined.

On December 10, in Belgrade, Hungary and Yugoslavia signed a treaty of eternal friendship, with the approval of Germany.

Under German pressure, the Yugoslav government also joined the tripartite pact, however that turned out to be its downfall because public opinion was strongly against it and the government was swept out of office. **At that point, the Germans decided to occupy Yugoslavia and called on the Hungarian government to join in that move.** From then on, Hungary's situation was rapidly deteriorating. **Prime Minister Teleki was reluctant to go along with the German demand** and instructed the Hungarian Minister in London to find out what the British reaction would be.

The devastating answer came on April 2, with the threat of breaking off diplomatic relations between Britain and Hungary and, possibly, declaration of war. **Teleki did not see any way out of this hopeless situation and, on April 3, he committed suicide.**

Things began to speed up. On April 4, 1941, German forces, traveling through Hungary, entered Yugoslavia. Hungarian military units occupied the Bacska, the Baranya Triangle and the Mura regions. Britain broke diplomatic relations with Hungary.

On June 22, 1941, Germany invaded the Soviet Union. On June 25, Slovakia joined in the hostilities. On June 26, aircraft, presumed to be German but with Soviet markings, bombed Kassa. Next day, Hungarian aircraft bombed Soviet cities and Hungarian troops crossed the Soviet border.

Early in the war, the German forces were moving with lightning speed against the Soviet army, but at a very high cost in casualties. Germany began pressuring Rumania and Finland to increase their war effort. Subsequently, the size of the Rumanian forces was estimated at 1.8 million and Finnish forces at 401,000.

It goes without saying that Hungary also felt the German pressure, both in the military and economic spheres and the Hungarian political leadership was doing all it could to resist those pressures.

In November 1941, the British government declared war on Finland, Hungary and Rumania. On December 7, Japan launched a devastating aerial attack on American warships at Pearl Harbor. Both Germany and Italy declared themselves in state of war with the United States.

Soon, Hungary also followed suit, but the U.S. declaration of war was not delivered until June 5, 1942, when under increased German pressure, large Hungarian forces were deployed on the Soviet front. With the former *Little Entente* states closing ranks once again against Hungary, Hungary needed German assistance to resist. Consequently, Hungary was forced more and more to yield to German pressure.

In March 1942, Miklos Kallay was named Prime Minister of Hungary.

On November 8, 1942, American and British forces landed in North Africa. This event gave rise to hopes among the Hungarian leaders that an American-British landing in the Balkans may also occur. That hope prompted the Kallay government at the end of 1942 to seek contacts with the Western powers. Feelers were put out, mainly through Turkey, the Vatican, Switzerland and Sweden.

In January 1943, the bloody Battle of Stalingrad ended with Soviet victory and the Hungarian Second Army suffered a catastrophic defeat at Voronezh. A few weeks earlier, the Rumanian forces also suffered a major defeat.

The military developments accelerated the pace of Hungarian peace feelers in the West, especially in light of rumors of an impending British landing in the Balkans. Moreover, Hungary began conducting talks with its neighbors on the basis of the 1942 borders. When Benes learned of these secret talks, he broadcast the news over the BBC.

The peace feelers led nowhere. The same fate befell Vatican plans to establish a Central European bloc under the leadership of Otto von Hapsburg. The February 1943 plans of the Turkish foreign minister for a Central European and Balkan bloc also came to naught.

Hitler had learned of the various peace feelers and launched a bitter attack on Kallay's defeatist policies when he was visited by Horthy. Horthy came to his Prime Minisiter's defense and he did so again after his return to Hungary in a letter he sent on May 7 to Hitler.

The Western feelers, albeit more slowly, continued mainly through Barcza, the former Hungarian Minister in London, who was in contact, among others, with Allen Dulles. In June 1943, the Americans agreed to talks, among others, with Lipot Baranyay. Baranyay and Dulles agreed that Royall Tyler would serve as the American liaison, while Gyorgy Bakach-Bessenyey would represent the Hungarian government.

On July 10, 1943, American and British forces landed in Sicily. Two weeks later, Mussolini's rule came to an end.

Minister Barcza reported to Prime Minister Kallay that the Western powers want Hungary to declare an end of belligerency the moment Italy does so. Kallay, however was reluctant for fear that Hitler's forces would overrun Hungary. The leftist parties and the opposition in general demanded immediate action, even at the cost of German occupation. But Kallay did not want to act until the American and British forces reached the Hungarian border. Meanwhile, the idea of a landing in the Balkans, as promoted by Churchill, was dropped at the insistence of Roosevelt and Stalin.

On September 8, 1943, it was announced that the allies and Italy agreed on a ceasefire, while American and British forces landed at Naples.

On the same day, the British Ambassador in Ankara delivered the conditions for a possible ceasefire with Hungary. The gist of the nine points was that Hungary had to surrender unconditionally.

Following the conference of foreign ministers in Moscow from October 13 to October 19, 1943, Roosevelt, Churchill and Stalin met at Tehran between November 28 and December 1. They decided on landings at Normandy and in Southern France.

Hungary Loses Its Independence

Following the Italian capitulation, Hitler was afraid that Hungary may follow suit. He had his general staff prepare plans, code named *Margarethe*, for the military occupation of Hungary. On March 18, 1944, Horthy and his entourage were invited to Klessheim. The atmosphere was highly charged during the talks which were broken off several times. At 5 p.m., orders were issued to execute Project *Margarethe*.

It took 15 hours for the German military to occupy Hungary. The *Gestapo* arrested opposition leaders and pro-British politicians by the hundreds. The Kallay government resigned. The Germans wanted Imredy to form the new government but Horthy refused to appoint him Prime Minister. Ultimately, with the Germans' blessings, Dome Sztojay was named Prime Minister, but real power rested in the hands of Veesenmayer, the German Minister.

The Hungarian army's officers' corps was thoroughly purged, especially among the higher ranks. War production, agriculture and industry were brought under complete German control. Meanwhile, the opposition parties began to organize underground and established the so-called Hungarian Front to bring together all the anti-Fascist resistance forces into a single organization.

On June 6, 1944, the Western Allies landed in Normandy. In view of the new circumstances, Istvan Bethlen urged Horthy to replace the Sztojay government with one composed of military officers.

In August 1944, the Soviet army reached the Hungarian border. On August 15, the Western Allies landed in Southern France. On August 23, Rumania asked for a ceasefire. On August 24, Horthy was forced by the events to dismiss the Sztojay cabinet and named Colonel General Geza Lakatos Prime Minister.

On September 6, Soviet and Rumanian troops crossed the passes in the Southern Carpathians.

On September 18, Horthy decided to ask the Soviet Union for a ceasefire and sent a delegation to Moscow. Its members were Gabor Faragho, Geza Teleki and Domokos Szent-Ivanyi. Molotov insisted on unconditional surrender. On October 11, Molotov and Faragho signed a preliminary agreement of capitulation.

On October 15, the Germans captured the Regent's son. At 1:30 p.m., the radio broadcast Horthy's proclamation condemning the German occupation and announcing that he has requested a ceasefire. On October 16, yielding to German demands, Miklos Horthy resigned as Regent of Hungary. Ferenc Szalasi took over the government. On October 17, under German protection, Horthy left Hungary. He was taken to Hirschberg, Germany.

The Hungarian Front and the newly formed Liberation Committee began making plans for an armed uprising on December 1 and sent a delegation to the Soviet headquarters. But the uprising was thwarted by the *Gestapo* which arrested the leaders of the Liberation Committee, along with 30 military officers.

By December 1944, most of Hungary had come under Soviet military occupation. A provisional National Assembly was formed. It met on December 21 in Debrecen and elected a provisional government. Bela Dalnoki Miklos was named Prime Minister. In January 1945, the government sent a delegation to Moscow to sign an armistice agreement on January 20. The agreement did not recognize the validity of the Vienna arbitration decisions by the Axis powers and it ordered among others, complete evacuation of the occupied Czechoslovak, Rumanian and Yugoslav territories and return behind the borders as they existed on December 31, 1937. The armistice agreement also ordered Hungary to pay 300 million dollars in reparations, with 200 million dollars going to the Soviet Union and the remaining 100 million dollars to Czechoslovakia and Yugoslavia.

The Soviet military occupation of Hungary was completed on April 4, 1945. In May, Germany surrendered unconditionally.

D.

The Period since 1945

The Life and Struggles of the Hungarians in Slovakia between 1940 and 1945

We have given a brief review of the international developments between 1940 and 1945 to provide a perspective to the life and
struggles of the Hungarians in Slovakia. Their conditions were gradually deteriorating. This was true not only of the economic conditions
but particularly so because of the anti-Hungarian sentiments of the
Slovaks, fanned from above.

Even though the anti-Hungarian sentiments became fully
apparent only in 1945, their roots go back to the 1939 period. The
majority of the Hungarian authors traces it to the Vienna Decision of
1938. According to one author, "In the fall of 1939, Hitler's resettlement of national minorities in order to 'purify' the ethnic composition
of the various countries had raised great hopes in Pozsony."

In the spring of 1943, the *Gardista*, official organ of the
Hlinka Garda already foretold of the coming deprivation of rights
when it wrote: "We demand the expulsion of the Czechs, the deportation of the Jews, the roundup of the Gypsies and the stripping away of
the Hungarians' rights." This demand was published on April 19,
1943.

In December 1943, Benes and Klement Gottwald, secretary
general of the Communist Party, reached an agreement establishing
the principle of a Czechoslovak national state and its subsequent
realization. Smutny, the secretary of Benes, reporting about a visit to
Pozsony by Colonel Chapuisat, representative of the International
Red Cross, quoted him as saying, "the Germans and Hungarians are
hated here."[470]

Janos Esterhazy had to fight this anti-Hungarian discrimination all the time. Although he always emphasized in his speeches his sincere friendship and support for the newly independent Slovakia, he also raised the grievances against the Hungarians and demanded their rectification. Esterhazy sharply criticized Benes, who was in London at the time, for continuing to cling to his failed policies which had been based on the outcome of the treaty of Trianon.

In a major speech at the January 26, 1940, meeting of the United Hungarian Party, Esterhazy declared that those who want to create a new order in Europe after the end of the currently raging war will not be able to avoid the imperative of the conditions prevailing in the Carpathian Basin. **"Only the small group of people with a shared interest, greatly blinded but of little moral value, who had gathered around Benes and Hodza, are unable to see and learn the lessons of the failure of the principles and methods imposed in Versailles and Trianon. It is clear to everyone else that one must refrain even from the slightest attempt to reorder Europe in that manner. The Concept of St.Stephen recognizes only peoples or nations of equal rank -- ranked side-by-side and not above or below one another -- in the land of St.Stephen."**

With regard to the so-called gentlemanly principle, Esterhazy explained that "the only valid and lasting principle is the one that would raise everyone, in the noblest sense of the word, to the ranks of gentlemen (middle class). An integral part of this is the securing of freedom and independence for ourselves, as well as granting it to others."[471]

On March 14, 1940, Janos Esterhazy marked the first anniversary of Slovak independence with an editorial in the *Uj Hirek* newspaper. "Independent Slovakia came into being one year ago," he wrote. "More has been gained than the late, great leader of the Slovak nation, Father Hlinka would have dared to dream. The Slovak people have accomplished more than they ever hoped in their long struggle to free themselves from the Czech yoke.

"We Hungarians can truly appreciate what it means for a people, a nation, to attain its freedom. We only wish the celebrants would understand that now, as they are receiving every blessing from their rich cornucopia, they should not disparage our comradely sentiments developed over the years toward all our struggling and suffering fellow men."[472]

Speaking in the Slovak parliament on May 7, 1940, Esterhazy declared: **"Openly and bravely I acknowledge that we Hungarians** and Slovaks must look for what brings us together and not what separates us from each other. I stand here, before the Slovak parliament with clean conscience because ever since the beginning of my political career I have proclaimed and served the cause of friendship with the Slovaks."

Among the grievances, Esterhazy brought up the sudden dismissal of two Hungarian teachers after 28 and 33 years of service, without any disciplinary action. He demanded immediate investigation of this matter.[473]

Speaking at the June 21, 1940 meeting of the United Hungarian Party, Janos Esterhazy noted that "the 'peacemakers' at Trianon wanted to condemn Hungary and the Hungarian nation to death. It is thanks to the Hungarians' unwavering will to live that the death sentence could not be carried out.

"We want to believe," Esterhazy continued, "that the peace that will come will be true peace, sprung from from Christian brotherly love. The Hungarians in Slovakia had to live through many trials and tribulations during the last year-and-a-half. I beseech my Hungarian brethren who have been seasoned by all the suffering but their patience is understandably becoming short, I implore them not to falter for one minute."[474]

On August 30, Esterhazy met Minister of Interior Mach. On September 5, he announced the reform of Hungarian political party activities. The same day, the leadership of the United Hungarian Party gave Esterhazy a unanimous vote of confidence. On September 13, he addressed the organizing meeting of the Slovak Journalists Federation. On October 10, he spoke in the parliamentary debate on the census.[475]

On November 27, 1940, Esterhazy delivered an important speech in the Slovak parliament's debate of the new national security bill. He reiterated that "now that their party is about to be registered, the Hungarians of Slovakia will continue to meet their obligations toward the state and its representatives. The Hungarians of Slovakia have always had a positive attitude toward the independent Slovak state and I am convinced," Esterhazy continued, "that with proper understanding, this constructive positivism can be developed to the fullest extent. A just nationalities policy provides greater security than any Maginot Line because nothing will strengthen a state more than the sense of feeling at home, by its citizens, whether they belong to the majority or minority."[476]

On December 21, Esterhazy spoke in the parliament's budget debate and asked for rectification of the Hungarians' grievances.[477]

In his New Years Day article of January 1, 1941, Esterhazy declared that life is not easy for the Hungarians in Slovakia. "Still," he said, "on this day I wish to lay the veil of forgetting on everything that may provoke not only our just criticism but also our dissatisfaction because we have never deserved the harsh treatment we have received." And he quoted the wise aphorism of Ferenc Deak: "We must risk everything for the nation but we must not risk the nation for anything."[478]

At the February 28 meeting of the United Hungarian Party, Janos Esterhazy emphasized: **"We want peaceful accord with the Slovaks. We are guided by a single thought, one that does not know hatred, unequal treatment here in the Danubian Basin, among the sons of nations predestined to a common fate."**[479]

On the second anniversary of Slovakia's independence, Esterhazy wrote an editorial in the *Uj Hirek* newspaper. He raised the question, why did Czechoslovakia disintegrate after two decades? "The answer comes automatically," he wrote. "Because Czechoslovakia could never live up to its alleged 'historic destiny,' granted by the authors of the Paris peace treaties. Also, because Czechoslovakia had been forced on the stage of European history as an instrument of an imperial grouping whose political program consisted solely of vengeance, promotion of its own selfish interests, and the destruction and enslavement of the small nations. The larger half of the 14 million inhabitants of Czechoslovakia consisted of national minorities: Germans, Slovaks, Hungarians, Ruthenians and Poles. Yet, the Czech minority insisted on ruling over the non-Czech majority in such a drastic manner that it could not have any other fate than the one it had, along with the man who had personified it."

On the same occasion, the *Uj Hirek* greeted Esterhazy on his 40th birthday and paid tribute to his outstanding activities. The article mentioned that at an early age, in May 1931, at a meeting in the Szent-Ivany mansion, he had offered a 15,000 Crown prize for a popular work about the history of the Hungarian nation.[480]

On May 24, Esterhazy offered editorial greetings to *Slovenska Jednota*, the paper of the Slovaks in Hungary, which on that day became a daily newspaper in service of the cause and interests of the Slovak people in Hungary.[481]

On August 28, Esterhazy eulogized Istvan Floch, Editor of the *Uj Hirek*, at his funeral service in Pozsony's St.Andrew cemetery.[482]

On August 14, 1941, Janos Esterhazy delivered two lectures at the Summer University of Debrecen about the impact of minority life on the Hungarians and the life of the approximately 100,000 Hungarians in Slovakia.

Among the 63 members of the Slovak House of Deputies, Janos Esterhazy is the sole representative of the interests of the Hungarian minority. In addition, there are 150,000 Germans and 60,000 Ruthenians. The bulk of the Hungarians live in three significant linguistic islands, in Pozsony and vicinity, around Nyitra and near Nagymihaly.[483]

On September 2, 1941, Esterhazy spoke at the opening of the Madach Book House in Pozsony.[484]

Saving the Hungarian Soul

In June 1942, the Hungarian Parliament of Slovakia, the first gathering of the leaders of the Hungarian intelligentsia, met at the invitation of Janos Esterhazy. In his opening remarks, Esterhazy noted that **"a nation remains a nation only as long as it is guided, led and nourished by its own soul.** And let us continue right away," said, "It is being nourished by a unique nourishment, its Hungarian consciousness. As long as this soul is free to develop, it may lead and guide. As long as this soul can consciously enlist the forces of the nation into its service, the nation will survive. The soul of a nation does not grow from one day to another. The soul of the nation is being cultivated through centuries and millennia, shaped like granite by the erosive forces of wind and rain.

"A nation can be killed only if they kill its soul. We must always watch the intellectual currents of Hungary because that is the trunk of the tree from which our branch has grown." He quoted Istvan Gyorffy who had said: "It is the popular tradition that keeps us Hungarian and it is the international culture that makes us European. But if all we want is to be European, no matter how large a nation we may be, we would soon cease being Hungarian. We would merge into the great Western nation whose cultural influence is the easiest to absorb. And if we were to withdraw completely from under the influence of Western culture, our cultured and stronger neighbors would trample us under their feet and, again, we would diseappear."[485]

Also in the summer of 1942, Hungarian writers in Slovakia participated in the annual Budapest Book Fair. Elek Kornyei wrote this report about the Budapest visit of the leaders of Hungarian intellectual life in Slovakia:

"Our House of Books, with its shingle roof and porch decorated with Slovakian Hungarian folk motives, has a ceiling reminiscent of an open book. It carries a message from the past in the words of Berzsenyi, 'It is not the multitude but the soul that brings miracles.'

On the other side, a message of the present by our leader, Janos Esterhazy, about our fate in Slovakia, to the Hungarian nation: 'A Hungarian word in our land rings a festive tone in our souls.'"

On behalf of the writers, Anna Pozsonyi thanked Esterhazy for his services in the development of the Hungarian literary life in Slovakia: "Thank you for making it possible for us this year to introduce ourselves in Budapest under circumstances that became possible only through your generosity, Mr. Chairman. Thank you for helping call attention to the fact that in our land, too, the Hungarian words can be heard, the Hungarian rhymes resound and the flame of enthusiasm for Hungarian literature is burning in the hearts."[486]

The tenth anniversary of Janos Esterhazy's entry into politics was celebrated by the Hungarians of Slovakia on December 12, 1942, in Otatrafured. The festivities began with Mass, attended by Janos Esterhazy, his sister, young daughter and son, along with several leaders of the United Hungarian Party.

The Mass was followed by greetings by well-wishers in the great hall of the Grand Hotel. Telegrams from Hungarian Prime Minister Miklos Kallay, Istvan Bethlen and other Hungarian dignitaries were read.

The most moving tribute came from the representative of the Family Division of Hungarian Party: "May you, Mr. Chairman, remain the hope and support of every Hungarian poor! May all your good deeds, healing touch, return manyfold on your dear family! May the caressing warmth of every Hungarian mother reach the one who first taught you, Mr. Chairman in resounding Hungarian to help our neighbors, the one who poured from her own noble soul into your heart the sensitivity for everything that is good, noble and beautiful."

Janos Esterhazy was deeply moved as he thanked for the warm greetings.[487]

Earlier, the Slovak parliament was debating a bill calling for deportation of the Jews. Ivan Komanec reported about it as follows: "The Slovak national assembly voted by acclamation, by raising of hands. The only deputy among the members present, of whom it was obvious that he did not raise his hand, was Janos Esterhazy the representative of the United Hungarian Party. He drew immediate attacks from the *Grenzbote* and the *Gardista* newspapers."[488]

The *Grenzbote* article expressing its disapproval of Esterhazy's No vote was entitled "Der Herr Graf stimmte nicht mit."[489]

A report by the Slovak Communist Party, delivered to Moscow by Karol Smidke contained this characteristic description of the attitude of the Hungarians in Slovakia: "One can say that in contrast with the Germans, the Hungarians have behaved very decently in Slovakia, the majority of them are democrats, many are leftist-oriented."[490]

The *Gestapo* wanted to arrest Janos Esterhazy because of his anti-Fascist behavior, but the German government was reluctant to take the risk that would have entailed because Esterhazy was popular in Hungary and his arrest might have led to anti-German demonstrations. His arrest was ordered only in the fall of 1944, after the extreme right wing came to power in Hungary.[491]

On September 2, 1943, Esterhazy delivered a major speech in a meeting of the United Hungarian Party's central leadership. "Four years ago yesterday," he began, "war broke out between Germany and Poland. Soon, the whole world was engulfed in flames. We live in a time when mankind invests all its knowledge into the development of techniques for the more perfect destruction of man."

Esterhazy then spoke of the Hungarian grievances and stressed that he would do everything to have them rectified. He added, however: **"I will take no step which might endanger even for one moment the domestic peace, domestic order or the possibility of an honest rapprochement among nations. We regard to the Slovaks with the greatest goodwill and the most sincere sentiments. After the war, as peaceful reconstruction gets underway, those of us who have lived and will continue living here in the Danubian basin will depend on one another."[492]**

On January 19, 1944, Esterhazy delivered a lecture at the Hungarian Academy of Science on "The Fate of the Minorities among the Nationalities." He emphasized the Hungarians in Slovakia will always remain true Hungarians.[493]

Esterhazy summed up the tasks of the new year in these words: "Mutual understanding, unity and absolute discipline across the board."[494]

On January 29, 1944, Janos Esterhazy was invited by three large Hungarian organizations to address a joint session in Budapest. His topic was "National Life in Minority Status."[495]

On March 25, 1944, Esterhazy eulogized Laszlo Aixinger, the long-time executive director of the United Hungarian Party. He spoke before a crowd of several thousand mourners in St.Andrew Cemetery in Pozsony.

These were his closing words: "On behalf of all the Hungarians in Slovakia, and at the same time in the name of the entire decent Hungarian nation, I express the deepest gratitude to Laszlo Aixinger for his loyalty, for his unselfish work and his perseverance. With these words, I say Goodbye to you Laci, my dear colleague."[496]

The Hungarians Face New Threats in Slovakia

Letters reaching Benes's circle in London in March 1944 from Slovakia told of demands to remove the Hungarians. "Remove the minorities! We reject feelers to the Sudeten Germans living in England. There is no difference between them. They have betrayed us. It is true of the Hungarians also." The publication reproducing this letter contained several letters written in the same vein.[497]

On August 4, 1944, Karol Smidke and M. Ferjencik traveled to Moscow and, on September 5, submitted the decisions reached by the Czechoslovak emigrants in Moscow and the Communist leadership to the Slovak National Council. The decisions called for a solution to the Hungarian problem by recommending expulsion of the Hungarians. That has been revealed by the minutes of the Moscow talks, as published in 1964: "In order to open the way, as agreed upon, for the Red Army when it enters Slovakia, a general national uprising must be arranged, the traitors' government in Pozsony must be driven out, a provisional governmental authority must be given to the Slovak National Council, and with the help of the Red Army, the Germans and Hungarians must be driven out of Slovakia's occupied territories."[498] It should be noted here that we have given a detailed account of the "National Uprising" in Part One.

With regard to the Hungarians, it is worth mentioning a memorandum that Slovak Minister of War Catlos sent to Moscow. He wrote: "As soon as the Soviet forces establish a foothold in the Krakow area, the moment will arrive for a successful surprise attack on Hungary, as well as the opportunity to conduct additional military action against the Germans. The Slovak military forces would prepare and facilitate the prompt and smooth movement of Soviet forces across Slovak territory and would join in an attack on Hungary.[499]

The Czechoslovak government in London, headed by Benes, sent a message on September 8 to General Viest in Slovakia: "In the event of Hungary's collapse or capitulation, the Slovak territories lost to Hungary must be occupied."[500]

On September 5, 1944, the Slovak National Council met to hear a report by Smidke and Ferjencik about their talks in Moscow. From then on, Slovakia's policies began to foreshadow the so-called Kassa Program, promulgated in April 1945, which deprived the Hungarians of their rights. The idea that the deprivation of rights was a consequence of the extreme right wing policies that prevailed at the end of 1944 in Hungary, has been sharply rejected by Hungarian historians because by the time of the pro-German *coup d'etat* in Hungary, in October 1944, Benes and the Slovak National Council have long agreed on the plan of deporting the Hungarians and confiscating their possessions. "The decree to confiscate German and Hungarian enemy property was prepared by the Slovak National Council at the time of the Slovak National Uprising."[501]

In October, 1944, the persecution of Hungarian peasants also began. "All the land of the Germans, Hungarians and all their traitor collaborators must be confiscated at once, without any compensation and given free of charge to Slovak farmers."[502]

Thus the formerly anti-Semitic wave was suddenly replaced by an anti-Hungarian orientation. According to the Hungarian view, the emigrants who were directing the resistance in Slovakia were responsible for the fanning of the anti-Hungarian sentiments. "By the time of the visit by the delegation of the Slovak National Council to London, in November 1944, there was already a consensus both in London and Moscow that transfer of the Hungarian population must be taken into consideration."[503] By the time the war ended, the principle of a national state and the demand for the expulsion of the Hungarians became the established policy.

The Persecution of Janos Esterhazy

Janos Esterhazy learned in mid-October 1944, following the pro-German *coup* in Hungary that the *Gestapo* wanted to arrest him. He went into hiding for a while. Wearing a disguise, he visited his family. They almost did not recognize him, sporting a long beard and his furcoat turned inside out.

December 1944, after the advance of the Soviet army forced the *Gestapo* to flee Slovakia, Esterhazy came out of hiding and returned to his office in Pozsony to await the arrival of the Soviet forces. His friends begged him to flee and surrender to the Western Allies. But he decided to stay with his Hungarian brethren whose interests he has represented from his early youth on.

It was agreed that the Esterhazy family would remain in Nyitraujlak because the air raids made travel on the roads very dangerous. On March 29, his house took a hit from the Soviet artillery. On March 31, the Soviet forces arrived. The Esterhazy home was taken over by plundering Soviet soldiers who did not leave the region until the end of April.

The Soviet forces reached Pozsony in April 1945. A few days after the German surrender on May 8, 1945, word came from Pozsony that the Soviet army kept Janos Esterhazy in custody for one or two weeks before he was released. He prepared one more memorandum on behalf of the persecuted Hungarian minority, defending it against accusations of fascism.

Esterhazy asked Gustav Husak the new Czechoslovak Commissar of Internal Affairs, for an appointment to deliver the memorandum. Husak did receive Esterhazy and accepted the memorandum, but then he had Esterhazy immediately arrested and jailed. The new Czechoslovak state accused him, along with the entire Hungarian minority in Slovakia, of being fascist and revisionist.

Esterhazy was held in the Spitalska street police jail. His sister Louise was denied permission to visit him. All property of the

Hungarian institutions in Pozsony was confiscated, including all the contents of the United Hungarian Party's offices. These measures were carried out by the new political police, in accord with the provisions of the Kassa Program.

The situation became so tense that Esterhazy's wife and two children had to leave Nyitraujlak and move to Budapest. Meanwhile, Janos Esterhazy was kept in jail while waiting for his trial. On June 22, his sister Louise managed with great difficulty to visit her older brother in the jail.

Esterhazy was aware that he may face a death sentence but was prepared to defend himself against the unfounded accusations. Another meeting between Esterhazy and his sister was scheduled for July 6 but events took a dramatic turn. On June 25, 1945, officers of the Soviet NKVD came to the jail, demanding that Esterhazy be handed over. The Czechoslovak police complied. Janos Esterhazy and Mihaly Csaky, vice chairman of the United Hungarian Party, were taken to a secret NKVD headquarters. One month later, the two men, along with several other leaders of the United Hungarian Party, were taken by the NKVD to the Soviet Union.

Louise Esterhazy was locked up in detention camp at Petronka. Later, she was taken with 2,000 other Hungarians, all labeled as dangerous Fascists, to Prtrelzka.

Meanwhile, there were contradictory reports about Janos Esterhazy's whereabouts. Some said, he was detained in Transylvania, according to other reports, he had been taken to Moscow.

Louise Esterhazy learned one day that she has been invited by the *Secours Catholique* to Paris to work as a translator-interpreter in Central European languages and that a passport and visa had been sent to facilitate her passage. She arrived in Paris on June 7, 1946 and learned that the report on Janos Esterhazy being in Transylvania was in error, due to a mixup of names, and her brother and his colleagues had been taken to Moscow.

During the Paris peace conference, Louise Esterhazy worked indefatigably, lobbying the various governmental delegations against the planned expulsion of the Hungarian minority. When speaking with the Canadian and Indian delegates, for example, she pointed out her brother's anti-Fascist behavior. She had a difficult task because Benes was trying to persuade them that the Hungarians were fascists. Ultimately, on September 30, 1946, the peace conference rejected the Czehoslovak proposal to deport the Hungarians.

In February 1947, Louise Esterhazy met in Paris V.Clementis the Czechoslovak Deputy Foreign Minister and asked him where her brother was being kept. Clementis replied, "Somewhere in the Soviet Union. We don't know where because we have not been told."[504]

Janos Esterhazy, emaciated by hunger and torture, was taken in 1946 to a concentration camp in the northern Soviet Union.

The Kassa Program and Its Impact on the Hungarians in Slovakia

We have noted in Part One that with the help of the Soviet Union, Benes had returned from London to Czechoslovakia. On April 5, 1945, the infamous Kassa Program was proclaimed. It became the legal basis for the cruel deprivation of the Hungarians' rights between 1945 and 1948.

The Kassa (Kosice) Program provided for the systematic and violent transformation of Czechoslovakia from a state of nationalities into a national state, with all of its consequences. It would require many volumes just to sum up those measures of the program which have stricken the Hungarians with unparalleled cruelty. We wish to present here in a nutshell only the highlights of the Kassa Program. Several publications have dealt with it in great detail, among them *Hungarians in Czechoslovakia*, by Francis S. Wagner, et al., which was the first comprehensive treatise of the Kassa Program, as well as Kalman Janics' frequently cited book.

The Kassa Program and the numerous decrees it had spawned, declared every Hungarian an enemy of the state and took away their Czechoslovak citizenship. The number of the impacted Hungarians was estimated at 800,000.

Hungarian public employees were dismissed at once. They were denied any compensation, including their vested pension rights. Private employees of Hungarian nationality were fired in a similar manner. The Hungarian language schools were closed down. The Hungarian cultural and social organizations, even sports clubs, were disbanded. Their property was confiscated and turned over to the state. Between 1945 and 1949, at least 40,000 Hungarians were condemned as war criminals and deported. All Hungarian-owned real estate was seized. Hungarian news publications were banned. The use of the Hungarian language was forbidden.

The other great problem was the issue of the **deportation** of the Hungarian minority. A Czechoslovak memorandum submitted to the Pottsdam Conference about the question of "transfer" was accepted only in part because only the deportation of the Sudeten Germans was approved, but not of the Hungarians. Therefore, a Hungarian-Slovak **population exchange** was negotiated with the Hungarian government and the resulting agreement was signed on February 27, 1946.

Under the terms of the agreement, the number of Hungarians in Slovakia designated to be transferred to Hungary would match the number of Slovaks in Hungary who would volunteer to move to Czechoslovakia. As a result, 73,373 Slovaks transferred, while the number of Hungarians was 68,407. Six-thousand Hungarians left voluntarily.

Another cruel and inhumane technique employed was the so-called "re-Slovakization." Many Hungarians were forced to declare themselves Slovak so that they may be permitted to secure their livelihood. This process had substantially reduced the number of the Hungarians. By 1950, only 367,733 were left.

The most drastic move was still to come. The Czechoslovak government had to find a way to get rid of an additional 200,000 Hungarians. It turned to the Paris peace conference of 1946 for approval. The roots of this move go back to the Pottsdam Conference where the United States proposed the establishment of a Council of Foreign Ministers, composed of the foreign ministers of the five permanent members of the United Nations Security Council. The Council of Foreign Ministers was charged with preparing the peace treaties and making recommendations for the settlement of the remaining territorial questions. Decisions by the Council were final.

The Paris Peace Conference

The Peace Preparatory Division of the Hungarian Foreign Ministry, under Istvan Kertesz, called on several institutions and experts to help prepare a memorandum. Its premise was that in contrast to the Paris peace treaties of 1918-1919, the new peace treaties should serve as the basis for a general rearrangement of Europe, rather than as punishment for the vanquished.

On July 4, 1945, the Hungarian provisional government delivered a memorandum to G.M.Puskin, the representative of the Soviet Union. The memorandum called attention to the atrocities by which the Hungarians in Czechoslovakia were being deprived of their rights. It also suggested that the territorial arrangements be based on the principles of ethnicity. The memorandum was not answered.

In August 1945, the Hungarian Foreign Ministry turned to the Budapest representatives of Great Britain, the United States and the Soviet Union. It was stated that Hungary is rejecting the idea of a population exchange, it would be acceptable only if linked with territorial compensations. The representatives of the Western powers did not respond to the Hungarian note, the Soviet representative refused to accept it.

In January 1946, Hungary sent a new note to the Allied Powers, followed by another and yet another. Soon thereafter, the Foreign Ministry prepared a draft document which included the territorial questions, especially that of Transylvania. The draft drew sharp attacks from the leftwing parties because of its "revisionist" tone, and it has never been delivered.

The inability of the Hungarian political parties to bring their views into harmony led to all kinds of difficulties. They agreed only in March 1946 to send a delegation to Moscow. With regard to Transylvania, they agreed to request the return of territories along the border with a purely Hungarian population.

The delegation, led by Prime Minister Ferenc Nagy, arrived in Moscow in April 1946. In the question of territories they were unable to accomplish anything.

In anticipation of the June meeting of the Council of Foreign Ministers, the Hungarian political parties agreed to request the securing of equal rights for the Hungarian minority in Czechoslovakia and the partial return of Transylvania. The Hungarian requests were rejected both in the June meeting and also at the London meeting of the Council of Foreign Ministers in September 1945. The Soviet Union recommended that the Vienna Decisions be set aside and Transyvlania in its entirety be given to Rumania. This Soviet position has never changed.

The United States position regarding the Vienna Decisions was identical with that of the Soviet Union. Only with reference to the territorial claims in Transylvania did the American position change repeatedly, always with less and less inclination to accept the Hungarian claims. The British were largely behind the American position but later they lined up with the Soviet Union.

At the May 7, 1946 meeting of the Council of Foreign Ministers, after much deliberation and many changes, the United States government accepted the Soviet position and withdrew its support for the possible revision of the borders of Transylvania. The Hungarian government was shocked by this decision but the Hungarian delegation in Washington and London was unable to do anything about it.

The Hungarian delegation to the Peace Conference, led by Foreign Minister Janos Gyongyosi, arrived in Paris in August 1946. As a consequence of the previous diplomatic negotiations, the delegation had no choice but to sharply reduce its claims. Essentially, the Hungarian goals were confined to securing citizenship rights to Hungarian minorities in the neighboring countries, to halting the further deportation of Hungarians from Czechoslovakia, an easing of the reparation burdens, and minor adjustments along the Hungarian-Rumanian border.

At the joint session of the Hungarian-Rumanian Territorial and Political Committee on August 31, 1946, Paul Auer presented the Hungarian position. He asked for the return of 4,000 square kilometers, involving about 500,000 people, 67% of them Hungarian, and towns along the border. He also recommended that the Szekely[505] land be granted autonomy, guaranteed by the United Nations. On September 5, with 10 Yes votes and 2 abstentions, the Committee accepted the May 7 decision of the Council of Foreign Ministers.

Clementis of Czechoslovakia proposed on September 10 that in order to widen the Pozsony bridgehead, five Hungarian villages across the Danube be transferred to Czechoslovakia. This move was supported by the Soviet Union, the Ukraine and Yugoslavia, but not by the United States and Britain. A compromise was reached, with the resulting transfer of Horvatjarfalu, Oroszvar and Dunacsuny to Czechoslovakia.

These decisions were approved by the November 1946 meeting of the Council of Foreign Ministers in New York, and were signed on February 10, 1947, in Paris. It has been demonstrated that once again, the guiding principle was not to create conditions which might lead to the development of a more favorable atmosphere for peaceful coexistence in the Danubian Basin. Once again, the principle of victor versus vanquished prevailed. Let the reader decide what the consequences were.[506]

Chiefly because of opposition by the United States and Britain, the Paris Peace Conference did not consent to the deportation of 200,000 Hungarians, as planned by Czechoslovakia, yet it failed to resolve the question because the eventual peace treaty just left the Hungarians in Czechoslovakia to their fate.

The peace treaty did not contain any provision banning the forced dispersal of the Hungarians. Such an action was commenced as early as August 1946, at a joint meeting in Pozsony of central and Slovak national organizations.[507] The deportations, lasting for 99 days, were carried out according to precise plans: "One or two villages were surrounded by military units. There were lists of families to be deported and they were ordered to start packing. The deportees were told that they have to leave their homes; their real estate, animals and agricultural implements were confiscated. There was no legal recourse against the deportation decision, the members of the family had to go, regardless of age or sex. The designated families were moved by military trucks to the nearest railroad station and put on trains to travel under heavy guard to Bohemia. The action lasted 99 days, ending on February 25, 1947. It was not halted even in the bitterest cold and the severe winter made everything much more difficult.[508]

Several Hungarian writers in Slovakia, including Gyula Duba, Laszlo Dobos, Viktor Egri, as well as others, recorded many cruel details of the deportations. The Hungarian press also reported extensively about the issue and soon the deportations came into the focus of international attention.

Janos Esterhazy Sentenced to Death

After more than two years in Soviet prison, on September 17, 1947, Janos Esterhazy was sentenced to death by hanging, *in absentia*, by the Slovak National Court of Pozsony. Here is a contemporary account of the trial: "Acting under authority of the Czechoslovak law establishing the peoples courts, the Slovak National Court of Pozsony sentenced him, in his absence, to death by hanging. The trial was presided over by judge Karol Bedrna and the lay judges included Andrej Bagar, member of the Slovak National Theater and Dr. Cerno, a ministerial counselor.

"Esterhazy was charged with undermining the Czechoslovak Republic and services to Fascism. Dr. Cikvanova the court appointed defense attorney, a Czech women lawyer from Pozsony, announced at the beginning of the trial that she had received the charges only five days earlier and did not have enough time to prepare for the trial. She asked for a postponement. The court rejected the request.

"Next, the defense requested that witnesses be called because the court had not summoned a single witness. Specifically, the Czech defense lawyer wanted to have testimony from witnesses who could prove Esterhazy's anti-fascist behavior throughout the entire war and even before the war, when he rescued any number of Czechoslovak patriots from the *Gestapo* and helped them to go through Budapest to Belgrade and then to London. One person Esterhazy had helped to go to London was General Viest, the well-known Minister of War of the Czechoslovak government in exile, who became the military leader of the Slovak uprising in 1944. The court rejected this request, too.

"The judge gave a quick and superficial overview of the evidence against Esterhazy, such as the journals of the Slovak parliament which contained his speeches. It was characteristic of the court's attitude that for lack of any serious evidence, the judge brought up the fact instead of saying Bratislava, Esterhazy had been using the city's Hungarian name, Pozsony.

"Another charge was that in August 1943, in Poprad, Esterhazy had called Tiso's Slovak republic a swindle and said the entire state had been built on a confidence game. Thus, even the most daring, almost foolhardy criticism of Fascism was presented by the judge as evidence against the accused.

"The defense attorney said in her summation that the court has failed to prove a single charge because Janos Esterhazy did not undermine the republic. There is incontrovertible proof of that in the fact that Esterhazy was not present at the time of the Zsolna decision, on October 6, 1938, declaring Slovakia's autonomy, nor was he present on March 14, 1939, in Pozsony, when the national assembly seceded from Czechoslovakia and declared Slovakia's independence.

"This contrasts with the statement Esterhazy gave during the 1938 Czechoslovak crisis to the *Slovak*, the organ of the Hlinka Party, clearly and decisively declaring that he was working for the securing of the minority rights of the Hungarians in Czechoslovakia within the framework of the Czechoslovak republic.

"The defense attorney also pointed out that Esterhazy's statements in the parliament during the war were no proof at all of a fascist behavior because he spoke during the budget debate and his speeches did not hide any fascist ideology. On the contrary, everything he said was a declaration of democratic principles and Christian humanity. He demonstrated this the most eloquently when alone in the Slovak parliament he voted against the anti-Jewish laws, provoking sharp attacks from the *Volkischer Beobachter*, the *Grenzbote* of Pozsony and other newspapers.

"The defense attorney further noted that Esterhazy had been selflessly helping Czechoslovak patriots on their way to London through Budapest and Belgrade. She pointed out that there was no real collaboration between Esterhazy and Henlein, the leader of theSudeten German Party, nor between Esterhazy and Jozef Tito. The United Hungarian Party under Esterhazy's leadership was nothing but an organization for the defense of the interests of Hungarians in Slovakia.

"In view of the foregoing, the defense attorney asked the court to take into account mitigating circumstances and judge Esterhazy by the same standards that have been employed with regard to all other members of the Slovak parliament. With a few exceptions, they have been all acquitted.

"Following the defense summation, the court retired. It came back 15 minutes later and announced the death sentence, based on

Title Three. The entire trial lasted three hours. After the death sen tence was announced on September 17, 1947, an old leader of the Slovak communists, a man of high moral standards, declared: 'This is sheer murder.'" (The rest of the report has been censored.)[509]

This so-called trial and death sentence enraged not only the Hungarians living in Czechoslovakia but also numerous Czech and Slovak patriots. Professor Charles Koch, a leading opposition figure from the Nazi period, called the sentence a judicial murder.[510]

Janos Esterhazy's sister, Louise learned of the death sentence by reading about it in *The New York Herald-Tribune*. On September 17 she sent a telegram to President Benes, protesting her brother's trial and condemnation in his absence. She asked the president to have her brother brought back to Czechoslovakia so that he may be tried again in a free, democratically conducted trial. She asked that the power which had taken her brother from Slovakia exercise the same generosity it had extended to other important Slovak personalities, such as Catlos, Spisiak or Sokol, who had been allowed to go home.

Benes promised Louise Esterhazy that Janos Esterhazy would be given an opportunity freely to defend himself in a new trial against the charges against him. Louise Esterhazy received Benes's response in November 1947 through the Czechoslovak embassy and she thanked the president through embassy Counselor M.Klvana.

In January 1948, Louise Esterhazy was invited to the Czecho-slovak embassy where the Counselor informed her that President Benes and his wife had received her letter of thanks. However, in February 1948, she was told that Benes, claiming poor health, ten-dered his resignation. A paralysis was preventing him from perform-ing his duties, so there was nothing more he could do in the matter of Janos Esterhazy. On September 4, 1948, Benes died.

Janos Esterhazy's younger sister, Mariska, had remained in Nyitraujlak with her husband Ferenc who was of Polish origin, and their children. On May 10, 1949, she sent a telegram, then a letter, to her sister Louise, telling her that Janos Esterhazy has been brought back to Pozsony and is being kept in the courthouse lockup. Ferenc, his Polish brother-in-law, was permitted to visit him. A well-intentioned court official informed him that the death sentence was still in force and could be carried out within 48 hours. Only an amnes-ty would help, he said.

Janos Esterhazy's first question was about his family. Ferenc told him that his son, Janos was in Switzerland, his daughter Alice was in Budapest with her mother. His mother and his sister Louise were doing well in Montreser, France. Mariska, Ferenc and their children in Nyitraujlak were also all-right.

Janos Esterhazy was visibly relieved by the news. Since he had been taken away, this was his first contact with his family. He was obviously weak and had to sit down in his cell. He said he has just learned that he had been sentenced to death in his absence. Ferenc assured him that they will immediately submit a petition for clemency to the president.

Esterhazy told his brother-in-law that he had contracted tuberculosis in the Soviet Union and he would have died before long if he had stayed in the concentration camp. Ferenc comforted him, saying he was sure amnesty would be granted. The two men were both laughing and crying as they parted.

That same afternoon, Mariska came by taxi to Pozsony so that as Janos Esterhazy's younger sister she could to sign the petition for amnesty. In the evening, she traveled to Prague to see two friends, one of whom was of Jewish origin. Next day, he delivered the petition to the president.

Another friend of Mariska was received by Srobar, a Slovak who had participated in the resistance. He remembered Janos Esterhazy's anti-Hitler behavior. He took a copy of the petition and brought it to the council of ministers which happened to be in session. Srobar declared, it would be an assassination to execute Esterhazy. He recalled that in 1941 Esterhazy had voted against the deportation of the Jews and rescued many people by securing asylum for them.

The family was waiting in a hotel where Srobar called and told them that at the order of President Clement Gottwald, the execution would not be carried out and a decision will be made later about what to do with Esterhazy. That saved his life. Soon, he was transferred to the Red Cross Hospital and placed under medical supervision. Mariska went to Pozsony at once to visit her brother. On June 21, 1949, Louise received her first long letter and out of it learned what has happened to her brother since June 22, 1945.

The day after, on June 23, 1945, the NKVD took him and Mihaly Csaky from the Czechoslovak jail to its secret jail in Kempelen Street. He was repeatedly beaten while there and was afraid that members of his family might also be mistreated. Toward the end of 1945, he learned that he was to be taken to Hungary. Two days later, he was put on a train bound for Budapest, along with Mihaly Csaky, Tibor Neumann, Janos Jabloniczky, Lajos Parkanyi and other leaders of the United Hungarian Party. From Hungary, after a long, tiring journey, they arrived in Moscow where they were taken to the Lubyanka Prison. There, Esterhazy was locked into a solitary cell, tortured and interrogated day and night. After a while, he was taken to a camp where, in 1947 he became extremely ill in the severe cold. The camp hospital diagnosed his illness as tuberculosis.

In 1948, orders came from Moscow that Janos Esterhazy be given good nourishment and built up because he would go on a lengthy journey. By 1949 he recuperated sufficiently to be declared ready to travel. On February 12, 1949, he was put on a train but it was only in April that he arrived at the Czechoslovak border where he was taken into police custody and brought to Kassa, then to a hospital in Pozsony. His condition gradually improved in the hospital.

In June 1949, his sister Louise and their mother sent a petition for amnesty to the president and to Foreign Minister Clementis. At the end of July, Mariska wrote to Louise that their brother has been returned to the prison hospital for treatment. Mariska sent her brother a small parcel every day to supplement the hospital food. Meanwhile, word came that the president had rejected the petition for full amnesty but commuted the sentence to life in prison.

In November 1949, Janos Esterhazy was transferred to Leopoldov prison where he was kept until March 5, 1950. On March 6, he was taken to Mirov prison in Moravia, then on August 23, to Ilava prison in Slovakia. On March 4, 1954, Esterhazy was transferred again, this time to the Rocov u Louny prison in the Czech region. On April 11, 1955, he was taken to Bory (Trestnica na Borech) near Plzno, on June 2 to Leopoldov, on May 4, 1956, to Mirov in Moravia. Despite the frequent transfers, miraculously the parcels had reached him and so did the letters once every three months. Later on, the letters became more scarce. Occasionally, Mariska was able to talk with his brother across an iron grill.

In July 1951, Louise Esterhazy was named Secretary of the Hungarian Refugee Committe which had been founded by Father Imre Gacser.

In the summer of 1951, Alice and Louise's mother were deported, alongh with countless other Hungarians, from Budapest to the Great Hungarian Plain where they were to suffer a great deal from hunger and cold. In 1952, Alice was arrested by the AVO secret police. For a while she was imprisoned in Budapest, later she was taken to a concentration camp in Melykut.

Meanwhile Mariska kept besieging the authorities to have her brother transferred to a general hospital. Her husband, Ferenc, went to South Africa in order to earn money and support his family. Whatever had been left of the family home in Nyitraujlak was taken away from Mariska and she moved into a tiny apartment in the village.

In 1954, Janos Esterhazy learned from Mariska that his daughter, Alice managed to leave Hungary and was staying in Vienna with her uncle, Laszlo Esterhazy and his family.

In January 1956, Mihaly Csaky was freed. Louise met him in Paris and he told her that Tibor Neumann and Janos Jabloniczky had died in the Soviet prison camp.

On February 24, 1956, Louise's mother suffered a cerebral hemorrhage and on February 27, she died. Mariska traveled to the Leopoldov prison to tell her brother Janos of the death of their mother. They cried over their loss together.

Janos Esterhazy was still hoping that one day he may yet see his family. Unfortunately, however, the stormy times had spread them all over the globe. His son, Janos was working in New Zealand and his daughter, Alice was in Manhattanville College in the United States.

Nothing was more characteristic of Janos Esterhazy's deep religious faith and noble spirit than that on every day of the week he prayed for a different member of his family and on Sundays he prayed for his enemies.

In that period, between 1950 and 1955, Janos Esterhazy put up a heroic struggle to restore his health to live to see the day when he regains his freedom. The poor nourishment and the bitter cold did not help. And in the fall of 1956, the warden of Mirov prison took away the privilege of receiving an occasional food parcel from his family.

His fellow prisoners, both in the Soviet Union and in the Czechoslovak prisons, reported that Janos Esterhazy bore the sufferings of imprisonment and all the physical pain with superior courage and spiritual serenity. He drew this strength from his deep faith and was able to radiate it to his fellow prisoners. They said he was always ready to comfort them and ease their misery with his gentle humor and sympathy.

The 12 years of imprisonment have finally broken his health. In February 1957 his condition turned critical and he sent word to his family about the impending end. Mariska asked for permission immediately to go to Mirov and see her brother. On February 24, 1957, she was escorted to him by four Czech physicians who were also prisoners. Discreetly, they left brother and sister alone. He told her that the doctors, who had been condemned also, were like best friends to him. They had been looking after him day and night. He appeared to be calm, serious, even though occasionally he would crack a joke. He wished he would be taken to the Nyitra hospital. But the warden persisted in refusing every request by the family. "I will not give you my prisoner, dead or alive," was his answer. The family tried once more in Prague to have him transferred to a general hospital. All in vain. And the end was inexorably approaching.

On March 8, 1957, the prison warden sent a terse telegram to the family, informing them that "Janos Esterhazy has died on March 8. His remains will be cremated and will not be released to his family."

Mariska went to Mirov at once to prevent the cremation and to try to have her brother's body released to her. The warden told her that the body had been taken already to Olomonc to be cremated. She asked the warden at least for the urn so that she might take it to Nyitraujlak to be interred in their father's grave, which had been the wish of her brother. Once more, the warden refused: "I told you once before that I will not release him, dead or alive."

A *Requiem* was celebrated in Paris by Father Roman Rezek, director of the Hungarian Catholic Mission, assisted by Father Michel Riquet. But the great son of our land was mourned by thousands of Hungarians all over the world.

The *Requiem* Mass in **Paris** was attended by many Hungarians emigres and French dignitaries and representatives of various institutions. The French Foreign Ministry, the Assembly of Captive European Nations, the International Rescue Committee, the National Catholic Welfare Conference, as well as fellow emigre groups were also represented. The family was represented by Louise Esterhazy, a member of the executive committee of the Cultural Association of Hungarians from Czechoslovakia.

The Hungarians of **New York** celebrated a *Requiem* Mass in St.Stephen church on March 30. It was attended by representatives of emigre organizations of Hungarian minority groups, such as the National Committee of Hungarians in Czechoslovakia, the Scientific Society of the Highlands, the Society of Hungarians from Subcarpathian Ruthenia, the American Transylvania Federation, Council for the Liberation of Southern Hungary. Of the other Hungarian emigre groups, there were representatives from the American Hungarian Federation, the Hungarian National Council, the Hungarian Veterans Organization, the Hungarian Branch of the American Friends of the

Federation of Anti-Bolshevist Nations, leaders of the American Hungarian Catholic League. Following the Mass, condolences were received by Alice Esterhazy, daughter of Janos Esterhazy and recording secretary of the Cultural Association of Hungarians from Czechoslovakia.

The **Cleveland** branch of the National Committee of Hungarians in Czechoslovakia also celebrated a *Requiem* Mass on March 30 for the soul of Janos Esterhazy.[511]

We might note that a few months after the death of Janos Esterhazy, his sister Mariska and her daughter Erzsebet went to Olomonc to view his urn. They were shown in the crematory a niche holding 18 urns, including that of Janos Esterhazy. These urns contained the ashes of his fellow prisoners -- Czechs, Slovaks, Hungarians -- who had to walk the same way of the cross and whose familes were also denied that most elementary of rights, giving a decent funeral to their loved ones.

In Remembrance of Janos Esterhazy, the Politician, the Hungarian, the Man

"Janos Esterhazy died on March 8, 1957 in Mirov prison in Czechoslovakia. It would be more accurate to say that he died a hero's death, falling in the struggle to which he had dedicated his life. His grave is surrounded not only by the Hungarian minority of the Highlands, but the entire Hungarian nation, extending to him the respect and affection due to national heroes and mourning him in their hearts. He was given a tragic destiny by the Allmighty, the same tragic destiny with which He punishes, or perhaps rewards those who have been predestined to greatness.

"The era in which he lived was characterized by ideological chaos, hypocrisy and decadence. It was in the year of Trianon that he turned from youth to manhood, that was the time when the soul is the most impressionable, when impressions leave the most lasting mark. He grew up during a period of world war which was fought in the name of democracy and self-determination -- principles in whose name one out of four Hungarians were forced to live under a foreign state. That event and the subsequent sense of just rebellion against the injustice of Trianon may have been the most determining factor in shaping his entire life.

"His public life began in the early 1920s when Geza Szullo, the leader of the Hungarians in the Highlands chose him as his political heir. Geza Szullo's recommendation was received with universal approval on the part of the Hungarians in the Highlands and, before long, Esterhazy was named chairman of the Christian Socialist Party. His parliamentary career coincided with the period when there became increasingly apparent in Prague the signs of disintegration which was a natural consequence of the chauvinistic Czech national policies.

"He demonstrated his political maturity by sparing no energy in fighting for the right of self-determination of the Hungarians, while taking the greatest care to remain on the high ground of public morality even amidst the most severe struggle.

"In choosing his political allies, Esterhazy was looking at the historical perspective, rather than momentary gain. **He never forgot that the many small nations of the Danubian Basin will either stand together or fall together -- as demonstrated by events -- therefore even the deepest conflicts must be eliminated without violating national sensibilities, so that that the atmosphere of cooperation based on understanding may be brought about.** He paid particular attention to that in the relationship of the Hungarians and Slovaks, knowing very well that because of their geographic location, these two nations occupy a key position in any Danubian cooperation.

"The ferment of the 1930s did not bring the desired results, it was drowned out by the roar of the cannons of the second World War.

"The Hungarian minority remaining in the independent Slovakia was relatively small in numbers. Janos Esterhazy chose to stay with them. In the turmoil of the second World War, his position outgrew its original Hungarian dimensions. His struggles shifted from politics to ideology. It was not Esterhazy, the politician, but Esterhazy, the man clinging to his Christian ideology, who was able to and dared to take a stand against the Satanic forces arising in the guise of Naziism and Communism.

"Esterhazy knew from the very beginning that cooperation with Naziism would be morally impossible and would lead to political disaster. But he also knew that cooperation with Communism, while resisting Naziism, would be likewise morally impossible and would also lead to political disaster. He saw this clearly at the time when many in the Western world, political leaders included, deceived themselves by believing that some sort of ideological compromise with Communism is possible and when these Westerners were urging all resistance fighters to cooperate with the communists.

"It was not easy in those times to hew to the straight path. History provided a tragic justification of the rightness of his cause and his own passing was no less tragic.

"In 1945, he was taken away by the Russians. He spent three long years in Soviet forced labor camps. He came home broken in body but unshaken in spirit only to face a death sentence by the infamous Czechoslovak peoples court. The judge refused to weigh his behavior during the war. He was not interested in what defense witnesses had to say, he just pronounced the sentence which was probably dictated from the Hradcany palace in Prague. The amnesty changed it to life in prison.

"He was condemned first of all because he was Hungarian, a fearless and uncompromising representative of his people, and because he was a true Christian. The lords of the Kremlin and the Hradcany palace knew that the man who dared openly to proclaim during the terror of the Swastika (cross) that "we Hungarians know only one cross, the Cross of Jesus Christ," that man would never surrender either to the hammer and sickle, or to the Czechoslovak peoples democracy. They knew that men like him must be liquidated by any means possible. There is just one thing they failed to take into account, that the children of martyrs are counted by the hundreds of thousands. And in 1956, the children of the Hungarian martyrs passed their first trial on the world stage."[512]

As we look back at the great Hungarian martyrs of the years of 1930-1950, three men come to mind immediately: Count Pal Teleki, former Prime Minister of Hungary; Baron Vilmos Apor, the Roman Catholic Bishop of Gyor, and Count Janos Esterhazy, leader of the Hungarian Party of the Highlands.

Pal Teleki became a victim of the imperialistic policies of Hitler's Germany. Vilmos Apor sacrificed his life in the defense of nuns who were seeking refuge in his Bishop's Palace from Stalin's hordes. Janos Esterhazy became a martyr at the hands of Hitler's Nazis, Stalin's Bolsheviks and the self-centered, chauvinistic system of Benes.

Their martyrdom was not in vain because "the children of martyrs are counted by the hundreds of thousands."

Conclusion

In Part Two, we have attempted to sketch in their broad out-lines the struggles of the Hungarian inhabitants of the Highlands, later of the independent Slovakia, for the right of self-determination solemnly proclaimed by President Wilson, for their minority rights, for the peaceful revision on the basis of mutual agreement of the injustices imposed by the peace treaties of Paris and Trianon.

At the end of Part One, in the discussion of the Slovak efforts for autonomy and independence, we touched upon the conclusions that could be drawn from the stormy events of the post-1918 period. We emphasized that those conclusions could be, in general, equally applied not only to the Slovaks but to the other inhabitants of the Danubian Basin -- Hungarians, Germans, Poles, Ruthenians -- as well. To underscore that statement, we cited a Slovak publication, issued in the West, which called the fate of Slovakia a typical example of the problem of small nations. According to the article, the more than sixty-year coexistence of Czechs and Slovaks has been a decep-tion and just as harmful under the rule of Masaryk and Benes, as under the Communists.

We have noted in that respect that how well a state takes care of its minorities is one measure of how far democracy has come in that state. We have also emphasized that according to the Hungarian view, the political leadership of Benes has miserably failed before the court of history. This has been clearly demonstrated by the fact that over a period of twenty years he was unable to secure the loyalty of his national minorities, not even that of the Slovaks, even though he kept calling them a "sister nation." Is it any wonder then that for twenty years it took the greatest difficulties and violent measures to keep this jerrybuilt artificial state alive, and even with that, it barely missed setting of a continent-wide conflagration?

Gigantic errors were made at the very birth of the Benes system. At the very beginning, its planners turned against the ideas of

President Wilson, who had a great foresight. For a detailed discussion of that, please refer to Note #22 at the end of Part One. President Wilson, as we have seen, was inclined toward the plan to establish an Austro-Hungarian federation, as recommended by his Commission of Inquiry. Then British Prime Minister Lloyd George, one of the architects of the Paris peace treaties and one of the best qualified witnesses in this question, spoke in a similar vein.

In his Memoirs, published by *The Daily Telegraph* in 1938, Lloyd George stated that originally, the allied powers had no intention of breaking up the Austro-Hungarian Monarchy. On the contrary, he wrote, "Their only intention was to adjust the borders of the Monarchy in favor of Italy, Serbia and Rumania, and to establish a federated state in the rest of its territory, with the fullest autonomy for all nationalities." According to Lloyd George the people interested in the fate of the Monarchy, presented the great powers with a *fait accompli* and that is why the original plan could not be realized.

We have discussed in some detail the identity of those responsible for the *fait accompli*. It was made possible largely with the the massive propaganda, based on empty promises and untruths, the illness of the well-intentioned President Wilson, and the activities of Secretary of State Lansing and French Foreign Minister Pichon, both of whom had been strongly opposed to the Monarchy.

On February 5, 1919, Benes did not hesitate to make a solemn promise that Czechoslovakia will not oppress the national minorities which will come under its rule. On the contrary, he said, it is their intention to grant full rights to the minorities. Accordingly, on May 20, Benes submitted a memorandum to the Peace Conference, listing point-by-point the high-sounding promises which were never kept.

We have seen in both Parts what became of those promises. Of course, Benes and his friends and Western well-wishers denied that the grievances were valid and tried to portrait them as empty excuses and means for the undermining of the republic. That became the basis for the condemnation of large numbers of people, including Janos Esterhazy. It is sufficient at this point to refer to the final report of Lord Runciman, the impartial British diplomat who stated, among others: "Even at the end of my mission, I saw no intention to remedy these grievances... The Nazi power has given them new hope. I consider it a natural development that they would turn to their ethnic kin and want to be transferred to the German empire... Should certain transfer of land be unavoidable, and I think it is, it should be carried out at once."

Benes would not hear of such moves until he was confronted by the German arms. The same happened with regard to the Slovaks and the Hungarians. Benes would listen to the Hungarian grievances only when he was already under pressure. This was demonstrated, for example, by the totally candid statement by Bakach-Bessenyei before Kobr, the Czechoslovak Minister in Budapest, on April 6, 1938, when he blamed the *Little Entente* for failing to reach out a hand to Hungary before it was too late: "All opportunities have been buried by now and the Danubian nations face an unrelenting fate very soon. In one form or another, they will become satellites of Germany. It will happen to Czechoslovakia because of the Sudeten German problem. Hungary will become a satellite of Germany on account of their comradeship in arms. Rumania and Yugoslavia will find themselves in the same situation because of economic pressure."

The greatest responsibility rests on the Benes system, but it must be shared also by the great powers, which they will have to recognize sooner or later, just as Lloyd George became aware of and tried to explain the failures. They are responsible because, contrary to Wilson's concepts which were guided by foresight and the interests of the future, rather than vengeance, they lent a helping hand to the creation of a nonviable system and its maintenance to the very end, to the point where their own interests became endangered by a European war.

Thirdly, the nationalities living in the Danubian Basin are also responsible because, instead of showing more patience, more goodwill, mutual understanding and, if necessary, willingness to compromise in the solution of their mutual problems, they believed the empty promises of the great powers which were playing them off one against another, and were competing for the favors of the great powers.

Let us now take a closer look at those whom we have just pronounced responsible for the fate that befell the peoples of the Danubian Basin.

The Benes system must respond to the judgment of history and one needs not be a prophet to tell that it is only a matter of time. That procedure has begun a long time ago, primarily among his compatriots and colleagues, greatly supported by the Slovak patriots also. The small nations concerned over the future of the Danubian Basin must do everything in their power to banish that spirit forever from their joint homeland.

Who could take the **great powers** to task for their responsibility? A great power is always looking for its interests and acts accordingly. All that can happen that after a while the great power becomes aware of the fact that, for example, its policies toward the peoples of the Danubian Basin have been in error and, on the long run, contrary to its own interests. When that happens, the great power has the option of reviewing and revising its policies. The peoples of the Danubian Basin can very effectively contribute to this with their informational activities. It is, after all, in their interest to help revise a faulty policy which has reached a dead end.

Naturally, the third group we mentioned, the **peoples of the Danubian Basin** can do the most because they would be serving, above all, their own interests. But by no means should they attempt to blame each other because that would just take them back into the old, worn rut.

We have repeatedly stated in this work that, in our opinion, the destiny of the peoples of the Danubian Basin must be held jointly in their hands because, as we have clearly seen, that is how they stand or fall. That is why Janos Esterhazy said on September 2, 1943, "We maintain the best intentions and most sincere sentiments toward the Slovaks. After the end of the war when the time comes for peaceful construction, those of us who have lived and continued to live in the Danubian Basin, will have to depend on each other."

Esterhazy also said, on October 28, 1939: **"Every person, even the most virtuous among us, is too weak successfully to struggle with the weight of his conditions. If at no other time, this is the time when we have to build muscles on the solidarity derived from the mutual interdependence of small nations, otherwise we might lose a valuable facet of our national identity. It is in our common interest with the Slovaks to create harmonic cooperation within the borders of the state, as well as among all the peoples of the Danubian Basin, to secure peaceful existence and pursuit of happiness even for the smallest ones among us."**

There is evidence that some Slovaks also share these views. Stefan B. Roman the late chairman of the Slovak World Congress, who died in 1988, said: "It is clear for us that the foundations of a free Europe can be established only through the cooperation of the oppressed nations of Central and Eastern Europe. Recrimination and chauvinism will not lead to a better future for the nations of Central Europe. That is why we deem it necessary to seek cooperation with every neighbor of Slovakia, as well as their representatives in the free world."[513]

We have noted in the Introduction that it is of paramount importance to become reconciled in spirit. We must be aware and we need to be thoroughly educated to the fact that this serves not only Hungarian or Slovak interests of which one or the other may take advantage. We must understand and we have to use every means to bring it into public consciousness that this is in the interest of both nations -- we are dealing here with a common Hungarian-Slovak destiny -- which is to serve the survival of both of them.

Representatives of the Central and Eastern European nations who live in the West have a significant historic mission to fulfill. They are not bound by the system ruling the mother country, which can preclude any dialog not in the interest of the regime, even if it were to serve the real future interests of the nation. Such dialogs can have but one prevailing theme: acceptance and further development of the common destiny with the neighboring peoples, which must serve the ultimate survival of their people. If representatives of these nations, living in the West, are willing to undertake and carry out this mission without any reservation, then the dream of Janos Esterhazy may be fulfilled. The dream which has been his intellectual heritage, expressed so clearly in his address already cited:

"Let us develop a peaceful and constructive cooperation, based on equal rights, among the peoples and nations which mutually depend on each other. This is equally in the interest of the Hungarians, Germans, Slovaks and Ruthenians who have lived here for centuries."

NOTES TO PART TWO

(159)*Kuruc* was the name given to Hungarian nationalists fighting the Austrian Hapsburg rule. Hungarians who became loyal to the Hapsburgs were called *labanc*.

(160)Information about the origins of Janos Esterhazy was taken from the following sources:

Kemeny, Lajos, "Az Esterhazyak Pozsonyban." *A Toldy Kor 1943-as Evkonyve.* 1943.

Editorial in *Uj Hirek.* Pozsony. March 14, 1941.

Gotaischer Geneologisches Taschenbuch der Graflichen Hauser, 1931. pp. 148-158.

(161)Speech by Janos Esterhazy at Otatrafured on December 14, 1942, when he was greeted with great enthusiasm by the Hungarians of Slovakia on the tenth anniversary of his election, in the same town, to the presidency of the National Christian Socialist Party. *Magyar Hirlap.* December 15, 1942.

(162)Arato, Endre, *Tanulmanyok a szlovakiai magyarok eletebol, 1918-1975.* Budapest: Magveto Konyvkiado, 1977. p.29.

(163)Olvedi, Janos, *Napfogyatkozas; magyarok Szlovakiaban.* New York: Puski, 1985, p.38.

(164)Borsody, Istvan, "Masaryk es az uj Europa, Egy felvideki magyar emlekei." *Uj Latohatar.* v.XXXIX, No.1, March 25, 1988, pp. 21-22.

(165) Bibo, Istvan, *Valogatott tanulmanyok.* v.I., 1935-1944. Budapest: Magveto Konyvkiado, 1986. pp. 508-509.

(166)*Archives Diplomatiques, Paris, Europe 1918-1929, Hongrie.* v.59. pp. 181-192.

(167)PDR FRH II. Doc.no. 221, 224, 529, cited in Szarka, Laszlo: "Kisebbsegvedelem, reciprocitas, revizio. Megegyezesi kiserletek a nemzetisegi kerdes teren." in *Hungaro-Bohemislovaca 2.* Budapest: 1988. pp. 49-50.

(168)ibid p.53.

(169)Masaryk, in his talks with Jozsef Szent-Ivany, confirmed his readiness to give up the territories inhabited by Hungarians, under certain conditions. First among these was construction of an East-West railroad line. (Magyarorszag a parizsi konferencian, Hungarian Foreign Ministry, 1947, v.4, p.163.)

Also, a very interesting statement Masaryk made early 1923 before Dr. Ede Palyi, a Hungarian journalist, to the effect that "originally it was not our intention to take away from Hungary territories with a Hungarian majority... I am prepared to announce that negotiations may be held to return such territories under appropriate conditions." (Dr. Palyi, Ede, *Mikep szereztem en meg a csehek ajanlatat az elszakitott magyarok bekes visszaadasara.* Budapest: 1927. pp.19-27)

Igor Hrusovsky, a Slovak member of the Czechoslovak parliament also spoke with Palyi on behalf of Masaryk and sketched a map of the territories which might be returned. This map has been reproduced in Dr. Palyi's book.

Masaryk also told F.Rainiss, the Prague director of the Hungarian State Insurance Company: "I am prepared, even today, to negotiate about peaceful revision." (Magyarorszag a parizsi konferencian, op.cit. p.168.)

Mihaly Karolyi wrote in his memoirs: "A truly liberal democrat did not approve the detachment of purely Hungarian territories without the consent of the population." (Karolyi, Mihaly, *Faith without Illusion.* New York: 1957. p.171.)

(170)Raschhofer, Hermann, ed., *Die Tschechoslovakische Denkschriften fur die Friedenskonferenz von Paris, 1919/1920. Berlin: 1938. p.185.*

(171)Buza, Laszlo, *The Legal Status of National Minorities According to the Peace Treaties and Other International Agreements.* Budapest: 1930.

(172)Olvedi, Janos, *A magyar kisebbseg Csehszlovakiaban.* p.280.

(173)Turczel, Lajos, "A kisebbsegi helyzet kialakulasanak korulmenyei Csehszlovakiaban 1918 utan." *Irodalmi Szemle.* 1966. 3.

(174)Kovacs, Endre, *Korszakvaltas.* Budapest: Magveto Konyvkiado, 1981. p.366.

(175)Arato, Endre, *Tanulmanyok a szlovakiai magyarok tortenetebol, 1918-1975.* Budapest: Magveto Konyvkiado, pp.87-89.

(176)Olvedi, Janos, *Napfogyatkozas.* op.cit. pp.41-42.

PART TWO

(177)Szilassy, Bela, "A felvideki magyarsag elete a ket vilaghaboru kozott."
Elszakitott magyarsag. Buenos Aires: 1956, p.16.

(178)'48 refers to the March 15, 1848 revolution in Hungary.

(179)Regarding the formation and activities of the Hungarian parties in Slovakia, see
Szilassy, Bela, op.cit.; Sirchich, Laszlo: *A felvidek az ezereves magyar
allamtestben, magyarok Csehszlovakiaban. Tanulmanyok.* Cleveland, 1979.;
Arato, Endre: *Tanulmanyok a szlovakiai magyarok tortenetebol,* op.cit.;
Szvatko, Pal: *A visszatert magyarok. A felvideki magyarsag husz eve.* Buda-
pest, 1938.; Merei, Gyula: *A magyar polgari partok programmjai 1867-1918.*
Budapest, 1971.; Darvas, Janos, "Politikai eletunk husz eve. Magyarok Csehszlo-
vakiaban. *Az orszag utja.* Budapest, June 1938.

(180)*Pragai Magyar Hirlap.* November 29, 1932.

(181)ibid December 16, 1932.

(182)ibid December 29, 1932.

(183)ibid January 1, 1933.

(184)ibid June 29, 1933.

(185)ibid July 15, 16, 1933.

(186)*Hirado.* September 28, October 5, 1933.

(187)*Pragai Magyar Hirlap.* December 24, 1933.

(188)*Hirado.* December 24, 1933

(189)*Pragai Magyar Hirlap.* March 17, May 3, 1934.

(190)ibid May 23, 1934.

(191)ibid June 20, 27, July 11, October 4, 1934

(192)ibid October 21, 1934.

(193)ibid October 25, 1934.

(194)*Hirado*. December 25, 1934.

(195)*Pragai Magyar Hirlap*. February 10, 12, March 6, 13, 28, April 4, 1935.

(196)ibid April 27, 1935.

(197) ibid June 27, 1935 and *Hirado* 27, 1935.

(198)ibid September 22, November 15, 29, 1935.

(199)ibid November 30, 1935.

(200)Nittner, Ernest, *Documente zur Sudetendeutschen Frage*. p. 128.

(201)Wojatsek, Charles, op.cit. ref.to. Culen Konstantin: "Po Svatopluki druha nasa hlava" (Zivot Dr. Josefa Tisu) Middletown JEDNOTA, 1947, 169-170.

(202)*Pragai Magyar Hirlap*. December 6, 1935.

(203)Adam, Magda, *Magyarorszag es a Kisantant a harmincas evekben*. Budapest: Akademiai Kiado, 1968. p.83.

(204)Orszagos Leveltar. Kum.res.pol. 1935-7-228 and 1936-171896. cited in Adam, Magda, *Magyarorszag es a kisantant*. op.cit., p.108.

(205)Adam, Magda, *A muncheni egyezmeny*, op.cit. No.10.

(206)ibid No.11.

(207)ibid No.3.

(208)ibid No.9 and 23.

(209)*Pragai Magyar Hirlap*. January 14, 1936.

(210)ibid February 20, 1936.

(211)ibid February 29, 1936.

(212)ibid March 26, 1936.

(213)ibid April 23, 1936.

(214)*Hirado*. May 5, 1936.

(215)ibid June 23, 1936.

(216)Nittner op.cit. p.148.

(217)Orszagos Leveltar, Horthy kabinetirodajanak anyaga. B.I.7. in *Horthy Miklos titkos iratai*, comp. Miklos Szinai, Budapest: 1962. Doc.No.32. pp. 157-167.

(218)Adam, Magda, *A muncheni egyezmeny*. op.cit. No.30.

(219)Battle of Mohacs in 1526, a devastating defeat of the Hungarian army by the Ottoman Turks, followed by 150 years of Turkish occupation.

(220)ibid No.32.

(221)*Hirado*. September 30, 1936.

(222)*Pragai Magyar Hirlap*. September 3, 1936.

(223)*Hirado*. October 9, 1936.

(224)*Pragai Magyar Hirlap*. October 16, 1936.

(225)*Hirado*. November 5, 1936.

(226)*Pragai Magyar Hirlap*. November 12 and 15, 1936.

(227)ibid December 3, 1936.

(228)ibid December 15, 1936.

(229)ibid December 20, 1936.

(230)Adam, Magda, *A muncheni egyezmeny*. op.cit. No.54.

(231)ibid No.82.

(232)Orszagos Leveltar. Kum.pol.1938 7/7-541 and 7/7541 (1920).

(233)ibid Kum.res.pol. 1938-49-483.

(234)ibid Kum.res.pol. 1938-49-486.

(235)ibid Kum.res.pol. 1938-49-485.

(236)Adam, Magda, *Magyarorszag es a kisantant.* op.cit. p.165.

(237)*Pragai Magyar Hirlap.* January 30, February 17, 19, June 5, 16, 20, 22, October 6, 16, November 11, 1937.

(238)Adam, Magda, *A muncheni egyezmeny.* op.cit. No.95.

(239)ibid No.96.

(240)ibid No.98.

(241)ibid No.99.

(242)*Pragai Magyar Hirlap.* November 18, 1937.

(243)*Pragai Magyar Hirlap.* November 18, 1937.

(244)Orszagos Leveltar. Kum.res.pol. 1938-17-154.

(245)Adam, Magda, *A muncheni egyezmeny.* op.cit. No.104.

(246)ibid No.124.

(247)Gehl, Jurgen, *Austria, Germany and the Anschluss, 1931-1938.* London: Oxford University Press, 1963, pp.191-195.

(248)Rich, Norman, *Hitler's War Aims.* New York: Norton, 1970, v.1, pp.180-187.

(249)Macartney, C.A., *October Fifteenth: A History of Modern Hungary, 1929-1945.* 2nd ed. Edinburgh: University Press, 1961, v.1, p.109.

Among the political efforts to ease the tension between Hungary and the Little Entente, we should note an early March, 1938, visit by Gusztav Gratz to Prague. The Hungarian diplomat's visit, which took place just before the *Anschluss*, was regarded by many as having a semi-official character. He met President Benes, Prime Minister Hodza and Foreign Minister Krofta. With regard to the question of national minorities, Benes said he was planning to introduce reforms to grant far-reaching rights but has no intention of making those reforms subject of

272

international agreements. The Czech leaders flatly refused to discuss the question of boundaries. And when Gratz pointed to Czechoslovakia's difficult international situation, Benes gave a sarcastic response, saying that "the Czech people have already spent centuries swallowed up by the Holy Roman Empire and would survive even more centuries living in the stomach of another German Empire." (Orszagos Leveltar. Kum.res.pol. 1938-7-1455.)

(250)DGFP Washington, D.C., U.S.Govt.Printing Office, 1949. 1964. Series D, v.I, No.19.

(251)Adam, Magda, A muncheni egyezmeny. op.cit. No.121, 152, 182.

(252)Pragai Magyar Hirlap. February 23, 1938.

(253)ibid February 27, 1938.

(254)DGFP. Series D. II. 135.

(255)Pragai Magyar Hirlap. February 11, 12, 1938.

(256)ibid March 22, 1938.

(257)ibid March 30, 1938.

(258)ibid March 31, 1938.

(259)ibid April 2, 1938.

(260)ibid April 7, 1938.

(261)DBFP Third Series, I-IX. London, 1949-1955 I. 114, and Orszagos Leveltar. Kum.pol. 1938-7/25-897.(1235)

(262)Orszagos Leveltar. Kum.res.pol.k939-7/a-277.

(263)ibid Kum.res.pol.1938-49-304.

(264)Laffan, R.G.D., Survey of International Affairs, 1938.v.II.London: Oxford University Press, 1951. 95. in Wojatsek, Charles, From Trianon... op.cit. App.6.

(265)Pragai Magyar Hirlap. April 26, 1938.

(266)ibid May 11, 1938

(267)DBFP Third Series. v.1. Doc.No.164, 95-96.

(268)*Pragai Magyar Hirlap*, April 26, 27, 28, 29, 30, 1938.
In a statement for the MTI Hungarian Telegraphy Agency, Henderson declared: "The main result of my visit is that now I can fully understand and appreciate Hungary's national efforts and goals. Thinking people everywhere must understand that permanent peace in Central Europe can be maintained only if we remedy the wrongs perpetrated by the peace treaties and will not do injustice to other nations." (*Pesti Naplo*. April 26, 1938.)

(269)ibid May 4, 1938.

(270)Orszagos Leveltar. chiffre. 1938.

(271)ibid Kum.pol.1938-7/28-897.

(272)*Pragai Magyar Hirlap*. May 13, 1938.

(273)Orszagos Leveltar. Kum.pol.1938-7-25-897.

(274)Adam, Magda, *A kisantant...* op.cit. p.231 and Ciano, *Tagebuch 1937/1938*. p.164.

(275)*Le Temps*. May 16, 1938 and *Pragai Magyar Hirlap*. May 19, 1938.

(276)Orszagos Leveltar. Kum.res.pol.1938-7-438 and Hoensch op.cit. p.62.

(277)*Pragai Magyar Hirlap*. May 21, 1938.

(278)ADAP Serie D., Bd.II, Doc.No.184, 185, pp.246-256.

(279)DBFP. Third Series v.1., Doc.No.259, pp.338-339.

(280)*Pragai Magyar Hirlap*. May 22, 1938.

(281)ibid May 24, 1938.

(282)Orszagos Leveltar. Kum.res.pol. 1938-7-489.

(283)*Weltgeschichte der Gegenwart in Dokumenten*. pp.59-61.

(284)*Pragai Magyar Hirlap.* May 28 and 29, 1938.

(285)ibid May 31, 1938.

(286)ibid

(287)ibid June 1, 1938.

(288)Orszaggyulesi Naplo. 1935-40. v.XIX. June 1, 1938.

(289)AMZV PZ Budapest, 1938, 52402.

(290)*Pragai Magyar Hirlap.* June 3, 1938.

(291)ibid June 2, 1938.

(292)ibid June 3, 9, 1938.

(293)ibid June 11, 1938.

(294)ibid June 14, 1938.

(295)ibid June 23, 24, 1938.

(296)ibid June 25, 1938.

(297)ibid June 28, 1938.

(298)ibid July 1, 1938.

(299)ibid July 3, 1938.

(300)ibid July 5, 1938.

(301)ibid July 12, 1938.

(302)ibid July 14, 1938.

(303)ibid July 15, 1938.

(304)ibid July 21, 1938.

(305)ibid July 23, 1938.

(306)Orszagos Leveltar. Kum.res.pol. 1938-49-685 (605).

(307)ibid Kum.res.pol. 1938-49-63.

(308)ibid Kum.res.pol. 1938-2/7-2297.

(309)ibid Kum.res.pol. 1938-23.

(310)ibid Kum.res.pol. 1938-17-569.

(311)ibid Kum.res.pol. 1938-17-598.

(312)ibid Kum.res.pol. 1938-49-582.

(313)*Pragai Magyar Hirlap.* July 24, 1938.

(314)*The Times.* July 25, 1938.

(315)*Pragai Magyar Hirlap.* July 24, 1938.

(316)ibid July 27, 1938.

(317)ibid July 28, 1938.

(318)*The Daily Telegraph.*l July 26, 1938, and *Pragai Magyar Hirlap.* August 2, 1938.

(319)PRO.,FO., 371/21426, 133 and Wojatsek, Charles, op.cit. pp.109-110.

(320)*Pragai Magyar Hirlap.* August 4, 1938.

(321)ibid August 13, 1938.

(322)Orszagos Leveltar. Kum.pol. 1938-7/4-72.

(323)PRO., FO., 800/306, September 2, 1938.

(324)ibid 800/306, 108.

(325)AMZV desle Budapest, 1938. 837.838.

(326)Orszagos Leveltar. Kum.res.pol. 1938-49-579; Kum.res.pol. 1938-49-685(674); Kum.res.pol. 1938-49-688; Kum.res.pol. 1938-49-685; Kum.res.pol. 1938-49-715; Kum.res.pol. 1938-49-714; Kum.res.pol. 1939-16/a-726, and Kum.pol. 1938-2/7-2744 which shows most clearly the Hungarian position concerning the justification of the demand to Prague for a "more far-reaching statement." Copies of this document were sent to the Hungarian legations in London, Berlin, Warsaw, Prague, Belgrad and Bucharest.

(327)Daily Herald. August 24, 1938.

(328)Orszagos Leveltar. Kum.pol. 1938-2/7-2244.

(329)DGFP, C, III. No..336.

(330)Gehl, Jurgen, op.cit. pp. 173-174.

(331)Orszagos Leveltar. Kum.res.pol. 1938-7-792.

(332)DGFP, D, II., No.367, 383 and ADAP Serie D, v. II, 383, Doc.No.486-487.

(333)ibid

(334)ibid

(335)Pritz, op.cit. p.664.

(336)Hoensch, op.cit. p.52.

(337)Pritz, op.cit. pp. 665-667.

(338)ibid pp. 666-667.

(339)Sakmyster, Thomas L., The Hungarian State Visit to Germany of August, 1938: Some New Evidence on Hungary in Hitler's Pre-Munich Policy." in Canadian Slavic Studies, 3 (1969). This article contains the minutes of the Ratz-Hitler meeting from the so-called "Ratz Memorandum." The Memorandum itself is in the Collection of Hungarian Political and Military Records, 1909-1945, U.S. National Archives, Washington, D.C., microcopy T973, roll 15, pp. 1 and 6 of the Memorandum.

(340)DGFP, D, II. No.395.

(341)Hory, Andras. *A kulisszak mogott.* Vienna: 1965, p.33 and DGFP, D, II, No. 402.

(342)*Pragai Magyar Hirlap.* August 30, 1938.

(343)ibid August 30, 1938.

(344)ibid September 1, 1938.

(345)ibid September 3, 1938.

(346)ibid

(347)ibid September 2, 1938.

(348)*8 Orai Ujsag.* September 3, 1938.

(349)*Pragai Magyar Hirlap.* September 4, 1938.

(350)ibid September 7, 1938.

(351)ibid September 6, 1938.

(352)Hoensch, op.cit. p.81.

(353)Adam, Magda, *A muncheni...* op.cit. No.322.

(354)*Pragai Magyar Hirlap.* September 7, 1938.

(355)ibid September 10, 1938.

(356)*Lord Runciman to the Prime Minister. Correspondence respecting Czechoslovakia, September 1938.* September 21, 1938. Miscellaneous No.7. Cmd.5847. London: His Majesty's Stat.Off. 1938, cited in Wojatsek, Charles, op.cit. Appendix 8.

(357)Mnichov v dokumentech I. Praha 1958, 120,127.

(358)Orszagos Leveltar. Kum.res.pol. 1938-7-806.

(359)ibid Kum.res.pol. 1938-7/25-897 (2940).

(360)ibid Kum.res.pol. 1938-7-804.

(361)Adam, Magda, *A muncheni...* op.cit. No.340.

(362)ibid No.341.

(363)Orszagos Leveltar. Kum.res.pol. 1938-7-809.

(364)Adam, Magda, *A muncheni...* op.cit. No.343.

(365)Adam, Magda, *A kisantant...* op.cit. p.226.

(366)*Weltgeschichte der Gegenwart in Dokumenten.* 67. dok.

(367)Adam, Magda, *A muncheni...* op.cit. No.351.

(368)ibid No.346.

(369)ibid No.359.

(370)ibid No.347.

(371)ibid No.358.

(372)*Pragai Magyar Hirlap.* September 19 and 23, 1938.

Since the Prague government's censorship had prevented publication of the proclamation in the Hungarian newspapers, Janos Eszterhazy, Geza Szullo and Andor Jaross issued an appeal, addressed to "Hungarian Brethren!" On account of the censorship, they chose this way to speak to the Hungarians in Czechoslovakia:

"We know that we live in increasingly difficult times. Our fate is harsh but the nation summons every Hungarian to persevere, to work and to have discipline and a confident spirit. We are sending a message to every dwelling where Hungarians live:

"Brethren! We are watching over you! You are not defenseless! We want you to know that you are not alone. Not only we, but the whole world is looking. Let us defend each other! We are waging a determined struggle for a happier and better future, for a free national existence! Hungarian Brethren! Persevere! Be faithful to the nation! Have faith!

With Hungarian comradeship and brotherly greetings.

(signed by Janos Esterhazy, Geza Szullo and Andor Jaross)

(373)Oszagos Leveltar. Kum.res/pol. 1938-11/7-3017.

(374)ibid Kum.pol. 1938-7/7-3265 (3292) -- Regarding Cadogan's notes, see SBFP Third Ser. III.77.

(375)Adam, Magda, *A muncheni...* op.cit. No.365.

(376)ibid No.368.

(377)DBFP Third Ser.II. 928 and 937.

(378)Adam, Magda, *A muncheni...* op.cit. No.376.

(379)ibid No.378.

(380)Orszagos Leveltar. Kum.chiffre.-bejovo-Varso. 6051/173 and 6055/174.

(381)DBFP Thir Ser. II. 1004, 986, *Neue Dokumente zur Geschichte der Munchener Abkommens.* 44.dok.

(382)Adam, Magda, *A muncheni...* op.cit. No.380.

(383)ibid No.381.

(384)ADAP Serie D, vol. II. 554 dok. pp.689-690.

(385)ibid vol.II. 583 dok. pp. 716-724.

(386)Orszagos Leveltar. Kum.pol. 1938-7/43-2541 and Kum.chiffre.1938-kimeno-Varso.

(387)ibid Kum.chiffre-bejovo-Varso-6215/229 and Landau, Z.-J.Tomaszwski, Monachium, No.316, 218 and No.441-442 377.

(388)Kral, V., *Die Deutschen in der Tschechoslowakei 1933-1947.* Praha: 1964, p.221 and Kral, V., *Spojenectvi ceskoslovensko-sovetske v europske politice 1935-1939.* Praha: pp.345-346, and Landau, Z. op.cit. 468-469, 410.

(389)Orszagos Leveltar. Kum.chiffre.1938-kimeno-London.

(390)ibid Kum.pol. 1938-7/7-3265(3293).

(391)ibid Kum.pol.chiffre-1938-kimeno-Varso-5995/105.

(392)ibid Kum.chiffre-1938-kimeno-Berlin-6245/159.

(393)*Weltgeschichte der Gegenwart in Dokumenten.* 99 dok.223-225.

(394)*Weltgeschichte...* op.cit. pp.207--208.

(395)ADAP Serie D, II. 671, and Orszagos Leveltar. Kum.res.pol.1939-7/a-918.

(396)*Allianz Hitler-Horthy-Mussolini.* 38.

(397)Orszagos Leveltar. Kum.res.pol.1939-7/a-937.

(398)ADAP Serie D., II. 670.

(399)DBFP II. Anlage C.

(400)Orszagos Leveltar. Kum.res.pol.1939-7/a-957.

(401)ibid 1939-7/a-959.

(402)ibid 1938-7/7-3265 (3475)

(403)ibid Kum.pol.1938-7/7-3265 (3476).

(404)ibid Kum.res.pol. 1939-7/a-994.

(405)ibid Kum.res.pol. 1939-7/a-991.

(406)ibid Minisztertanacsi jegyzokonyvek, October 7, 1938.

(407)ADAP Serie D, v.IV. Doc.No.61, pp.65-68.

(408)Orszagos Leveltar. Kum.res.pol. 1938-7-Komaromi targyalasok jegyzokonyve.

(409)ADAP Serie D, v.IV, Doc.No.62, pp.68-71.

(410)Orszagos Leveltar. Kum.pol. 1938-7/7-3265 (3755).

(411)ibid Kum.chiffre-bejovo-Roma and DBFP Third Ser. III. No.26.

(412)Orszagos Leveltar. Rum.res.pol. 1939-7/8-1210.

(413)ibid Kum.chiffre.1938-bejovo-Roma.

(414)*Pragai Magyar Hirlap.* November 4, 1938.

(415)DBFP Third Ser.III.202.

(416)Orszagos Leveltar. Kum.chiffre-bejovo-Roma, and DBFP Third Ser. III.220.

(417)Hoench, op.cit. p.173. See also pertinent information cited in Part One.

(418)France. Ministere des Affaires Etrangeres. *The French Yellow Book. Diplomatic Documents, 1938-1939.* London: Hutchinson and Co., Ltd., 1940. p.25.

(419)Orszagos Leveltar. Kum.pol. 1938-7/7-3265 (3451).

(420)ibid Kum.pol. 1938-7/7-3265 (3497) and DBFP Third Ser. III.174.

(421)ibid Kum.chiffre. 1938-bejovo-Roma.

(422)ibid Kum.chiffre.1938-bejovo-Roma.

(423)ibid Kum.chiffre.1938-kimeno-Berlin.

(424)ibid Kul.chiffre. 1938-bejovo-Roma.

(425)ibid

(426)DBFP Third Ser. III. 202.

(427)Craster, H.H.E., ed. *Speeches on Foreign Policy by Viscount Halifax.* London: Oxford University Press, 1940, p.204.

(428)Chaszar, Edward, op.cit. p.60.

(429)Great Britain Parliament. Parliamentary Debates. House of Commons. Fifth Series. London: His Majesty's Stat.Off., 1938-1939. v.341, p.477.

(430)Chaszar, Edward, op.cit. pp.4-8. See also on the following pages a detailed analysis of the question, with ample references to source material.

(431)Felvideki Magyar Hirlap. December 4, 1938.

PART TWO

(432)ibid

(433)ibid

(434)ibid December 24, 1938.

(435)Orszagos Leveltar. Kum.res.pol. 1939-33/a-442 and Kum.chiffre. 1939-Praga-kimeno-5028/3.

(436)Bolgar, Elek, comp. *A nemetek magyarorszagi politikaja titkos nemet diplomaciai okmanyokban, 1937-1942* and Orszagos Leveltar. Kum.chiffre. Berlini kovetseg szamjeltaviratai 1939. I.18. Doc.No.25, pp.73-82.

(437)ADAP Serie D, v.IV, Doc.No.158

(438)DGFP Serie D, v.IV, Doc.No. 168, p.213.

(439)Orszagos Leveltar. Kum.res.pol. 1939-33/a-74. Regarding the Kozma-Bonnet talks in Paris, see: Orszagos Leveltar. Kozma Miklos iratai 27 cs. Naplojegyzetek, March 4,7,8,11, 1939.

(440)ibid Kum.chiffre.1939-Praga-bejovo-5291/35 and ADAP Serie D, v.IV. Doc.181, pp.198 and Orszagos Leveltar. Kum.res.pol. 1939-33a-155.

(441)DGFP Serie D, v.VIII.

(442)Orszagos Leveltar. Kum.pol. 1939-21/7-2377.

(443)Macartney op.cit. p.336.

(444)*Uj Hirek*. January 1, 1939.

(445)ibid January 8, 1939.

(446)*Felvideki Magyar Hirlap*, January 20, 1939.

(447)*Uj Hirek*. January 28, 29, 1939.

(448)ibid February 9, 1939.

(449)ibid February 11, 1939.

283

(450)*Magyar Nemzet*. February 28, 1939.

(451)*Uj Hirek*. February 28, 1939.

(452)*Felvideki Magyar Hirlap*. March 16, 1939.

(453)*Uj Hirek*. March 21, 1939.

(454)ibid April 9, 1939.

(455)Magyar Tudomanyos Akademia. Tortenettudomanyi Intezet. *Diplomaciai iratok Magyarorszag kulpolitikajahoz, 1936-1945*. Laszlo Zsigmond, ed. Budapest: 1963. Barcza to Csaky, March 18, 1939; Barcza to Csaky, March 19, 1939. 3:614-6, 619.

(456)ADAP Serie D. v.IV, Doc.No.10, 215, 219, 222; and Orszagos Leveltar. Kum.rs.pol. 1939-33/a-447.,-74-319.

(457)*Esti Ujsag*. May 14, 1939 and *Felvideki Magyar Hirlap*. May 13, 1939.

(458)*Uj Hirek*. June 20, 1939.

(459)*Felvideki Magyar Hirlap*. July 23, 1939.

(460)*Uj Hirek*. July 27, 1939.

(461)ibid August 8, 1939.

(462)ibid September 7, 1939.

(463)*Magyar Nemzet*. September 12, 1933.

(464)*Uj Hirek*. October 12, 1939.

(465)ibid October 24, 1939.

(466)ibid October 29, 1939.

(467)ibid November 30, 1939.

(468)ibid December 23, 1939.

(469)ibid January 1, 1940.

(470)*Dokumenty z historie ceskoslovenskej politiky 1939-1943.* Otahalova Cervinkova, Praha, 1966. Smutny's note on August 4, 1943, p.720. Cited by Janics, Kalman op.cit. p.96.

(471)*Uj Hirek.* January 28, 1940.

(472)ibid March 14, 1940.

(473)ibid May 9, 1940.

(474)ibid June 23, 1940.

(475)ibid August 30, September 5, 13, October 10, 1940.

(476)ibid November 28, 1940.

(477)ibid December 22, 1940.

(478)ibid January 1, 1941.

(479)*Pesti Hirlap.* February 29????????, 1941.

(480)*Uj Hirek.* March 11, 1941.

(481)*Magyar Hirek.* May 24, 1941.

(482)*Uj Hirek.* August 29, 1941.

(483)ibid August 15, 1941 and *Kisebbsegvedelem 1941.* No. 5-6, pp.36-37.

(484)*Uj Hirek.* September 2, 1941.

(485)*Magyar Hirlap.* June 28, 1942.

(486)ibid

(487)ibid December 15, 1942.

(488)*Historicky Casopis.* Bratislava, 1969/3, p.352, cited in Janics, Kalman, op.cit. 35-36.

(489)*Grenzbote*. May 19, 1942, Vol.72, No.133. Copy in author's possession.

(490)*Nove Slovo*. Bratislava: August 21, 1969, cited in Janics, Kalman, op.cit. p.36.

(491)Notes among the papers of the late Louise Esterhazy, sister of Janos Esterhazy, in the author's possession. Hereafter: Louise Esterhazy papers.

(492)*Magyar Hirlap*. September 5, 1943.

(493)*Pesti Hirlap*. January 20, 1944.

(494)*Losonci Hirlap*. January 9, 1944.

(495)ibid January 30, 1944.

(496)*Magyar Hirlap*. March 26, 1944.

(497)Precan, Vilem, *Slovenske narodne povstanie*. Bratislava: 1965. Letter from a non-Communist resistance group, March 14, 1944 p.102. Cited in Janics, Kalman, op.cit. 101.

(498)Precan, Vilem, op.cit. p.331, cited in Janics, Kalman, op.cit.p.102.

(499)ibid p.262, cited in Janics, Kalman, op.cit. p.103.

(500)ibid p.468, cited in Janics, Kalman, op.cit.p.108.

(501)Janics, Kalman op.cit.p.111.

(502)*Cesta ke kvetnu*. Praha, 1965. (Collection of Documents) Minutes of the meetings between Benes and the delegation of the Czech Communist Party in Moscow, p.268. Also, address by Marek Culen on October 13, 1944, cited in Janics, Kalman op.cit. p.113.

(503)Husak, Gustav, *Svedectvo o Slovenskom narodnom povstani*, 1964. p.548, cited in Janics, Kalman op.cit. p.117.

(504)Louise Esterhazy papers.

(505)Szekely, an ancient branch of the Hungarian people, descendants of the earliest inhabitants of Transylvania.

(506)Kertesz, Stephen O., *The Last European Peace Conference -- Paris, 1946 -- Values in Conflict*. Lanham, MD: University Press of America, 1985.

and Kertesz, Stephen O., *Between Russia and the West. Hungary and the Illusion of Peace Making, 1945-1947*. South Bend, IN: University of Notre Dame Press, 1984.

and Fulop, Mihaly, "A Kulugyminiszterek Tanacsa es a magyar bekeszerzodes." *Kulpolitika*. 1985, No.4, pp.124-156.

(507)The meeting was called pursuant to decree No. 88/1945 by the President of the Republic.

(508)Janics, Kalman op,cit. p.228.

(509)Contemporary press report from Pozsony, dated October 5, 1947. Copy in author's possession.

(510)Louise Esterhazy papers.

(511)*Felvideki Tudomanyos Tarsasag Ertesitoje, 1957* No.1.

(512)ibid

(513)Prejav presedu SKS. Stefan B. Roman na osmom Generalnom Zhomazdeni SKS. Bulletin c.76 and c.80.

BIBLIOGRAPHY

DOCUMENTS

Acten zur Deutschen Auswartigen Politik, 1918-1945. (*ADAP*) Serie D. Baden-Baden, 1950-1953.

Allianz Hitler, Horthy, Mussolini. ed. Lajos Kerekes, Budapest, 1965.

Archives diplomatiques. Paris. Europe 1918-1929. Hongrie.

Documents on British Foreign Policy 1919-1939. (*DBFP*) Series III. London, 1949-1952.

Documents on German Foreign Policy 1918-1945. (*DGFP*) Series D. Washington, DC, 1951-1954.

Papers of Lujza Esterhazy. Private collection, unpublished. Copies of several documents in author's possession.

France. Ministere des Affaires Etrangeres. *The French Yellow Book. Diplomatic Documents 1938-1939.* London, Hutchinson and Co. Ltd. 1940.

Gt. Brit. Parliament. *Parliamentary Debates. House of Commons.* Fifth Series. London. H.M. Stat. Off. 1938-1939.

Mnichov v dokumentech.1.Zrada zapadnich mocnosti na Ceskoslovensku. Ministertsve zachranich, Praha. 1958.

Papers and Documents Relating to the Foreign Relations of Hungary. (PDR FRH) ed. Francis Deak and Dezso Ujvary. Budapest, 1939, 1946.

Orszagos Leveltar. Kulugyminiszteriumi iratanyag. (National Archives of Hungary. Documents of the Hungarian Foreign Ministry) (OL KUM)

Papers Relating to the Foreign Relations of the United States. Paris Peace Conference, 1919. (FRUS PPC) Washington, D.C., 1942-1947.

Public Record Office. Foreign Office. v. 371. 1919-1937. (PRO FO)

Weltgeschichte der Gegenwart in Dokumenten. Bd.1. Munchen, 1953.

MONOGRAPHS

Adam, Magda, *Magyarorszag es a kisantant a harmincas evekben*. Budapest: Akademiai Kiado, 1968.

Arato, Endre, *A magyar-csehszlovak viszony otven eve. Torteneti attekintes*. Budapest: Kossuth Konyvkiado, 1969.

Arato, Endre, *Tanulmanyok a szlovakiai magyarok eletebol, 1918-1975*. Budapest: Magveto Konyvkiado, 1977.

Bibo, Istvan, *Valogatott tanulmanyok*. v.1, 1935-1944. Budapest: Magveto Konyvkiado, 1986.

Bohm, Jaroslav, *La Grande Moravie*. Prague: Czechoslovak Academy of Science, 1963.

Bolgar, Elek, comp., *A nemetek magyarorszagi politikaja titkos nemet diplomaciai okmanyokban (1937-1942*. Budapest, 1947.

Bonsal, Stephen, *Suitors and Supplicants, The Little Nations at Versailles*. Port Washington, NY: Kennicat Press, Inc., 1946.

Borsody, Istvan, *Magyar-szlovak kiegyezes*. Budapest: Officina (1945?).

Buza, Laszlo, *A kisebbsegek jogi helyzete a bekeszerzodesek es mas nemzetkozi egyezsegek ertelmeben*. Budapest, 1930.

Butvin, Jozef, et al., *Dejini Slovenska slovom i obrazom*. II. Bratislava, 1981.

Chaszar, Edward, *Decision in Vienna, The Czechoslovak-Hungarian Border Dispute*. Astor, FL: Danubian Press, 1978.

Ciano, Galeazzo, *The Ciano Diaries*. New York: Doubleday, 1946.

Craster, H.H.E., ed., *Speeches on Foreign Policy by Viscount Halifax*. London: Oxford University Press, 1940.

Deak, Francis, *Hungary at the Paris Peace Conference; The Diplomatic History of the Treaty of Trianon*. New York, 1942.

Dukes, Frantisek, *Dejini Slovenska a Slovakov*. Bratislava, 1946.

Durcansky, Ferdinand, *Pohl'ad na slovensku politicku minulost*. Bratislava, 1943. Cited in Istvan Borsody, *Magyar-szlovak kiegyezes*. op.cit.

Dvornik, Francis, *The Making of Central and Eastern Europe*. London: Polish Research Center, 1919.

Franchet d'Esperey to Barthelot, March 19, 1919. Ministere de la Guerre, Etat Major de l'Armee. Archives historiques, *Campagne contre Allemagne, 1914-1918*. 27 N 89.

Franchet d'Esperey to Clemenceau and Foch, March 10, 1919. Ministere des Affaires Etrangeres. *Correspondence des Affaires politiques, Roumanie*.

Gehl, Jurgen, *Austria, Germany and the Anschluss, 1931-1938*. London: Oxford University Press, 1963.

Grebert, Arved, *Dr. Jozef Kirschbaum. Politik a Diplomat*. Koln, 1984.

Hajek, Milos, *Old Mnichova k Breznu*. Praha, 1959.

Hodza, Milan, *Federation in Central Europe*. London, 1942.

Hodza, Milan, *Kozep-Europa orszagutjan. Hodza Milan valogatott irasai.* II.v. comp. Rudinszky Jozsef. Bratislava, 1938.

Hoensch, Jorg, *Der Ungarische Revisionismus and die Zerschlagen der Tschechoslovakei.* Tubingen: J.C.R. Mohr, 1967.

Horthy, Nicholas von, *Ein Leben fur Ungarn.* Bonn, 1953.

Hory, Andras, *A kulisszak mogott.* Vienna, 1965.

House, Edward Mandell, *Papers, 1891-1938.* Yale University Library.

Husak, Gustav, *Svedectvo o Slovenskom narodom povstani.* 1964.

Janics, Kalman, *A hontalansag evei. A szlovakiai magyar kisebbseg a masodik vilaghaboru utan, 1945-1948.* Bern: Europai Protestans Magyar Szabadegyetem, 1979.

Juhasz, Gyula, *Magyarorszag kulpolitikaja, 1919-1945.* Budapest: Kossuth Konyvkiado, 1969.

Kallay, Nicholas, *Hungarian Premier. A Personal Account of a Nation's Struggle in the Second World War.* New York, 1954.

Karolyi, Mihaly, *Faith without Illusion.* New York, 1957.

Kertesz, Stephen O., *The Last European Peace Conference, Paris 1946. Values of Conflict.* Lanham, MD: University Press of America, 1985.

Kertesz, Stephen O., *Between Russia and the West, Hungary and the Illusions of Peace Making, 1945-1947.* South Bend, IN: University of Notre Dame Press, 1984.

Kirkconnel, Watson, *Canada, Europe and Hitler.* London: Oxford University Press, 1939.

Kirschbaum, Joseph M., *An Outline of Slovakia's Struggle for Independence.* Toronto: Canadian Slovak League, 1964.

Kirschbaum, Joseph M., *Slovakia, Nation at the Crossroads of Europe.* New York, 1960.

Kis, Aladar, *Magyarorszag kulpolitikaja a masodik vilaghaboru eloestejen.* Budapest, 1963

Kovacs, Endre, *Korszakvaltas.* Budapest: Magveto Konyvkiado, 1981.

Kovtun, George J., *The Czechoslovak Declaration of Independence. A History of the Document.* Washington, DC: Library of Congress, 1985.

Kral, V. *Die Deutschen in der Tschechoslovakei, 1933-1947.* Praha, 1947.

Kral, V. *Spojenectvi ceskoslovensko-sovetske v europske politice 1935-1939.* Praha.

Laffan, R.G.D., *Survey of International Affairs, 1938.* v.II. London: Oxford University Press, 1951.

Landau, Z., *Monachium.*

Lansing, Robert, *Papers, 1890-1933.* Washington, DC: Library of Congress, Manuscript Division.

Lettrich, Josef, *History of Modern Slovakia.* New York, 1955.

Lias, Godfrey, *Benes of Czechoslovakia.* London: George Allen & Unwin, Ltd., 1940.

Macartney, C.A., *October Fifteenth: A History of Modern Hungary, 1929-1945.* 2nd ed. Edinburgh: University Press, 1961.

Masaryk, Thomas G., *The Lectures of T.G.Masaryk at the University of Chicago, Summer 1902.* London.

Medvecky, Karol A., *Slovensky prevrat*. III., Trnava, 1930-1931.

Mikus, J.A., *Slovakia, A Political History, 1918-1950*. Marquette University Press, 1964.

Mikus, J.A., *La Slovaquie dans le drama de l'Europe*.

Merei, Gyula, *A magyar polgari partok programmjai, 1867-1918*. Budapest, 1971.

Nittner, Ernest, *Dokumente zur Sudetendeutschen Fragen*.

Nowak, Karl, *The Collapse of Central Europe*. Westport, CT: Greenwood Press, 1970.

Olvedi, Janos, *Napfogyatkozas; magyarok Szlovakiaban*. New York: Puski, 1985.

Olvedi, Janos, *A magyar kisebbseg Csehszlovakiaban*.

Palyi, Ede, *Mikent szereztem en meg a csehek ajanlatat az elszakitott magyarok bekes visszaadasara*. Budapest, 1927.

Perman, Dagmar, *The Shaping of the Czechoslovak State*. Leiden: Brill, 1962.

Precan, Vilem, *Slovenske narodne povstanie*. Bratislava, 1965.

Puspoki-Nagy, Peter, *On the Location of Great Moravia: A Reassessment*. Pittsburgh, PA: Duquesne University, Department of History, 1982.

Puspoki-Nagy, Peter, *A tenyek erejevel*. New York: Puski, 1985.

Raschhofer, Herman, ed., *Die Tschechoslovakische Denkschriften fur die Friedenskonferenz von Paris, 1919-1920*. Berlin, 1930.

Rich, Norman, *Hitler's War Aims*. New York: Norton, 1970.

Rumpler, Helmuth, *Das Volkermanifest Kaiser Karl's von 16 Oktober 1918; Letzter Versuch zur Rettung der Habsburgerreiches*, Wien: Verband fur Geschichte und Politik, 1966.

Schafarik, Pavel Jozef, *Slawische Alterthumer*.

Szinai, Miklos, comp., *Horthy Miklos titkos iratai*. Budapest, 1962.

Szvatko, Pal, *A visszatert magyarok. A felvideki magyarsag husz eve*. Budapest, 1938.

Sirchich, Laszlo, *A Felvidek az ezereves magyar allamtestben; a magyarok Csehszlovakiaban. Tanulmanyok*. Cleveland, OH, 1979.

Taborsky, Edward, *President Benes between East and West, 1938-1948*. Stanford, CA.: Hoover Institution Press, 1981.

Thompson, S. Harrison, *Czechoslovakia in European History*. 2nd ed. Princeton, 1953.

Il Ventesimo bollettino del congresso slovacco. Rome, June 1975.

Wagner, Francis S., et al., *Hungarians in Czechoslovakia*. New York: Research Institute for Minority Studies, 1959.

Weizsacker, Ernst von, *Erinnerungen*. Munchen, 1950.

Wojatsek, Charles, *From Trianon to the First Vienna Arbitral Award*. Montreal: Institute of Comparative Civilizations, 1980.

Zubek, T.J., *The Church of Silencee in Slovakia.*, Whiting, IN, 1956.

MONOGRAPHS IN SERIALS - ARTICLES IN PERIODICALS

Adam, Magda, "A muncheni egyezmeny letrejotte es Magyarorszag
kulpolitikaja, 1936-1938," in *Diplomaciai iratok
Magyarorszag kulpolitikajahoz, 1936-1945.*
vol.II, Budapest: Akademiai Kiado, 1965.

Baumgarten, Vladimir, "Federalism vs. the Policies of
Opportunism; The Careers of Milan Hodza," in
The Central European Forum. vol.1,no.1. Astor, FL:
Danubian Press, Inc., Spring 1938.

Baumgarten, Vladimir, "Slovakia's 1944 Uprising Reexamined," in
The Central European Forum. vol.1,no.2. Astor, FL:
Danubian Press, Fall 1988.

Bogdan, Kriaman, "The Belgrade Armistice of November 1938," in
Slavonic and East European Review. vol.LXVIII, no.110,
1970.

Borsody, Istvan, "Masaryk es az uj Europa. Egy felvideki magyar
emlekei," in *Uj Latohatar.* vol.XXXIX, no.1, March 1988.

Darvas, Janos, "Politikai eletunk husz eve. Magyarok
Csehszlovakiaban 1918 utan," in *Orszag Utja,* June 1938.

Durcansky, Ferdinand, "Mit Tiso bei Hitler," in *Politische Studien,*
vol.7, no.80, 1956.

Fulop, Mihaly, "A Kulugyminiszterek Tanacsa es a magyar
bekeszerzodes," in *Kulpolitika.* No.4., 1985.

Jellinek, Yeshayau, "The Treaty of Trianon and Czechoslovakia:
Reflections," in *War and Society in East Central Europe*.
vol.6. New York: Columbia University Press, 1982.

Keller, Hans, "Die Kurze Jahren der Slovakischen Republik,
1939-1945," in *Geschichte historisches Magazin*. No.69,
St.Gallen, Schweiz, Marz/April 1985.

Kemeny, Lajos, "Az Esterhazyak Pozsonyban," in *Toldy Kor
evkonyve*. 1943.

Pritz, Paul. "A kieli talalkozo; forraskritikai tanulmany," in
Szazadok. 1974.

"Ratz Memorandum," in *U.S. National Archives, Collection of
Hungarian Political and Military Records, 1909-1945*.
Washington, DC. Microcopies T 937, roll 15.

Roos, Hans, "Polen und Europa. Studien zur Polnische
Aussenpolitik, 1931-1939," in *Tubinger Studien*, no.108,
Tubingen, 1957.

Sakmyster, Thomas L.,"The Hungarian State Visit to Germany of
August 1938: Some New Evidence on Hungary in Hitler's pre-
Munich Policy," in *Canadian Slavic Studies*.vol.3.1969.

Szarka, Laszlo, "Kisebbsegvedelem, reciprocitas, revizio.
Megegyezesi kiserletek a nemzetisegi kerdes teren," in
Hungaro-Bohemicoslovaca. vol.2. Budapest, 1988.

Szilassy, Bela, "A felvideki magyarsag elete a ket vilaghaboru
kozott," in *Elszakitott magyarsag*. Buenos Aires, 1956.

Szvatko Pal, "A csehszlovak-szudetanemet kiegyezes kiserlete," in
Magyar Szemle. vol.III, no.71. May 1937.

Smutny, Jaromyr, "Papers," in *Archives of Russian and East
European History and Culture*. Columbia University.

Turczel, Lajos, "A kisebbsegi helyzet kialakulasanak korulmenyei
Csehszlovakiaban 1918 utan," *Irodalmi Szemle*.vol.3,1966.

PERIODICALS, NEWSPAPERS AND YEARBOOKS

Affari Esteri
Ceskoslovensky Casopis Historicky
Daily Herald
Esti Ujsag
Felvideki Magyar Hirlap
Felvideki Tudomanyos Tarsasag Ertesitoje
Gazeta Polska
Grenzbote
Historia
Historicky Casopis
Kisebbsegvedelem
Losonci Hirlap
Magyar Nemzet
Pesti Hirlap
Pragai Magyar Hirlap
Prager Montagsblatt
Slovak
Szazadok
Times
Uj Hirek
Uj Szellem
Venkov

ABBREVIATIONS

ADAP - *Akten zur Deutschen auswärtigen Politik, 1918-1945*, Serie D.

AMZV - *Archiv ministerstva zahranicnich veci Praga*. Pliticke zpravy (PZ) 1920-1938.

DBFP - *Documents on British Foreign Policy, 1919-1939*, Series III.

DGFP - *Documents on German Foreign Policy, 1918-1945*. Series C. London. 1957-1962.

DGFP - *Documents on German Foreign Policy, 1918-1945*. Series D. Washington. 1951-1954.

FRUS - *Foreign Relations of the United States. Diplomatic Papers, 1938*. Washington, U.S.Govt.Print.Off. 1955.

PRO FO - Public Record Office. Foreign Office. 1919-1937.

OL - Orszagos Leveltar (National Archives of Hungary)
 KUM - Kulugyminiszteriumi iratanyag (Documents of the Hungarian Foreign Ministry).
 POL. - Political
 RES. - Restricted

PDR FRH - *Papers and Documents Relating to the Foreign Relations of Hungary*. ed. Francis Deak and Dezso Ujvary. Budapest. 1939, 1946.

INDEX